ROUTLEDGE LIBRARY EDITIONS:
SLAVERY

Volume 2

AFRICA'S SLAVES TODAY

# AFRICA'S SLAVES TODAY

JONATHAN DERRICK

LONDON AND NEW YORK

First published in 1975 by George Allen & Unwin Ltd

This edition first published in 2023
by Routledge
4 Park Square, Milton Park, Abingdon, Oxon OX14 4RN

and by Routledge
605 Third Avenue, New York, NY 10158

*Routledge is an imprint of the Taylor & Francis Group, an informa business*

© 1975 George Allen & Unwin Ltd

All rights reserved. No part of this book may be reprinted or reproduced or utilised in any form or by any electronic, mechanical, or other means, now known or hereafter invented, including photocopying and recording, or in any information storage or retrieval system, without permission in writing from the publishers.

Trademark notice: Product or corporate names may be trademarks or registered trademarks, and are used only for identification and explanation without intent to infringe.

*British Library Cataloguing in Publication Data*
A catalogue record for this book is available from the British Library

ISBN: 978-1-032-30942-2 (Set)
ISBN: 978-1-032-31654-3 (Volume 2) (hbk)
ISBN: 978-1-032-31664-2 (Volume 2) (pbk)
ISBN: 978-1-003-31074-7 (Volume 2) (ebk)

DOI: 10.4324/9781003310747

**Publisher's Note**
The publisher has gone to great lengths to ensure the quality of this reprint but points out that some imperfections in the original copies may be apparent.

**Disclaimer**
The publisher has made every effort to trace copyright holders and would welcome correspondence from those they have been unable to trace.

# AFRICA'S SLAVES TODAY

Jonathan Derrick

London   George Allen and Unwin Ltd.
Ruskin House   Museum Street

First published in 1975

This book is copyright under the Berne Convention. All rights are reserved. Apart from any fair dealing for the purpose of private study, research, criticism or review, as permitted under the Copyright Act 1956, no part of this publication may be reproduced, stored in a retrieval system, or transmitted, in any form or by any means, electronic, electrical, chemical, mechanical, optical, photocopying, recording or otherwise, without the prior permission of the copyright owner. Inquiries should be addressed to the publishers.

© George Allen & Unwin Ltd 1975

ISBN 0 04 326002 0

Printed in Great Britain
in 10 point Plantin type
by Cox & Wyman Ltd,
London, Fakenham and Reading

## Contents

| | | |
|---|---|---|
| Introduction | | *page* 9 |
| 1 | The Moors and their Slaves | 19 |
| 2 | Tuareg and other Sahara Slaves | 34 |
| 3 | Savanna Slaves | 55 |
| 4 | Black African Slaves and Serfs | 83 |
| 5 | The Old Slave-Trade | 110 |
| 6 | One-Way Trips to Arabia | 134 |
| 7 | Ethiopia's Modern Slaves | 150 |
| 8 | Colonisation and Forced Labour | 159 |
| 9 | Forced Labour in the White South | 167 |
| 10 | Forced Labour in Liberia | 194 |
| 11 | Modern Exploitation | 203 |
| 12 | Action on Slavery | 220 |
| Index | | 241 |

Acknowledgements are due to the Camera Press for all the illustrations in the book and to Paul Almasy (3 and 10), Corry Bevinton (9), Mauro Colasanti (6 and 7), Richard Harrington (2, 11 and 12), Peter Wrinch-Schulz (8), John Seymour (14).

*Introduction*

When Europeans and Americans think of slavery they think of Africa, for African slavery has been an important part of the history of three continents for five centuries.

Europeans enslaved millions of Africans for work in the Americas, and after the abolition of this trade other Europeans took action against other slavery and slave-dealing in Africa, until colonisation had the abolition of local African slavery as one of its aims. Action against slavery was an important aspect of colonial rule in Africa, and the last war of colonial conquest, in which the Italian victory over Ethiopia helped to pave the way for the Second World War, had as one of its official pretexts the continuation of slavery in Ethiopia.

So the continuation of slavery into modern times in parts of Africa is a late chapter in an old story. It is the subject of this book.

At one time or another slavery has been normal, and accepted, over much of the world. Slaves did the hard work in the ancient civilisations of Egypt, Greece and Rome. Within living memory, the Hitler and Stalin régimes have taken millions of people into what amounted virtually to slavery. But African slavery is a subject on its own.

What remains of African slavery today does not have the international importance that once attached to African slavery and slave-trading, but it is of interest partly because the past has had such lasting effects. The Atlantic slave-trade not only helped lay the foundations of British prosperity but also shaped the character and future of the West Indian islands and other parts of the New World and provided a cause for the American Civil War. Descendants of transported African slaves form the majority of the population in five independent countries and important minorities in a dozen others, including Great Britain. Their story enters at many points into what is taught to European schoolchildren and what adult Europeans read – the life and writings of David Livingstone, the story of the successful campaign of William Wilberforce and other Abolitionists, *Uncle Tom's Cabin* and *Gone With the Wind*, and many paperback novels. The African slave-trade has become part of 'general knowledge' outside Africa, and this must be one reason why reports of continued slavery in Africa arouse attention. This book examines in a small way what lies behind such reports.

In Africa, of course, the legacy of slavery and the slave-trade is immeasurable. To some extent it is a part of the whole enormous legacy of European penetration and conquest. The Arab slave-trade in Africa, considerably older than the European, has also left its mark on the north, west and east of the continent. Unfortunately the inherited psychological effects of slavery on a large number of people cannot be assessed, but in many parts of Africa where people formerly enslaved others for their own use or for export, mental attitudes bred by this clearly continue, as do similar attitudes in the USA. Even if slavery in Africa had vanished altogether, the impact of both local indigenous slavery (which was widespread all over the continent) and the European and Arab slave-trades would still be worth attention as their effects can still be felt today.

In fact, slavery has not disappeared in Africa; if there is little or no trace of it in most parts of the continent, in many places it vanished only very recently. In this book, the many places where slavery ended only in the past fifteen or twenty years, as well as the few places where it seems still to be going on today, are discussed. The number of such places is more than one might think.

That this should shock as well as surprise is natural. By an almost unparalleled moral revolution, European, American and world ethical opinion, so far as one can assess it, has turned wholly against slavery, which was tolerated and even praised through most of human history. Public and governmental opinion may accept or ignore many sorts of oppression, dictatorship and large-scale crime, but not slavery. The United Nations Charter and the Universal Declaration of Human Rights proclaim that there shall be no more slavery or slave-trading, and this corresponds to general thinking. Accusations of slavery in any country are always strenuously denied by the government of that country. So there is bound to be shock and concern at reports of continued slavery in Africa.

For that reason it is important not to have any exaggerated notions of Africa's residual slavery. This book will show that slavery is almost certainly not very common, that it is usually of local importance only, and that it continues for special reasons which make it impossible to regard it as a mere crime to be outlawed. Leaving detailed explanation of this until later, it is important at the outset to dispel any ideas of forced overland marches of slaves from raided inland villages to the coast, of barracoons for confining them and irons for branding them before a journey on a crowded ship to a distant land. Residual slavery in Africa is as far removed as possible from anything like this. It is a residue of the traditional slavery which existed for centuries independently of outside slave-trading, and it takes the form of a particular social order, not of systematic exploitation of a sort preventable by gunboats or police action.

Individual and small-scale slavery (an extension, quite common in Africa, of the universal crime of kidnapping) also exists in Africa. This, too, is nothing like what Africa has known in the past few centuries. Even the cases of enslavement of Africans in Arabia in recent times have amounted to very little by comparison with the past.

This study does not intend to show slavery as a major problem or scandal in independent Africa, nor does it aim to promote international campaigns over situations in which international efforts can help only marginally, though usefully. Africa has scores of problems which are far more urgent than a few remaining cases of slavery. But these are, even so, a proper object of the outside world's interest and concern.

That slavery is a matter that concerns the world as a whole has been recognised since the last century. Abolition of the slave-trade by Great Britain and later (reluctantly in some cases) by other European powers was only the start. It was soon felt that not only should European and other slave-trading be abolished (the British Government concentrated on this) and the slaves in the colonies of Europe be liberated, but that all slavery everywhere, including tribal slavery in Africa, should be ended. This concern was expressed most strongly by the missionaries and by the Anti-Slavery Society, founded in London in 1823 and active from then on, with a short break, in the campaign against slavery all over the world. The success of their campaigns meant that action against slavery was an important pretext for the colonisation of Africa by the British and other European imperialists. The Berlin Act of 1885, which was a step in the partition of Africa among the colonial powers (not, as is often believed, a final agreement on the partition), was also an international agreement on the abolition of slavery and the slave-trade. The Brussels Act of 1890 dealt more fully with this and laid down that action against slave-dealing and slavery was a world-wide obligation.

In a sense, these agreements were the forerunners of agreements, such as the Geneva and Hague Conventions, which have laid down international obligations on a number of vital matters. Co-operation on such matters has been further promoted by the establishment of such bodies as the International Labour Organisation, and is widely – officially, almost universally – accepted today as desirable. Unfortunately, in the late nineteenth century international agreements of this sort were inevitably of an imperialist nature. In those days the deduction that because slavery (for example) was wrong, Europe, or Britain, must send in troops wherever necessary to stop it was commonly made. Thus anti-slavery action, proposed and organised by men whose sincerity was manifest, was linked inextricably with colonial aggression and conquest, particularly by the British.

Before the era of colonial conquest, many independent African rulers, including the Bey of Tunis, the Sultan of Zanzibar, the Queen of Madagascar, and the rulers of Calabar and Bonny on the West Coast, had made agreements with Great Britain to abolish slave-trading and slavery. But these agreements were not treaties between equals, and were often the outcome of crude gunboat diplomacy. However much one may admire the concern to abolish slavery, and criticise the African rulers who had to be forced to order its abolition, the fact is that anti-slavery was a slogan of imperialism.

It is important to recall those days to remind oneself that they are past. The days when one nation or a group of nations could send gunboats to force an end to slave-trading or slavery in any part of the globe have long since ended. Modern African governments are sensitive over their sovereignty, and where questions of slavery are concerned recent history provides them with some reason for this. Any expression of international concern over slavery must be completely divested of the spirit of 1890. But if it is free from that spirit, it is legitimate and admirable, and believers in human liberty in any country can properly show interest in African slavery as in any other way in which people anywhere are deprived of their freedom.

Slavery is accepted all over the world as illegal and shameful, and the international obligation to end it is clearly laid down. The most important texts laying it down are the League of Nations' Slavery Convention of 1926 and the United Nations' Supplementary Convention of 1956. The first was signed at the height of the colonial era, when the obligation to end slavery affected mainly Great Britain, France and Belgium, as far as Africa was concerned. The second, however, was signed when the end of the colonial era was in sight (though it was to come sooner than expected), and independent African states have since signed it. So there is an international obligation, of a sort not influenced by European imperialism, to take action against slavery. The Anti-Slavery Society, which virtually wrote the text of the 1926 Convention, has continued since then to stress that obligation.

All this means that concern by outsiders about African slavery is legitimate and not improper 'interference'. It does not mean that action by outsiders is always possible or appropriate, or, indeed, that any simple action is possible in any particular case. On the contrary, the situations described in this book are such that no action by local governments or others can usually be recommended without proper close study of each situation.

Some of the situations, in fact, are such that when studying them the first question to be asked is the most basic question of all: 'What is a slave?'

It is one of those words whose meaning is generally known but cannot easily be defined. We know that the black workers on cotton plantations in the pre-war Deep South were slaves; we know that employees of Ford's at Dagenham are not; but it is less easy to tell where slavery begins and where it ends. As generally accepted, however, the word denotes a person who is treated as another's property. This is the meaning accepted by the 1926 Convention and the 1956 Supplementary Convention, and the best course is to adopt their working definition. The 'Supplementary Convention on the Abolition of Slavery, the Slave-Trade, and Institutions and Practices similar to Slavery' of 4th September, 1956, states (Section IV, article 7) that:

'For the purposes of the present Convention:
(*a*) "slavery" means, as defined in the Slavery Convention of 1926, the status or condition of a person over whom any or all of the powers attaching to the right of ownership are exercised, and "slave" means a person in such condition or status . . .'

One may as well adopt this definition, but how to apply it in actual situations? The ultimate proof of exercise of ownership rights is the buying and selling of human beings, but many slaves have lived all their lives as slaves of one master, and property can be held without the right of alienation. To tell who is a slave and who is not can be difficult because where no sales take place slaves may seem to be in a situation not very different from people in other sorts of subjection.

Slavery may, for example, merge into serfdom, which as commonly understood is different from slavery, and is different also from the situation of an employee. A serf is a man in a state of personal subjection to another man, bound to him by legal ties and obliged to work for him but not actually regarded as his property; commonly he is a farmer or a farm labourer tied by law to land which he works for his master. He may not always be easily distinguished from a slave or, on the other hand, from a sharecropper or tenant farmer. In certain countries, some sorts of farm tenancy are in fact similar to serfdom and not too far removed from slavery.

Because of this, and because the 1926 and 1956 Conventions and all the work of the Anti-Slavery Society have dealt with other practices similar to slavery as well as with slavery itself, it is reasonable to deal with serfdom in this book. Efforts are made throughout to distinguish genuine slavery from other practices, but there is bound, in complicated human situations, to be a fair amount of vagueness.

Of the practices similar to slavery, this book refers to pawning of human beings for debt and to abuses linked to adoption of children. What is said on these subjects is little and inadequate, for lack of data. For the same reason, and because this book is intended as a general introductory survey and cannot do full justice to any one topic, not much is said on the position of sharecroppers in certain countries, and the large subject of rural credit is left untouched. The money-lender is an important local figure in much of Africa, but I have not found data on how far he is able anywhere to reduce people to real debt-bondage. This happens in many parts of the world and a comprehensive study of indigenous credit for farmers and fishermen in Africa, and the state of dependence which may result from it, might reveal interesting things. Such a study is necessary but cannot be tackled here.

'White slavery' is not covered in this book. It is a subject on its own and probably does not fit into a book on African slavery very well. Sometimes prostitutes really are treated as slaves, but often their entry into the oldest profession and their later movements between cities or between countries are due to free choice or at least not to mere coercion. In black Africa, anyway, freelance prostitutes, often part-timers, are more typical than organised brothels.

Whether they appear in the coming pages or not, practices verging on slavery must be borne in mind because clear-cut distinctions between slaves and non-slaves are often impossible to make. Real situations often elude classification, and in the case of modern African slavery there is a special reason for vagueness. This is that slavery is illegal in all African countries. Where slavery is legally recognised one can tell who is a slave, but how does one describe the situation of people who seem to be exactly like slaves but who, in the eyes of the law, cannot be so because the law says nobody can be legally enslaved? Anti-slavery laws do not – for good reasons – force slaves to leave their masters to show that they are free. If they stay with their masters (as they often do) and if both they and their masters think in terms of 'slave' and 'master', while the law says there are no slaves, the situation can be confusing.

This is in fact a common situation. Abolition of local slavery has been mainly the work of colonial administrations, which abolished the legal status of slavery but were obliged to leave individuals in situations which might often seem ambiguous. Where necessary, independent African governments have followed the same (unavoidable) policy. So, for decades after the legal abolition of slavery, many Africans have been considered by others, and even by themselves, to be slaves. Sometimes it may be obvious that the old order has continued despite the new laws, and one can reasonably say that slavery still survives. But in other cases, ex-slaves may really be the 'servants' or 'retainers' that they are said to be. It may be hard to tell because the test – whether the slave/servant can leave the household if he wants to – may in practice never arise. Moreover, it is possible, in fact quite common, for groups of people descended from traditional slaves to be regarded as 'slaves' even if they do not belong to anyone. And even when that ends, the attitudes of slavery days may persist.

So the vagueness with which certain situations are described in this book is inevitable. The truth is that nobody can say in any country exactly when slavery has 'effectively' come to an end. Was it when the legislation took legal effect? Surely not, but then when was it? There is no good answer, and one has often to be imprecise and approximate. Recognition of this no doubt led to the inclusion of other practices in the international anti-slavery conventions.

Besides such practices, this book also examines forced labour and various modern forms of exploitation, including the form of which African migrant labourers are victims. These are clearly distinct from slavery, though recruitment of forced labour could resemble slave-trading at times. But they are mentioned partly because forced labour was so important in colonial Africa and partly to put slavery in perspective by showing that it has not been the only form of labour coercion in Africa, nor even, in all cases, the most disagreeable. Forced labour for railway-building and other projects in the colonial era affected Africans in a way that tribal slavery seldom, if ever, did, and this must be remembered when one reads of the colonial powers' action against slavery. Similarly, both the modern forms of exploitation briefly mentioned in Chapter Eleven and the small-scale kidnappings for slavery which quite often occur can be cited to put slavery in perspective. The slavery which still remains is not really very important, relatively speaking, as a burden on African people.

In fact, slavery certainly does not deserve as much attention by Africa's people and the outside world as the problems of nutrition, disease, housing, agricultural development and education, and other urgent problems facing millions. This book certainly does not intend to distract attention from those more pressing problems. Slavery is not insignificant, but it must be seen against the general African background. In a continent with a mortality rate among infants and young children often up to 50 per cent, with endemic malaria and wide prevalence of filariasis, meningitis and other diseases, and with millions of men seeking jobs in vain, the fate of a relatively few people still living in traditional slavery must seem relatively less intolerable. The slaves know this, for they see the hard lives of free people around them, not the Western sort of life. Those concerned about slavery should be sure that they realise the general context of African poverty and do not unconsciously imagine that slaves are the only unfortunates in a 'system' in which others generally live well.

Non-African readers need to have some picture in their minds of ordinary African life to understand the situations described in this book. There is very little written material, even by experts on Africa, to give a good idea of ordinary life in Africa to those who do not know the continent; books about African politics, history and anthropology, and the majority of articles on Africa in the European press, do little to describe the realities of life – such basic things as food and housing and health – as they affect the average African. Only if such things are grasped can slavery be understood in context.

Understanding does not mean acquiescence. Slavery is everywhere condemned, not because it involves special ill-treatment (probably no slaves have suffered as much as many non-slaves have in recent decades), but because it treats some people as the property of others. To understand the reasons for cases of continued slavery need not mean abandoning the intention that it should be abolished one day. As slavery seems to continue at least partly because of the exceptional poverty of parts of Africa, it is necessary to examine its context precisely in order to see how it can eventually be ended; and, perhaps, to avoid all appearance of wishing to attack maliciously the governments of some African countries. Such governments commonly do not like to hear slavery mentioned; they are rightly angered if slavery is mentioned out of context and in such a way as to suggest that nothing else ever happens in the country concerned; but if slavery is mentioned as a very old and natural growth arising partly from a general state of poverty whose existence is not denied, there is no question of governments being attacked for its existence – one cannot blame a government in power since 1960 for slavery dating from centuries ago, any more than one can blame the Churches for the continued existence of sin.

Slavery is discussed in the coming pages not from any political motive, nor to encourage any notion that it is one of Africa's major contemporary problems, but because it is a little-known, distinctive and not unimportant part of life in some parts of Africa and touches on other aspects of life there.

In preparing this survey, whose inadequacies are my own personal contribution, I have used a large amount of published material and the evidence of Africans and of travellers to Africa, including myself to a small extent. The published works are cited in the footnotes. I must thank Dame Margery Perham and Viscount Maugham for permission to quote from their works. The informants must remain anonymous because giving information for a book on slavery is regarded as an unfriendly act in some quarters.

I must express particular thanks to the Anti-Slavery Society and its secretary, Colonel Montgomery, for the interest shown in this book and the permission given for my use of the Society's library and its publications. I dedicate the book to that venerable Society on its 150th birthday, which falls at the time of going to press. Provided that it continues for as long as it is needed, may its days be short.

*Chapter One*

# The Moors and their Slaves

Are people still held in slavery in Africa – the continent which for so many centuries was known to Europe as a land of slavery and the slave-trade? This book shows that the answer is yes – there are slaves in Africa today, and there were many more only a short while ago. Just over two hundred years after the Somersett case in England signalled the start of the campaign against the slave-trade, and just one hundred years after the slave-market in Zanzibar was closed and made the site of a cathedral, slavery still survives in Africa.

Before describing this in more detail, however, it is as well to mention what does *not* survive in modern Africa: there are no more powerful slave-holding monarchs, like the old Kings of Ashanti and Benin; there are no more busy slave-ports, like the old Bonny and Kilwa, shipping thousands of Africans to new owners across the Atlantic and Indian Oceans; there are no more massive slaving expeditions into the interior, like those which Livingstone described in East Africa, disrupting the lives of millions for the sake of manpower for local and distant use.

In case anyone needs reminding about these past horrors, Chapter Five says a little about them. As far as modern Africa is concerned, all images of African slaves evoked by the writings of Wilberforce and Livingstone should be forgotten. Twentieth-century slavery in Africa is generally a very different thing: it is less widespread, but more prosaic, less easy as an object of crusading by Europeans.

Slavery in Africa today cannot be considered in isolation from the general human condition that exists there. This vast continent has about 350 million people of great diversity, among whom traces of slavery, serfdom and related practices occur to varying degrees in different places.

General statements about slavery are unlikely to be of much relevance in a continent with such a wide variety of people and places. Africa, for example, contains the vast and expanding Sahara

Desert, where only a few nomads live; Nigeria (the 'giant of Africa') with its 70 million or more inhabitants, including the Hausa and Yoruba and Ibo; Ethiopia with its Amharans and Tigreans who preserved independence and Christianity in their mountain home for two millennia; the great basin of the Congo or Zaire River and its tributaries, scene of some of the bloodiest events in Africa's recent history as well as some of her most remarkable native civilisations; the Indian Ocean coast with its old ports influenced for so long by the Arab and Muslim worlds; the northern regions of the continent which for thirteen centuries have been part of the Arab and Muslim worlds, but which include Egypt with its far more ancient culture; the great expanse of the Sudan, straddling the Nile valley from the marshy *sudd* of the Upper White Nile to the new lake behind Egypt's Aswan Dam; Sierra Leone and Liberia, homes of former victims of the Atlantic slave-trade who for long dominated the indigenous Africans of the area; the 'White South' of today, a great territory ruled by Portugal and by the local white communities of South Africa and Rhodesia, and including the wealth of the Transvaal and the aridity of the Kalahari Desert; and the giant island of Madagascar with its half-Malay population.

Classification of the peoples of Africa is a source of continued argument among scholars and the subject cannot be considered in detail here. However, as a rough guide, one can say that there are approximately 240 million Negroes in Africa today, living in the west, centre, east and south of the continent. About 110 million of them speak languages of the Bantu family. Indeed, they are often referred to as belonging to the Bantu race, though it is doubtful whether one can really discern racial groups, as opposed to linguistic groups, in the African population. The theory of a 'Hamitic' ethnic group, distinct from the Negro African group, was once common, but it now widely discounted. However, there are many peoples in Africa who are dark-skinned but definitely different from the black Africans, for example the Amharas and Gallas in Ethiopia; the Somalis; and the Beja and other northern and 'Arab' Sudanese. There are also the Masai of Kenya, different from everyone; the Fulani of West Africa, who may be related to some of the above but whose origin is a mystery; the Berbers and the Arabic-speakers\* in the Sahara and North Africa, few of whom are descendants of Arabian immigrants, the Egyptians, for example, being still very different from the Moroccans and the Tunisians.

One generalisation that can be made about Africa's people is that

\* Arabic is the most widely spoken mother-tongue in Africa, with Hausa in the west and Swahili in the east coming next.

most are settled farmers – though there is little similarity between the growers of cassava in the forest belt of West Africa, the growers of maize in the savanna (grassland) regions of the continent, and the growers of cash crops such as rice, cocoa, cotton, groundnuts and oil palms. Some of Africa's peoples, however, are nomadic herders, employees of large-scale agricultural and other enterprises, city dwellers, and town and country traders. Nevertheless, one experience is common to all – that of poverty, shortages and exploitation. It varies greatly, and a few do not know it at all. But such things as food shortages or imbalanced diets, inadequate farming techniques, endemic diseases, pressure on land, an infant mortality rate often as high as 40 or 50 per cent, growing unemployment, and frustrations and difficulties due to 'rising expectations' are found in all parts of Africa. No matter how much their lives may vary, cattle herders in Mali, sharecroppers in Ethiopia, fishermen in Ghana, cassava growers in the Congo Basin, and urban workers and unemployed in Lagos are all among the world's underprivileged majority.

It is against the background of the general situation of Africa that cases of modern slavery must be considered – whether they concern individual criminal actions or traditional servitude still surviving. It is above all in the Sahara Desert and its southern borderlands that traditional slavery, that is, where slaves are a separate and long-established part of society, still goes on. The Moors are perhaps the most famous example of these part-slave African peoples.

*Mauritania's 'white men', the Moors*
From the Atlas Mountains of Morocco to the mouth of the Senegal River the Sahara Desert reaches to the Atlantic, whose shores have therefore been unwelcoming to many Europeans who have since the fifteenth century, come from the sea. Generally these sailors have travelled on farther south, with the result that to this day, few parts of Africa are less known, less heard of in Europe than the western edge of the Sahara, comprising the territory of Spanish Sahara and the independent Republic of Mauritania.

This region has, however, a long recorded history, and has influenced not only the Barbary States but also Europe. Its early inhabitants were the fair-skinned Berbers (who are also found in Morocco and Algeria). In the eleventh century, Berber warriors from Mauritania conquered Morocco and Spain. They were called in Arabic 'the holy men', *al-Murabitun,* and are recalled in Spain as the Almoravides.[1] Later Shinqit, an oasis town in the north of modern Mauritania, became one of the leading cities of Islam.

The dominant people of this region are descended from the

Mauritania and its Neighbours

Sanhaja Berbers, who were converted to the Muslim faith a thousand years ago, and from the Arab invaders who came several centuries later. They speak a dialect of Arabic called Hassaniya, and are known to Europeans as Moors. (At various times a 'Moor' has meant a Moroccan, or an African, or a Muslim, but nowadays it is applied particularly to the main tribe of Hassaniya-speaking people in Mauritania and Spanish Sahara.) Since Spanish Sahara is almost uninhabited, most Moors are found in Mauritania, where they dominate the desert area which covers most of the state (the grassland region to the south is occupied by black African peoples). Like the Reguibats who also roam over the desert in Spanish Sahara, Mauritania, Morocco and Algeria, the Moors are nomads; they number about 1 million. They call themselves 'the white men', to distinguish themselves from the black African peoples who live in the grasslands, desert oases and their own encampments, where many are slaves; and they call their territory *trab-le-bidan*, or 'the land of the white men'.

The Moors, and neighbouring nomadic peoples of the desert, are some of the few groups left in Africa who have a system of slavery that differs very little from that of their ancestors. Although their French and Spanish rulers outlawed slavery, it is such an important part of their way of life that, as recent studies make quite clear, it still continues.

The desert of Mauritania and Spanish Sahara is almost entirely barren, although some parts have occasional vegetation where sheep, goats and camels can graze. Only the oases allow the cultivation of dates and other crops. The desert people are therefore forced to lead a migrant existence. There are three sorts of nomadic life among the Moors: one is confined solely to the use of camels, another (in the southern Adrar region, for example) includes sheep and goats, and a third includes cattle as well.[2] The herders of camels travel great distances since their animals, unlike sheep, cattle and goats, can go for long spells without water.

The Moorish nomads include a number of tribes, and a number of castes. The two most important castes are the warriors (*ahel-le-rkad*, men of the sword) and the men of religion (*ahel-le-klem*, men of the word).[3] It is thought that the distinction between them may be due partly to the distinction which existed between the original Berbers and the Arabs, the religious caste being more Berber, with the *murabit* (marabout, 'holy man') occupying something like the position he has among Berbers: that is as an outstanding religious leader who preaches a particular form of contact with God and who gathers disciples to follow him in this.

According to the social hierarchy of the nomads, beneath these two groups come the white Arab vassals, who traditionally paid tribute (either personal tribute, *horma*, or tribal tribute, *ghafr*) to the noble tribes, continuing to do so even after the French Administration had banned such tribute (on paper) in 1946. On a par with these Arab vassals are some sedentary or semi-sedentary peoples who are also subject, traditionally, to the nobles, for example the Imraguen, a strange tribe of fishermen found on the Atlantic coast. Below the tributary people come the travelling entertainers and smiths who, like other similar groups found in many Saharan tribes, are used for various services but are generally feared for their alleged occult knowledge and are socially despised. They are apparently of a different origin from the Moors.[4] Then come the *haratin* (singular *hartani*), the freedmen and the black non-slave people of the oases and other places of permanent settlement. Finally come the slaves. For them, as all over the Arab world, the local term is *'abid* (singular *'abd*).*

Writing about Mauritania a few years ago, A. S. Gerteiny said:

'Slavery was outlawed under colonial rule, and Mauritania's Constitution declares that all men are born free and are equal before the law, but slavery remains basic in a social and economic structure largely isolated from the outside world.

'The juridical abandonment of the term *'abd* (slave) and its replacement by the term *hartani* (freedman) for a black Moor does not hide the continued existence of slavery.'[5]

There are two kinds of slave among the Moors: the *'abd-le-tilad*, who belongs to a tent like others of the nomadic household who live and travel in the tent; and the *'abd-le-tarbiyya*, who is a slave acquired by his master after infancy. There are also a few descendants of the slaves brought from Arabia centuries ago, but today they are not only different from the other slaves, but are even considered as a respected aristocracy. The true slaves are generally black, since they probably originated in the great savanna belt of West Africa (sometimes called the Sahel or, more confusingly as there is a country of that name, the Sudan). But, as a result of marriages and liaisons between white owners and black slave girls, and the liberation and favourable treatment of at least some of the offspring, a black Moor today may be one of the aristocracy of the desert, even a chief.

A study carried out by UNESCO about the time of the independence of Mauritania (1960) said that about one-quarter of the Kounta (one of the largest Mauritanian tribes) were slaves.[6] The warrior caste owns the most slaves, although the religious caste has many. (It has been alleged that a number of Muslim black Africans from other countries, such as Mali and Senegal, have become slaves after going to Moorish marabouts for religious teaching,[7] but this is unlikely.)

Slaves are partly, but not exclusively, responsible for the cultiva-

* *'abd* has in fact many shades of meaning; it implies subjection but not necessarily property, though it is the common word for those regarded as property.

tion of the oases, where the land belongs to the white nomads. During the nomads' absence, they are responsible for keeping the farms going, and therefore they play a vital role in keeping the nomads supplied with food. One important aspect of Saharan slavery is the interdependence of the noble nomads and the slaves who do manual work for them. Other slaves, however, move about with their nomadic masters, living in their tents and doing all sorts of work for them, for example 'the most menial kind of manual labour' (as L. C. Briggs puts it),[8] or domestic work such as the brewing and serving of the mint tea which the Saharan nomads consider so important.[9]

The work is very hard, at least on occasion, but life in the desert is hard for everyone, and the tent-slaves are often treated kindly; sometimes they are brought up with the children of their owners and can even be 'milk-brothers' of those children. Such slaves are frequently freed, even when they are still young and therefore useful.[10] But while they are slaves they are regarded as property: they cannot marry and their children belong to their owner rather than to them.

Slaves brought in from outside, by purchase or capture, have a more difficult time. According to Briggs they are 'often sold again, and they enjoy no special privileges but are mere chattels'.[11] They used to be bought mainly from the salt merchants.*

*Why slavery still goes on*
According to A. S. Gerteiny, slaves in Mauritania 'are minors for life; their master is their tutor'.[12] But slavery need not always involve ill-treatment; indeed, slavery and ill-treatment should be distinguished, slavery being 'the status or condition of a person over whom any or all of the powers attaching to the right of ownership are exercised'.[13] The only general sort of ill-treatment that a slave in Mauritania experiences is the ban on family life for them.

The Moors are Muslims, and the Islamic religion regards the freeing of a slave as a worthy act. Some Muslims today maintain that their religion does not tolerate slavery at all, but the traditional opinion of Muslims, as of a great many Christians until recent times,

---

* Salt is traditionally one of the most important products of the Sahara, and there are large salt-pans in the Taoudeni region just east of the Mauritanian border with Mali. From there the salt, mined by slaves, used to be exported northwards to Morocco and southwards to the Niger valley, and until this century the traders took slaves from the Niger valley to sell to the Moors. Today trading in slaves is rare – but it may not be extinct, as will be explained shortly.

was different. The Moors, however, follow the Koran, and sometimes free their slaves.[14] The Haratin farmers who live at the oases with slaves are partly descended from other slaves and ex-slaves. They give part of their crops to the nomads who own the farms, and pay (or used to pay) tribute to them, thus remaining dependent on them. Some freed slaves remain in the service of their former masters.[15] Moreover, the nobility, as already noted, is not racially exclusive; Moorish nomad society becomes 'darker', so to speak, as one moves south towards the savanna regions of the Senegal valley, where black African peoples, such as the Fulani (or Pular or Peul), Toucouleur (or Tokolor or Halphoolaren) and Soninke (or Sarakolle), live as farmers and herdsmen.

The slaves and the Haratin are probably all Arabic-speaking, but a recent report shows that they have retained their own songs and dances, which are different from those of the Moors and no doubt originated in the Sahel.[16] But since they are deprived of a family life of their own, they are bound to be 'assimilated' eventually.

Moorish slavery is part of a social system necessitated by the conditions of desert nomad life. While the noble castes despise agricultural work, historically they had no time to do it – some were busy with religious duties, others with fighting, for the harsh conditions of desert life and the fierce rivalries which existed led to frequent raids. These raids were sometimes made over vast distances and according to only a rough set of rules. The last big raid was carried out by the Reguibats in 1934, and it was only about then that the French finished their 'pacification' of Mauritania, thus depriving the warrior caste of work. Today, the necessity of moving on with the herds makes it impossible for the nomads to stay on their oasis farms, so the farming work must be done by other people.

What keeps the Moors' system of social subordination going? Perhaps that is the wrong question to ask. In the West one is so used to old traditions changing that it seems odd when they do not. It does not seem so odd in other parts of the world, where the question asked is rather: Why should anything change?

One obvious answer to that is that things should have changed because the French administration banned slavery and was generally antipathetic to hierarchy and social subordination. But not all the French colonial officials felt like this; many of them, like their British counterparts, probably admired the Arab and nomadic way of life. Besides, there was one important practical reason for not abolishing slavery too quickly. Because the desert is so vast it is difficult to exercise any control over it. The French, therefore, had to leave the Arabs much as they were, ruling in co-operation with them. This meant recognising their rulers and leaving their social system intact, in return for allegiance to France.

In these circumstances such a total revolution as the ending of slavery would imply was impossible. It would have been so strongly resisted that warfare would have filled sixty years of the French period instead of only thirty. The slaves themselves would not have helped such a measure. They were scattered among numerous households and oases, and had no power to resist their owners. They might not even have wanted to resist them. A nomad camp is like a ship in a stormy sea – life is too precarious to make mutiny worth while unless one is driven beyond endurance. The tent-slave, tired of his lot, could see nothing in front of him except the desert stretching away to the horizon; the only alternative to a hard life was death. The French authorities with their anti-slavery laws were far away; the master was near by. For most slaves the idea of taking action to make their proclaimed freedom real must have seemed like madness. And if the French had tried to enforce the liberation of slaves, they would have been faced with the problem of where to put them, for the slaves would have had nowhere to go, no work to do, no cogent alternative to their traditional way of life.

To a great extent this is still true. The Mauritanian Government insists that there are no slaves, and its determination to ensure that there really should be none is not only as strong as one could expect, but it goes beyond the bounds of prudence. The Government has imposed its will firmly on the nomads, sometimes at least with the aim of freeing slaves.[17] But slaves so freed must go far away from their former owners, and often have nothing to do. Others no doubt know that this would happen if they were freed, and so prefer to remain as slaves.

It always sounds suspicious to say that slaves are content to remain as slaves, for everyone knows how such arguments were dishonourably used to justify the worst horrors of the 'Middle Passage' and the West Indian plantations. But the victims of those horrors were deliberately shipped to entirely new places just so their owners could profit: slave society in the New World was an artificial, imposed slave society. In this sense, slavery in Saharan society is different: only in the case of slaves being taken to dig for salt at the Taoudeni mines in the heart of the desert for a few months each year can Saharan slavery be compared to New World slavery.

Serious studies of Saharan peoples by unbiased experts confirm this. They also show that, in Mauritania, although slaves quite often leave the nomads' camp when they are near the towns or the grasslands, they tend to remain in contact with their masters and even reliant on them. Indeed, many do not leave, even when they can.

Mauritania is not simply a land of camels and date palms and nomads. Extensive iron-ore mining at Zouerate, near Fort Gouraud, has made her one of the world's leading exporters of iron-ore, and mining of copper at Akjoujt has just started. Zouerate, the port of Nouadhibou (Port Étienne), and the fantastically designed new capital Nouakchott, are centres of modern, partly Europeanised existence; and so too is Akjoujt in the far north and in a more populous area than Zouerate. Thus there are places where escaped slaves might be able to find work and start a new life. The Haratin, also, sometimes settle in the towns to form what Gerteiny calls 'a disgruntled, destitute and unmanageable urban proletariat'.[18]

Aided by the steady southward drift of the Moors, slaves and Haratin also escape to the savanna areas to the south. Some have emigrated to Senegal and Mali for good, while others (Haratin) go to Nioro, Bamako, Dakar and other places for seasonal work, returning to their fields and palm groves for the rest of the year.[19]

A glance at the rest of Africa, however, will show that migration, particularly from the country to the town, occurs throughout the continent and has nothing to do with slavery. It is due to poverty and the desire for a better life – better in terms of enjoyment, sometimes, but mainly in terms of money and the goods money can buy, the white man and the wealthier African being emulated by the mass of Africans, who think that they too can become rich in the towns. The fact that Haratin as well as slaves go to centres of 'modern' life in Mauritania indicates that such movements may not be due to slavery, still less to ill-treatment, though ill-treated slaves will no doubt take full advantage of the nearness of a place of refuge. Mlle Germaine Tillion, the French ethnologist who has studied the Sahara very thoroughly in recent years, says that the proximity of towns helps to ensure the good treatment of nomads' slaves.[20]

Many Africans who migrate to towns suffer, perhaps for years on end, the hardships of the unemployed, and those who migrate in Mauritania are no exception. But the example of other parts of Africa suggests that the hardships suffered by some who go to live in the towns do not deter others from going there. Slaves tend to remain in their homes and tents in Mauritania either because they have not the opportunity to leave (for example, for reasons of distance), or because they are reluctant to face the risks of the unknown when their present state at least ensures them a living, or because they have the lifelong habits and reactions of a slave and find it hard to imagine, still harder to face, a free life, or because they respect or feel loyal towards a particular master, especially if he has acted as their father.

This last factor is important, for reports suggest that some Saharan slaves who leave their masters still consider themselves obligated to them, and send them money. Sometimes this may be because they contract debts before they go or because they want to buy freedom for their relations still with the nomads. Sometimes a slave may be sent by his master to earn money by work or trade. But how can the master prevent such a slave from going to the authorities and being declared free? In fact, many who have the opportunity to do this do not take it because they feel that they still have ties with their owners.

Mlle Tillion relates a most extraordinary fact: that in France there are West African workers who are of servile status and who remit part of their earnings to their owners back home.[21] In that country there are thousands of West Africans doing the most menial jobs, such as sweeping the streets of Paris. Most come from Senegal, Mali and Mauritania, the poor countries relatively near to France. They send remittances home, which provide foreign currency for their countries and help to keep many families alive. And these families, it seems, include slave-owners.

Why do the slaves send this money? In France no one can force them to do so. But if it is expected of them, they may feel obliged to send it, and since many want to return home eventually, they cannot risk flouting the conventions of home. A slave may well regard his master and his master's family as his own family; few of us want to feel totally unattached. If he has been brought up in his owner's tent, he may feel as much obligation to him as a son does to his father. All these considerations may make a West African slave in France (quite likely to be Mauritanian) send money to a master thousands of miles away.

Mlle Tillion has also written – again without referring to any particular country – of 'the case of the two ageing sisters with practically no means of livelihood, whose only possession was a half-share in a slave which they had inherited and who supported them, thanks to his salary as a schoolmaster.

'For these two old women the half-share in the slave was all that stood between them and starvation. The slave himself would have thought and would still think, like the rest of the community in which he lived, that to abandon them would be dishonourable.'[22]

Whether this case occurred in Mauritania or not, such cases quite probably arise there, especially now that the mines pay such high wages that slaves can become richer than their masters. When this happens, it is not surprising that the slaves and ex-slaves who have settled in France, Senegal or other parts of Mauritania continue to feel attached to their masters whom they have left behind.

*The future for Moors' slaves*
All this illustrates the point that slavery in the Sahara is not like slavery in the Deep South. It is a natural and almost a necessary part of the life of the desert nomads, which has always required that some people should be free to move about with the camels and herds while others must keep the oases cultivated and prevent the desert from encroaching on the scarce farmland. Some of the conditions which originally gave rise to Saharan slavery have changed, but the slave/master relationship has become engrained.

The impression given by recent studies, however, is that traditional slavery is probably in decline. The development of towns and mining centres may affect nomadic life only very slowly, but it is unlikely that it will not affect it at all. It is also unlikely that the general drift in Africa towards more prosperous agricultural regions, towards towns, and (for a few) towards Europe, will not continue in Mauritania. Probably it will also occur in Spanish Sahara, where there is already a non-nomadic proletariat at El Aiún and where the phosphate mines could have the same effect as the mines in Mauritania. If people leave the desert life, even when they have been free there, the process could be self-perpetuating; as more and more slaves and Haratin leave the oases, so the desert encroaches further, and it becomes more difficult for the nomads to continue their traditional way of life. This process must have been hastened by the disastrous drought of the early 1970s.

In the long run, the danger of a collapse of nomadic life may be greater than the danger of continued large-scale domestic slavery. And one does not need to share the sentimentality of some travellers about the life of desert nomads to realise that the general abandonment of it would do little good. What alternative to it is there for most of the hundreds of thousands of nomads, slave and free, in Mauritania?

But, I suggest, there are three reasons why the enforcement of the Mauritanian Government's scheme to abolish slavery will be welcome. First, the mere fact that a large number of people are held in a menial, subject status where they are denied many rights – including the most important right of all, that is the right to marry and have a family life of their own – is disgraceful. 'Slaves are never married; they are bred', says Gerteiny, adding that in some tribes the children of a female slave automatically belong to the master of their father.[23] The mere fact that many Mauritanian slaves (perhaps not all) have no rights over their own children cancels out a great deal of the good treatment they may receive in other respects. The practical difficulties involved in liberation do not alter the shameful nature of slavery which gives an owner rights over his slave's children.

Second, the continued enslavement of black people by Arabs in Mauritania does not encourage the peaceful coexistence of the white and black communities in that country, even though probably only a few slaves are closely related to the free black people of the south. The two main communities in Mauritania are united only by Islam, and the efforts of the Ould Daddah Government to enforce the use of Arabic in schools has been strongly opposed by the black African community. Feelings of superiority on the part of the Moors, which may lie behind this move, must surely be perpetuated by their continued enslavement of some black people in their tents and oases.

Third, while slavery continues there can be no real guarantee against the capture or purchase of new slaves.

In 1962–3 André Chalard, a French schoolteacher at Tindouf (in the Algerian Sahara near the borders with Morocco and Mauritania), found that slavery was widespread there. He intervened on behalf of a slave family whose only daughter, Aouicha, a pupil at his school, was threatened with sale by her father's master. For his protests Chalard was expelled from Algeria. Together with Jacob Oliel, also expelled from Algeria for reporting on cases of slavery in contradiction to the Algerian Government's denial that slavery existed, he founded *Action pour l'Abolition de l'Esclavage* in Paris. This society, with a committee of distinguished people (including Mlle Tillion, the Africanist Théodore Monod, Pastor la Gravière, the veteran jurist and Nobel prizewinner René Cassin, the former minister Robert Buron, and another Africanist, the late Jean-Claude Froelich) does similar work to the Anti-Slavery Society in London. It made particular efforts to have Aouicha and her family freed from slavery. Chalard and his colleagues wrote ceaselessly to the Algerian authorities, who after a public meeting held by *Action pour l'Abolition de l'Esclavage* on 3rd May, 1966 at last sent news of the family. But although the Algerian Minister of Justice announced that her father, mother and two sisters had been freed from slavery, Aouicha herself in the meantime had been taken to Mauritania. She was no more than ten years old. Efforts to have her freed by the Mauritanian authorities were unsuccessful; one could hardly expect them to find one child in the desert.[24] If Aouicha has not been freed since then she may perhaps escape when she grows older. But, of course, it is less easy for women to escape, as greater care is probably taken to stop them fleeing, for they are valuable – besides satisfying their owner they can also produce new slaves.

One would like to feel that this sad case was the exception rather than the rule. It was not, for kidnapping – a sadly universal crime – is aided and encouraged by the presence near by of people willing to purchase kidnapped children as slaves. This happens quite often in the regions bordering the Sahara. Mlle Tillion mentions cases in the Senegal River valley of shepherd boys and girls of ten to twelve years of age being kidnapped and taken into Mauritania.[25]

The growth of towns and other modern centres may make such crimes more frequent, not less. Chapter Eleven shows how the poverty, the struggle for an easier life, and the breakdown of the family ties and old traditions which characterise African towns create new opportunities for all sorts of crime. Destitute people in the towns are easy victims for kidnappers. For this reason, hasty abolition of slavery may have the opposite effect to that intended. On the other hand, the existence of a 'market' for kidnapped people in nomad camps encourages odious crimes to an extent hard to tolerate. Obviously, prevention of kidnapping is a priority which cannot wait for total abolition of slavery. But crime is so difficult to prevent in Africa that, while there is demand anywhere for slaves, they will continue to be provided somehow.

Ways in which it might be possible to hasten the disappearance of slavery without harming the slaves themselves will be discussed more fully in the last chapter. In the case of Mauritania, one point to bear in mind is that any way will certainly be slow. The end of slavery among the Moors, very desirable for the reasons mentioned, will not come in a hurry.

*Notes*

1. E. W. Bovill, *The Golden Trade of the Moors*, pp. 72 ff.
2. A. S. Gerteiny, *Mauritania*, p. 14.
3. Ibid., pp. 47–8.
4. Ibid., pp. 50–6; Claude Bataillon *et al.*, *Nomades et Nomadisme au Sahara* (study for UNESCO), p. 70; L. C. Briggs, *Living Races of the Sahara Desert*, p. 80.
5. Gerteiny, op. cit., p. 52.
6. Bataillon *et al.*, op. cit., p. 31.
7. Gerteiny, op. cit., pp. 51–2.
8. L. C. Briggs, *Tribes of the Sahara*, p. 93.

19. Gerteiny, op. cit., pp. 58–65.
10. Briggs, *Tribes of the Sahara*, p. 235.
11. Ibid.
12. Gerteiny, op. cit., p. 52.
13. As defined in the 1926 Convention.
14. Gerteiny, op. cit., p. 52; Briggs, *Tribes of the Sahara*, p. 235.
15. Briggs, *Tribes of the Sahara*. p. 235.
16. Attilio Gaudio in *Jeune Afrique* (17th August, 1971).
17. G. Tillion in 'The Problem of Slavery', an eight-page pamphlet issued by *Action pour l'Abolition de l'Esclavage* and the Anti-Slavery Society, p. 3.
18. Gerteiny, p. 52.
19. Bataillon *et al.*, op. cit., pp. 76–7.
20. Ibid., p. 5.
21. Ibid.
22. Ibid.
23. Gerteiny, op. cit., p. 52.
24. Annual Report of the Anti-Slavery Society (1966–7), pp. 3–4; *The Anti-Slavery Society: Its Task Today*, p. 12.
25. 'The Problem of Slavery,' p. 4.

*Chapter Two*

# Tuareg and other Sahara Slaves

The Sahara Desert, which includes high mountains and jagged regions of black rock as well as large areas of sand, has other inhabitants besides the Moors. But life in the desert or on its borders is to some extent similar for all these different peoples. And it is similar for some of the inhabitants of the savanna lands south of the desert, for life is sometimes not much less harsh there than it is in the Sahara itself, and a nomadic existence is necessary for hundreds of thousands of cattle herders. It is among these nomads of the desert and the near by grassland regions that slavery has lasted particularly well.

Of all the West African nomads, those best known to Europeans are probably the Tuareg.* They have lived for centuries in the mountainous regions of the central Sahara (the mountains of the Ahaggar or Hoggar, the Tassili, the Adrar des Iforas, and the Aïr or Azbine) and in the sub-desert areas further south, in the territory now covered by the states of Mali and Niger. Nearly all the Tuareg today live in these sub-desert steppe lands, though the desert has been moving south after them. Only a few thousand still live in the deep desert of the Ahaggar mountains. But the territory of the Tuareg is not fixed; as nomads they roam over large distances, going south of the Niger River at its central 'bend' where Timbuktu is situated, and east over the Aïr plateau and beyond. As traders, many have gone to Kano in Nigeria.

It is a mistake to regard all parts of the Sahara as totally barren. Some tough plants and animals can survive in many parts of it, and there are large areas, not necessarily at the edges, where nomads who know the desert well can find grass for their cattle and sheep, water for themselves and their animals, and perhaps some wild animals to hunt. The Tuareg cultivate plots of land by the Niger River, at oases and in other places where millet, dates and other

* Strictly, 'Tuareg' is the plural form, the singular being 'Targui', but the former is commonly used for both singular and plural.

crops can be grown. As among the Moors, this farming is an important part of the work left to the slaves. Also as among the Moors, the white nomads have for generations obtained slaves from the south, and today large numbers of Tuareg – Tuareg in language and culture – are black.

The Tuareg are divided into several clans, such as the Kel Antessar who live north of the once legendary Timbuktu, and the Ioullemeden who roam over a wide area in modern Mali and Niger. The members of these clans have much in common; they all speak Tamashek, a language which is not closely related to the Arabic of the Moors but is a Berber language akin to that spoken in Morocco and Algeria. This fact, and various others, have made the question of the Tuareg's origin and history fascinating to the Europeans who have written about them. These writers, of whom the first to make

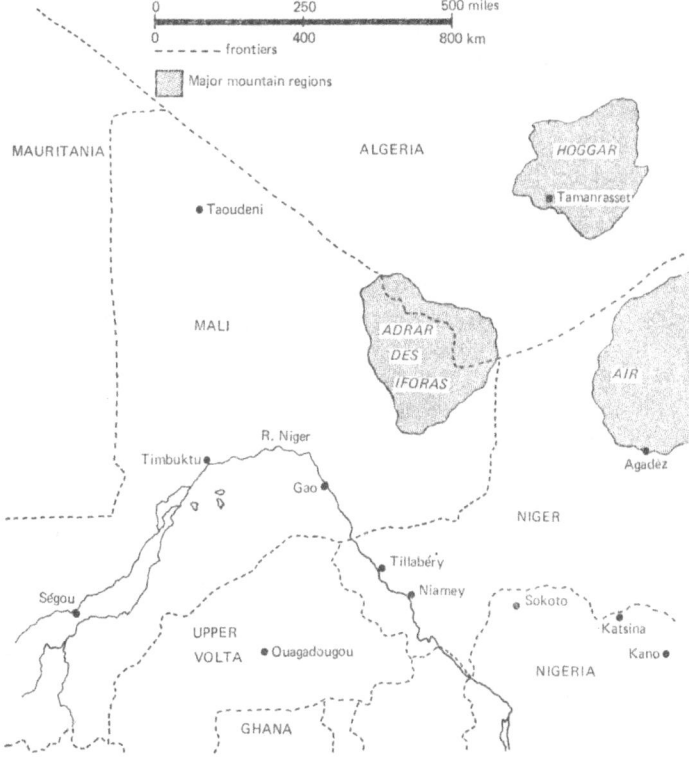

The Central Sahara

a close study was the Frenchman Henri Duveyrier in the mid-nineteenth century, have also been intrigued by the Tuareg's way of life and one particular custom of theirs: the wearing of the veil by the men and not, as among so many of their fellow Muslims, by the women.

In the nineteenth century, the Tuareg controlled the central Sahara desert and its trade. Their rulers, such as the Amenokal of the Ahaggar, had for the previous century or more dominated, politically as well as commercially, a large region of the Sahara and the Sahel (savanna), including the trade-routes leading northward from Timbuktu and Kano. They helped the caravans by digging wells for them and by acting as guides; but in return they expected tribute from them, though never more than the traders could pay without being ruined. The Tuareg clung jealously to their control of the desert trade, and this was no doubt one reason why they were hostile to Gordon Laing, the Scots traveller who went to Timbuktu in 1825–6 (though it was not they who killed him), and why in 1881 they caused the death amid great suffering of the French expedition of Colonel Flatters, whose aim, a railway across the Sahara, would have seriously affected their position. Colonial rule – which was French rule for all the area of the Tuareg – eventually did undermine their position, but it was not imposed at all easily on the former lords of the desert, who have shown in recent years that their independent spirit is not dead.

Slaves were an important element in the old trans-Saharan trade (see p. 46). The Tuareg bought or seized slaves from the black peoples of the south for themselves, too. This was largely stopped after the Tuareg were defeated by the French Saharan Camel Corps and the Foreign Legion at the Battle of Tit in 1902, and brought under French rule in the French Sudan (now Mali), Niger and the Southern Territories of Algeria; but domestic slavery continued among them, as it did in Mauritania further west. The French Colonial Government realised that the abolition of slavery could not be achieved easily or quickly, and that nomads could not simply be coerced into the sweeping changes that this would involve.

Tuareg society – like that of the Moors – has many divisions apart from that between free and slave. There are noble tribes and vassal tribes (for example, in the Ahaggar the latter pay tribute in dates, millet or baby camels to the Amenokal).* Then there are

---

* This monarch rules in the Algerian Sahara where he is the successor of the ruler well known to students of the life of Charles de Foucauld, the French hermit who knew the Tuareg and studied their language and life so well.[1] Traditionally, the Amenokal lived by tribute, rent being owed to him

tributary clans (called *Imrad* in Tamashek), warrior clans (called *Imouchar, Imajeren*), and religious clans (called *Ineslimen, Cheriffen*). Also, as among the Moors, there is a separate caste of blacksmiths (called *Enaden* in Tamashek) who are of mysterious origin and are feared and despised as an inferior caste, but are believed to have secret powers. And finally there are the slaves, whom the Tuareg call *Iklan*.[3]

The Tuareg of all classes are Muslims. Because they use the symbol of the cross, and have some names more typical of Christians than of Muslims, it has been supposed that they were once Christians or at least came into contact with Christianity at some time in their history. This is not improbable if the Tuareg lived in, or nearer to, the Berber regions of North Africa in the days when these were a leading centre of the Christian faith.†

The old activities of these blue-robed desert warriors, including their well organised *razzias* or raids and their control of caravan traffic, have ended. The Tuareg now live by stock-rearing and farming, as already mentioned, and by trade. For all these three activities, in both the desert and the grasslands, slaves are important.

About ten years ago a UNESCO survey of nomadic life in the Sahara found that the proportion of slaves among the Tuareg, who numbered 465,000, varied from region to region; one in seven was a slave in the Adrar, between one in six and one in three in the Ahaggar, and one in three in the Aïr.[6] Going further south into the grasslands, it was found that the proportion of slaves increased the further away the nomads were from the real desert; among the Ioullemeden one in two were slaves, and among the Tuareg of Gourma, south of the Niger bend, no less than three out of four were slaves.‡

So slavery is part of nomadic life not only in the Sahara itself but also in the savanna areas to the south, where life is easier than in

---

for pasture land and for the plots worked – often by slaves, but not always, as will be explained later – at points where the nomads halted.[2]

† This is a historical mystery, like the mystery surrounding the tomb of Queen Tin Hinan in the Ahaggar,[4] and that of the origin of the men's veils. E. W. Bovill, who became interested in the old trans-Sahara trade from the Nigerian end when he was serving there in the army in 1918–19, and later wrote two fascinating and scholarly books on the subject (*Caravans of the Old Sahara* and *The Golden Trade of the Moors*), said that 'no fully convincing explanation' had been put forward for the Tuareg's veils.[5] Many believe, however, that they are simply intended to keep dust and sand out of the faces of the men as they ride their camels.

‡ Johannes Nicolaisen (see note 15) gave at the same period a very different picture of the Aïr, where, he said, slavery was almost insignificant.

the desert (though still not very easy, especially after the repeated droughts of recent years) and where the possibilities of escape are far greater. But as in the case of the Moors, in the Sahara a slave does not necessarily try to escape even though he has the opportunity to do so. It is hard to attribute this to the fact that the only alternative to slavery is starvation, though it is true that large parts of the grasslands of Mali and Niger are almost as barren as the desert, so this alternative may be present for many.

Slavery has traditionally been a necessary part of the life of the nomads. The slaves cared for the cattle, sheep and camels, leaving the noble and vassal freemen of the Tuareg free to fight, raid and govern. This division of labour has become so hardened by custom, that the free men and women remain averse to manual work, although the free men still have work to do, for example in seeking pastures and acting as scouts.[7]

The slaves also do manual work for their Tuareg masters at desert oases, around wells, and along the Niger River. The nomads own the land and provide it for cultivation, sometimes making use of a *foqqara* – the remarkable underground water supply system used in the Sahara, with shafts leading down to the large supplies of water which lie below the surface. Cultivation, for example of wheat, barley, millet and dates, is not done exclusively by slaves. There are also ex-slaves who, on their release, are given land by their former owners. And there are also the Haratin, a group of people of (at least partly) ex-slave origin but different from the slaves and recent ex-slaves of known and fairly recent Sudanese origin.\* As already noted, they are also found in Mauritania further west, but there the term is applied, at least officially, to all the black people of traditional servile or menial status living among the Moors; whereas both there and further east it is commonly applied to a group of people separate from the Sudanese slaves and ex-slaves. They are black, but different in appearance from the Africans from the south, who often retain traces in their language and culture of their origin among the Bambara and other tribes in the Sudanic belt. It has been suggested, for example by L. C. Briggs, that the Haratin are descended from the original inhabitants of the Sahara region, the people who executed the famous cave paintings found all over the desert.[8]

Whatever their origin, today they are tenants of the Tuareg in many oases; in the Ahaggar they pay a third of their produce to the Amenokal. There are other sharecroppers farming land for Tuareg

\* The term 'Sudan' is here used as another term for the whole savanna or Sahelian belt of West Africa; it originally means 'Land of the Blacks'.

owners, sometimes paying a bushel of grain as rent for each plot of land.[9] According to Briggs,[10] the Haratin for some time have been coming to take over cultivation increasingly from slaves.

Freed slaves who have been allocated land by their ex-owners remain their sharecropping tenants – at least around Lake Faguibine near the Niger River, where they cultivate land belonging to families or chieftancies of the Kel Antessar Tuareg, their former owners. Along this river at its bend, black people have for long been in varying states of dependence, often as actual slaves, on the Tuareg nomads of the area.[11] 'Bela' is a collective name for these enslaved or subject black people.

The produce of the herds which the slaves look after, and of the land which they cultivate to some extent, is not used only to feed them and their masters. Some is also sold; the Ahaggar Tuareg sell the wheat and barley which they grow, and buy millet from the Sahel to the south.[12] So trade is also dependent on slave work, especially as salt, another important article of the desert trade of the Tuareg, is dug by slaves deep in the desert. Ten years ago a UNESCO survey described in detail the trade in salt and other articles of the Ahaggar Tuareg, making it clear that the actual work of trading was also left to the slaves. According to this survey, every April or May, slaves generally take a barter caravan north-eastwards to find salt. They then take the salt south to the Tamesna and Damergou areas to exchange it for arms, saddles, sandals, dry cheese, millet or dates. The size of these caravans has been diminishing; in the early 1960s there were 3,000–4,000 camels per year, compared with 5,000–6,000 in 1938. In the early 1960s each caravan had about 100 camels, one in every four or five carrying salt.[13] The Sahel drought and famine must have altered all this considerably.

The slaves who look after the herds are often left alone with them for some time, while the slaves who cultivate the plots are necessarily left alone for long periods. But they may not be any better off materially than the slaves who remain close to their masters. These, whether they do domestic or herding work, are said to be generally well cared for, except – and an important exception – for the definite hardships and dangers of the herd-watching job. Besides this job, slaves may serve food, pound millet and fetch cow-dung (for fuel) or wood, as Robin Maugham, a British visitor to a Tuareg camp near the Niger in French Sudan, noted in 1959.[14]

*The slave in the household*
Clearly the slaves' lot depends on that of the whole community, and it can vary greatly from year to year. When there is plenty of

rain in the grasslands, animals and their milk (partly for butter and cheese) are plentiful and trade can prosper; but normally, four years out of ten are dry and many of the animals die – in parts of Mali and Niger where many Tuareg live, seven whole years have recently passed without adequate rain.

While such changes of fortune affect a slave's daily life considerably, he always remains his master's property and is considered legally on the same level as a child, however old he may be.[15] He is not, however, without rights. Even the master's right of property is not absolute because he cannot normally sell a slave, who instead remains with him until his death when he is inherited within the family. If a slave is ill-treated he can change his master, at least sometimes; in the Ahaggar he can do this by choosing a new master and then cutting off part of one ear of a camel belonging to that man, after which he (the slave) is automatically taken by the camel's owner as compensation for the damage to the beast, and the original owner cannot reclaim the slave.[16] The old owner will consider this a disgrace to him, best avoided. A slave on good terms with his master may be given she-goats by him. These are in full property, except that his children cannot inherit them as his master reclaims them on his death.

As among the Moors, to some extent the children of Tuareg slaves are treated as part of the master's family. But there is one great difference between the two peoples: whereas the Tuareg slaves may marry and their children are considered as at least partly their own, among the Moors there is a ban on marriage and family life. The Tuareg slave must get his master's consent for the marriage, but if he agrees to it the master will often advance the 'bride-price' (this is paid to the bride's family by the bridegroom at a marriage among the Tuareg, as among black African peoples).[17] However, the slave himself can be part of the bride-price offered by a free man getting married.[18]

Tuareg slaves can be involved in a complicated set of relationships. In many ways, as in the matters of marriage and the bride-price, the master is considered as a father. When a married woman owns slaves (as happens often because Tuareg wives have considerable independence), her husband seems to be considered as having something like a stepfather's relationship to them; a man is not supposed to marry the slave of his divorced or dead wife, this being legally seen as incestuous.[19]

According to a study made ten years ago by Johannes Nicolaisen, the confusion between real and legal parentage works both ways.[20] A slave girl who nurses a free Tuareg child (female) and considers her as her own, may come to be regarded as the real mother, and her real children as the other child's brothers and sisters. If this happens it naturally follows that the child of a slave is not necessarily a slave himself. Nicolaisen notes, in fact, that it is easier for a Tuareg noble to marry a slave girl than a Tuareg vassal tribeswoman, for marrying the latter would upset the political structure, and his child by the slave wife can be a noble. While the Koran's ruling that the offspring of a free father and a slave mother should be considered as legitimate may not always be followed by the Tuareg, there is no rigid caste system. Indeed, Nicolaisen thinks that slavery is not really a caste or social class among the Tuareg at all; a leading chief of the Tassili Tuareg was of a slave family.

It may be rare for a slave to be sold outside his owner's family, as Nicolaisen said, but it is not unknown. In the late 1950s L. C. Briggs claimed that Tuareg slaves were 'chattels which can be bought, sold and inherited'.[21] About the same time, Robin Maugham (now Viscount Maugham) proved that they could be bought, in the most conclusive way – by buying one. He described this, and what he saw of Tuareg slavery around the Niger bend, in his book *The Slaves of Timbuktu*. Visiting that once fabulous town, he found that the Bela were often slaves of the Tuareg. Many lived in grass huts on the outskirts of Timbuktu. 'They may work on their own, growing millet or water-melons; they are probably aware that by law they are free men; but they still owe allegiance to their masters.'[22] Many people told him that the Bela were so used to thinking of themselves as slaves, and the Tuareg were so used to treating them as such, that the old relationship remained unchanged; slaves did not take the opportunity of getting the French administrator to declare them free.[23]

Maugham met people who talked to him freely of the buying and selling of Bela slaves. One ex-slave in his sixties, Assali ag Zeda, described how he had been sold in his youth and had escaped later, but had paid his master for formal manumission to make doubly sure of his freedom.[24] Another ageing man, Bu'ana Salah ag Alijumaa, who had been a slave all his life, described the old open slave-market at Timbuktu.[25] An aristocratic Tuareg named Salehoun said: 'We used to sell our Bela just like cattle. You'd drive your herd of sheep into market and the Bela as well and sell both of them together.'[26] The French, said another noble, had stopped open slave-trading, but slaves still changed hands in private. Maugham and his travelling companion then went to a camp outside the town and bought a slave, whom they immediately freed as arranged.[27]

Maugham found that the life of Tuareg slaves was harsh, and

heard many stories of cruelty towards them, as well as of open and brutal efforts by Tuareg masters to recover runaway slaves. Specific cases of this in the Niger bend area were described, including one of a Tuareg attacking a family of ex-slaves in the Gourma area to punish them.[28] He also heard of a Bela slave at the Taoudeni salt-mines who had been captured by a Reguibat. Then there was the story of a chief who had taken some Bela to Mecca and sold them in Saudi Arabia to pay for his stay and his return journey.[29] This was not the only case of its kind. The most famous case was that of Awd el Joud, slave or servant of a chief of the Kel Antessar Tuareg, Mohammed Ali ag Attaher (see p. 141). Even when they did not suffer like this, Tuareg slaves were often maltreated by their masters, as stories told to Maugham made clear. As in other slave societies, everything depends on the individual master.

*The French and the Tuareg*

If buying and selling of slaves was still possible in 1959, raiding for them had probably ended some time before, apart from isolated kidnappings. Briggs met a woman who had been captured in the Aïr in a raid over thirty years before.[30] This was possibly one of the last of the great desert *razzias*, which ended in this region in 1928.

That date, it will be noted, was long after the establishment of French rule. In fact, it was almost as difficult to impose effective rule in the Tuareg's stretch of the desert as it had been in Mauritania; the Méharistes (the Saharan Camel Corps), the Legion and other forces found it difficult to patrol such a vast area effectively, and the Tuareg resisted French rule strongly. In 1916–17 they rebelled, together with other peoples of the desert, particularly the Arabs of the Senussi order in Italian Libya. Charles de Foucauld, who was considered as a *marabout* by the Ahaggar Tuareg, was killed at Tamanrasset in the course of this rebellion. It covered a very large area, and the fighting in the Aïr uplands was particularly severe.

After suppressing the uprising, the French tried to hasten the emancipation of slaves, which had been proclaimed but not enforced. But they never wanted to change completely the Tuareg's way of life: slavery had in practice to be tolerated. What the French tried to do was to improve the condition of the slaves. They introduced medical treatment, with the result that the slaves benefited more than their masters (presumably because they were often sedentary while their nomadic masters might be away when medical teams came). They also encouraged efforts to have slaves set free and given cattle or land. There was also a tendency towards liberation of at least some slaves in the Sahel, where the Tuareg population has been migrating for decades and where the proportion of slaves has been the highest. All this was more helpful than freeing the slaves without providing for their future. But the people so freed could easily remain dependent on their former masters, as already shown. The number of slaves, however, fell. The Kel Antessar, once 90 per cent slave, in recent times came to be divided into three main groups: former masters, with their tent slaves; ex-slave herdsmen, sometimes as rich as the former masters; and ex-slave farmers.[31]

Not all freed slaves obtained real economic freedom, and not all slaves seriously tried to obtain any freedom. The French Administration could not everywhere be as powerful as the Tuareg slave-owners and it had to work together with the slave-owners to some extent. In the eyes of the Tuareg and the other local peoples, as Maugham found, manumission by a master was more valid than liberation ordered by the French.

The construction of roads, the starting of new wage-paying enterprises, and other sorts of colonial development brought about some changes. But, with the exception of the large agricultural scheme of the *Office du Niger* in the area of the Niger's 'inland delta' upstream from Timbuktu, such projects have been insignificant in the middle Niger area where most Tuareg live, and have remained insignificant there until today. Strangely, there were more modern economic projects in the last stages of French rule in the desert than in the savanna, mainly because of the discovery of oil in the Algerian Sahara and the nuclear test programme there. These projects created job-opportunities in new areas, Tamanrasset being one of these centres of activity.

Only the Haratin and freed black slaves, among the Tuareg of the Algerian Sahara, took up these opportunities. The Administration tried to stop them leaving the nomad camps and oases, but many continued to do so, with the result that in the early 1960s it was reported that the Ahaggar Tuareg risked losing their shepherds, caravan drivers and domestic servants. The noble Tuareg did not want to do manual work, although some who had been to school obtained office jobs in Tamanrasset (and no doubt this has continued). But in the early 1960s their traditional position began to be seriously threatened. In the last years of their rule in Algeria, the French enforced new reforms, including the granting of legal titles of ownership to sharecropper tenants of the Tuareg. In 1960 tribute was legally abolished, and the Amenokal was given an allowance in lieu of his tribute. In fact, payment of tribute continued,[32] but with the reforms and the introduction of paid labour (which could make oasis-dwellers 'rich') the desert Tuareg's situation changed. But only to a certain extent. In 1963 it emerged that the introduction of wage-paid labour was not leading to the emancipation of slaves at all.

*After independence*
Jacques Pucheu, a French teacher at Tamanrasset and one of a number of French observers who have witnessed slavery recently in the Algerian Sahara, said that in 1963 there were about 2,000 slaves in the Tamanrasset area, including some who worked at the nuclear-fission plant at In Ekkor. On 20th July, 1963 he wrote to the Algeria President, Ben Bella, saying: 'Many slaves work at the present time at the atomic energy base of In Ekkor. I know their Tuareg masters, they live directly off their wages and take two-thirds of their pay packets.' He mentioned one slave, 'O', who, three years before, had been sold for 100,000 old French francs and was still enslaved, though he had repaid this sum to his master many times over.[33]

This state of affairs seems all the more remarkable when one recalls that the free Tuareg of the Ahaggar then probably numbered not much more than 2,000, and had been losing power and influence for many years. In spite of this, it seems, slaves who could have won some real freedom by their earnings at In Ekkor paid two-thirds of their wages to the free Tuareg. This is an enormous proportion, even if it includes rent for oasis land, as it could have done despite the French efforts a few years before to make the oasis cultivators owners of their land. It is very likely that the freemen became dependent on the slaves after these obtained jobs at the nuclear installations, and that it was not mere physical force that made the slaves subsidise their nomadic 'masters' and shore up the threatened nomad way of life.

The continual migration of Tuareg southwards means that their desert way of life may not last much longer. Its end has been hastened in the most brutal way in the Adrar des Iforas mountains by the war which was fought there for several years in the 1960s between rebel Tuareg and the Malian Government of Modibo Keita. This was one of the 'forgotten wars', hardly noticed by the outside world; but reports which did emerge suggest that the Malian régime suppressed the Adrar Tuareg with the utmost ferocity, killing huge numbers of them. The Adrar Tuareg resisted fiercely, according to their old traditions, and were supported to some extent by other Tuareg in the Niger Republic, the frontier being no problem for them. But by the time Keita had been overthrown in an army *coup d'état* in 1968, they had been fairly thoroughly defeated. Major Silas Diarra Diby, a notable butcher of the Tuareg during the fighting, later quarrelled with other senior officers and was gaoled by them; now he is reported to have died in one of the terrible desert prison camps maintained by successive Malian régimes.

Other Tuareg in Mali were not involved in these events, and Tamashek is listed as one of the national languages of that state. Nowadays nearly all Tuareg live in Mali and Niger. In Niger a black Tuareg, Mouddour Zakara, is a leading politician; when he accompanied his President, Hamani Diori, on an official visit to Britain in 1969 (he was then, appropriately, Minister for Nomadic Affairs), he impressed the British with his imposing presence and nomadic garb.

It is impossible to assess exactly how many black Tuareg remain in conditions of near-slavery in Niger and Mali. The Mali Government in 1964 made a fairly thorough reply to the slavery questionnaire issued by the UN Special Rapporteur on Slavery, Dr Awad; but his report in 1965 did not add much to the information gathered by the UNESCO survey a few years earlier. That survey, as already noted, found that the trend had for long been towards the emancipation of nomads' slaves. But this is bound to be a slow process because there is not much work available for freed slaves once they have left their masters. The region over which Tuareg nomads roam is one of the poorest in the whole of Africa. Agriculture and stockbreeding remain the major sources of income – and not very good ones – for most of the population. Wage employment is limited, though some is offered in towns like Niamey, and in Nigeria, and at the uranium-mines in the Aïr, while the 'Liptako-Gourma' regional development plan envisages long-term possibilities. For the present, these schemes are less important than the catastrophic drought which has recently hit the whole area.

Since 1970 rainfall has been insufficient all over the Sahel, from Senegal to Chad, and in some parts of Mali there has been no proper rain for seven years. In 1972–3 a total drought brought the threat of famine to these areas. Thousands of cattle died, and in Niger and Chad people began trekking south to seek a new life. In Mauritania, where four-fifths of the cattle have been killed by the drought (and it is certain that numbers of people have also died), the situation has been particularly bad. In Mali it is bad too, especially as the military régime went on collecting cattle-tax on dead cattle long after the drought became disastrous, only suspending it very belatedly. The drought has been serious in Northern Nigeria too, causing failure of food crops, though this area is relatively better off than Mali or Chad in terms of income and communications.

When conditions are as bad as this (and they will not improve overnight), it is almost frivolous to pay too much attention to slavery. The release of slaves has obviously been hampered, and the re-enslavement of some ex-captives made easier, by the threat of famine. One can safely assume that the Tuaregs' remaining slaves have not chosen this period to exchange a situation where, to some extent, they can at least eat, for the hazards of a new life where in practice freedom means very little. Those slaves who have been sent to the towns to earn money probably prefer to remain attached to their masters in the nomad camps since this gives them some security. Thousands of Niger and Mali Tuareg have moved into Nigeria. And even when the present emergency has passed, the region will remain in a state of perpetual emergency. Slavery cannot be isolated from the general problems caused by this.

*The Sahara Desert 'middle passage'*
Besides the slavery practised by its nomadic dwellers, the Sahara Desert has witnessed over the centuries a terrible trade in slaves from south to north, surpassed only in the numbers involved, not in human suffering, by the Atlantic slave-trade. Probably the occasional slave is taken across the desert even today, but the old, large-scale trans-Sahara slave-trade ended early this century.

In the nineteenth century British Governments tried to stop this trade, appointing consuls at the desert trading centres of Murzuk and Ghadames and putting pressure on the Bey of Tunis to abolish slavery, which he did as early as 1846. It was a desire to abolish the trans-Sahara slave-trade that prompted the British Government to send Richardson and Barth on an expedition from Tripoli to the lands south of the desert in 1850, an expedition which lasted five years and led to Heinrich Barth's excellent, three-volume description of Hausaland, Bornu, Timbuktu and other Sudanic regions.[34]

There were four main Sahara trade-routes in the nineteenth century: from Timbuktu to Morocco, past the Taoudeni salt-mines; from Kano to Ghadames via the Aïr; from Bornu, the old and strong kingdom west of Lake Chad, to Tripoli via the Fezzan; and from Wadai, a powerful sultanate east of Lake Chad to Cyrenaica via the Kufra oases.[35] The second and the fourth were the most important during that century, particularly the second whose terminus was Kano (earlier Katsina had been more important). In that old trading city much has been preserved from the days of its eminence in the trans-Saharan trade, of which Barth has left a vivid description in his study. At the northern end caravans assembled at such places as Sijilmassa, on the southern slopes of the

Moroccan Atlas, and Ghadames.[36] Murzuk was the chief slave-market of the Sahara in the early nineteenth century. Besides slaves, the north-bound exports assembled at Kano and other places included cloth, hides, leather goods, ivory, kola nuts (a stimulant permitted to non-alcoholic Muslims) and civet. Imports from across the Sahara included British cotton prints, silks, muslins, writing paper, Italian beads, sword blades, needles, razors, snuff-boxes, and North African carpets and red caps.[37]

For the slaves, the crossing of the Sahara was a fearful ordeal. 'The men, who were mostly youths, were coupled with leg-irons and chain by the neck,' writes Bovill, 'but the women and girls were usually allowed to go free. Only the strongest survived the desert march, and these were little better than living skeletons by the time they reached Fezzan.'[38] Skeletons of many slaves were to be seen along the trade-routes.

The slaves for this trade were often caught in raids on the 'Pagan' (i.e. non-Muslim) tribes of what is now called simply 'The Plateau' in Nigeria. Some slaves were castrated, and as (according to Barth) only one in ten survived that operation, many more slaves were caught than were sold, and many more were sold than reached their destination. As the same was true of the transatlantic slave-trade (where castration seems, however, not to have been current), the effect on Western Africa of these two slave-trades, whose sources of supply overlapped, can be imagined. Eunuchs are familiar figures in many old accounts of Turkey, Egypt and other Near-Eastern countries (and, as Bovill points out, the Vatican). If the famous Egyptian mamelukes were often white, other eunuchs, used as soldiers or harem guards in many places, could be black. So were many inmates of the harems.

Generally, African slaves were in demand from Morocco eastwards throughout the Muslim world. In Morocco the famous Black Guard was made up of captive Africans (like other slave armies, it was used because the slaves, cut off from home and family, had no loyalties to anyone but their ruler and master). Many of the slaves who reached the Mediterranean were sent on to Constantinople, but the black slave element was particularly important on the southern shores of the Mediterranean, and today many Moroccans, Algerians and Tunisians are of black African descent. They have not lost all trace of their African origins; in the Kabyle (Berber) region of Algeria there is a secret religious cult of partly African non-Muslim origin.

With abolition of slavery in Tunisia in 1846 and Northern Algeria in 1848, imports of slaves to these areas declined. Slaves continued to be taken across the desert to Libya and other parts of the Ottoman Empire, which did not abolish slavery until 1889 and then only reluctantly.[39] The most easterly slave-route remained in use until the Italians conquered Libya in 1911 and until the French overran the large territory to the south, which they called Chad after the lake. But the French conquest there was very incomplete, despite the main campaigns which ended in 1913. Further west, the conquest of Hausaland by the British, and of most of the rest of the Sahel and nearly all of the Sahara by the French, meant that the old slave-caravans ceased to operate before 1914. But, if these are now no more than a dreadful memory, small-scale slave-trading may not have ended.

In Morocco, abolition of slavery was carried out fairly effectively after the French occupation in 1912. Soon after the independence in 1956, the secretary of the Anti-Slavery Society, Commander Fox-Pitt, visited Morocco and heard a lot about slavery in Mauritania to the south, but not in Morocco itself. The only slaves there, he gathered, were old family retainers who did not want to go (the usual pattern). 'I heard no evidence to make me think that there was any slave-trade in Morocco or anything but residual cases of slavery', he wrote.[40] But a few years later, Briggs claimed that Negro slaves were smuggled regularly into Morocco, and some were smuggled into the oases in the north of the Algerian Sahara 'only twenty-five years ago'; perhaps a few were still being smuggled, he added, but this would now be a 'clandestine luxury trade'.[41]

The territory of the slave-owning Moors and Reguibats extends into the Saharan areas of Algeria and Morocco – the case of the slave girl Aouicha, discussed in Chapter One, occurred near the disputed (now settled) frontier between Algeria and Morocco. And the kidnappings which, as already noted, are all too common on the southern edges of the desert could provide slaves to sell in the north even today, control of the frontiers being almost impossible. And in the Maghreb (Morocco, Algeria and Tunisia) 'white slavery' sometimes fully deserves its name: prostitution, except among the Ouled Naïl of Algeria who go in for it voluntarily because it is a respected tradition for their girls, can take the form of well-organised exploitation; and during the Algerian war there were protests at girls being physically imprisoned in the French forces' field brothels. It is possible that black African girls met with similar treatment, since the red-light district of Sidi bel Abbès in Algeria, headquarters of the Legion until 1962, was called the *Village Nègre*.

In Libya, with its smaller population and (today) a puritanical régime, such 'white slavery' is probably less common. Stories of

The Sahara and the Maghreb

European girls falling victim to such treatment in the Arab world usually relate to the Levant and the Arabian Peninsula. But it was in Libya that the old trans-Sahara slave-trade went on for the longest period; it was only in 1929 that the last slave-caravan crossed the desert to Libya.

Such slave-caravans reached Tripoli and Benghazi until the Italian conquest, and early in the First World War slaves from the Lake Chad region, taken through Libya and across the Mediterranean, were publicly on sale in what is now Yugoslavia.[42] The Italian occupation had little immediate effect except on the coast, for inland it was almost immediately challenged by an uprising of the Arabs of the Senussi order who felt that their trading activities, as well as their independence, were being threatened by the Italians.*

* The Senussi order is a Muslim religious order which was founded in the early nineteenth century by an Algerian, Mohammed ben Ali el-Senussi; warlike and fervent, it aroused a wide following in Libya and established a series of fortified monasteries to the south, along the Wadai trade-route. The Senussis came to control this route and to be involved in the slave-trade.

During the First World War they began a fierce revolt which was not suppressed until the early 1930s, and then only by a brutal campaign of total warfare waged by the Fascist Government. Unfortunately, the Senussis were defending slavery as well as independence, and it was because they controlled much of the desert that a slave-caravan reached Murzuk, the old centre of the desert slave-trade, in 1929: less than fifty years ago.[43]

Was even this the end? In 1929 it was reported that a 'slave-farm', run on scientific lines to breed slaves, was in existence at the Kufra oases. As it stands, this report should not be believed – it is hard to see how one runs a 'slave-farm', and such a thing could not be concealed at major oases. But behind the report may lie some continued small-scale slave-dealing. In the early 1950s came less improbable, but still barely credible reports of German Afrika Korps deserters dealing in slaves from hideouts in the Tibesti mountains, in Chad near the Libyan border.[44] A Dutch writer, Dr M. G. Schenk, said in 1954 that African Mecca pilgrims sometimes sold servants not (as is known to have occurred) in Saudi Arabia, but in the Tibesti mountains while *en route* to Arabia; but Europeans in Chad said it would be impossible for such traffic to go on undiscovered.[45]

*The Toubous: no more slaves now*
In the Tibesti mountains, far from the sea and from all areas of dense population, live the Toubou or Teda. They are found in thinly scattered settlements in the partly desert, partly savanna regions to the south and east in the Chad Republic, the regions of Borkou and Ennedi. They are dark-skinned, rather like the Africans to the south; they resemble the Haratin in some ways but have a different blood group and language (the latter forms a separate group with those of the Zaghawa to the south and the Kanuri, the people of the old state of Bornu). It is thought that the Toubous may be at least partly descended from the early inhabitants of the Sahara.

Like the Ahaggar Tuareg, the Toubous lead a nomadic existence and follow the Muslim religion (this, however, only very recently). They differ from both Tuareg and Moors in having no hierarchy of noble and vassal tribes. Another interesting fact is that nomadic life has actually increased in recent years among the Toubous, while agricultural activity has declined. Moreover, slavery has virtually ended among them, although a subject class of people of black African origin called Kamadja, dwell among them, but they are said to be really free men now. The UNESCO survey said[46] that these Kamadja remained subject to the nomadic Toubous, looking after their oasis farms in the Tibesti and Borkou while the nomads themselves (often, however, leaving their wives at the oases) were on the move, rearing their camels and cattle.

Briggs reported in the late 1950s that there were still slaves among the Teda; he applied the term Kamadja to the local Haratin, saying freed slaves became assimilated to these.[47] Elsewhere he wrote that the situation of these slaves was similar to that of the Ahaggar Tuareg's slaves.[48] He noted that some were very badly treated – some had the ligaments of their toes or feet cut. About the same time a British traveller, Nigel Heseltine, saw old ex-slaves at Ounianga, east of the Tibesti on the route from Faya to the Kufra oases, 'with calves shrivelled because their Achilles tendons had been cut when they were young to prevent them from running away'.[49] But he also said that the children of slaves were by then (about the mid-1950s) more than half-free, and in the Faya area he noted: 'The same problem has arisen here as elsewhere in the Sahara: namely, who is going to work the land now that there are officially no more slaves? For the Saharans, whether Arab, Tuareg, Mauretanian (*sic*) or Gorane, tilling the soil, and above all drawing water to irrigate it, is the work of slaves'.[50]

This, indeed, is a serious Saharan problem. The abolition of slavery is bound to create problems for all. It can destroy the social fabric which, however hard for the slaves, did keep the desert, and hence death, at bay. The ending of slavery among the Tedas may well lead to the abandonment of the oases and fields and the subsequent advance of the desert. Briggs certainly thought so fifteen years ago: 'The gradual suppression of slavery has been another important factor in this case, for it has progressively reduced the supply of cheap labour willing to cultivate the soil, a task that no true Teda nomad would ever dream of stooping to unless perhaps his very life depended on it'.[51]

Since then, the advance of the desert has probably been hastened by the war in Northern and Eastern Chad, which began before 1968 with a widespread revolt of several tribes, including the Toubous, against the régime of President Tombalbaye. During the suppression of the revolt, in which French troops played an important role, the ruler of the Toubous, the Derde, went with other rebels to Libya. It seems that the operations in Chad, in which the Legion took part, had some success against the insurgents, whose political leaders are, or were, the Chad National Liberation Front (FROLINAT). It is now clear, however, that fighting in the Tibesti is not over yet; while one can safely assume that the Toubous have suffered severely. After the return of peace they will probably have to concentrate more than ever on their herds and their trade (the selling of goats, salt, dates, tomatoes and the buying of millet, tobacco, tea), because of the hastened decline of their farming.

The example of the Toubous shows that the end of slavery is not the end, but the beginning of the general problem of an improved existence for the Saharan nomads. The same problem affects the Moors, the Tuareg, and other peoples of the Sahara.

*The Chaamba and others*
The most famous of all the smaller Saharan tribes – at least among the French who ruled them – are the Arab Chaamba people, who served for decades in the French Saharan Camel Corps (*Méharistes*). Numbering only a few tens of thousands, they live in the Saharan territory of Algeria, scattered over a wide area north and north-west of the Ahaggar, and they speak Arabic – but, unlike many Arabic-speakers of North Africa, they may be direct descendants of immigrants from Arabia. Like the Moors, Tuareg and Toubous they are semi-nomadic, growing dates at oases as well as roaming over large areas; in recent decades some have become very successful long-distance traders.[52]

Some of the Chaamba have left their nomadic way of life and settled down as farmers. But traditionally they had slaves to cultivate their fields according to the usual Saharan pattern. In the twentieth century many of these slaves have been freed, but have remained at the oases as farmers. At El Golea some ex-slaves are *khammès* (sharecroppers, paying a fifth or some other proportion of their crops as rent-in-kind) of Chaamba land-owners. El Golea, however, is in the heart of the Algerian oil area, and wage employment at the oil wells has helped the slaves to run the land and palm groves more independently, though still not owning them. Farm labourers' wages have been pushed up by the oil companies' competition.

A dozen years ago Chaamba slavery was still a going concern. As in other parts of the Sahara, the slaves were often black Africans, taken from the Sudanic belt and sold to the Chaamba at slave-markets in Ghardaia and In Salah. 'Although the Negro slaves of the Chaamba were all freed many years ago by French decree,' said Briggs, 'their material status, like that of the freed slaves of the Tuareg, remains very little changed in practice'.[53] They helped look after the goats, made baskets, and sometimes acted as sorcerers and magicians, like the smiths among the Tuareg.[54] They had their own organisation, a secret one which no doubt helped them to maintain their reputation as possessors of occult power.

Since Briggs wrote his book, the oil wells have expanded further.

This development, and the adoption of farming and business by some nomads, may have reduced the impact of slavery among the Chaamba.

Probably most of the other tribes of the Sahara have recently included slaves, even if they do not still include some. Traditionally, the Rebaia, a tribe of the Algerian Sahara about 14,000 strong, had slaves. South of Touggourt in the same region, the Ouargla well-diggers, called Ghattasin, a people of mysterious origin, seem to be traditionally serfs, but perhaps not slaves (most have now abandoned their traditional calling to work at the near-by oil fields). As mentioned earlier, the major serf group in the Sahara is that of the Haratin.[55]

So the Sahara Desert and its borderlands remain bastions of slavery even in the twentieth century. Slavery has been an essential part of the precarious life of the desert nomads, and this makes it impossible to think of abolishing it by decree overnight or sending expeditions to suppress it. (Chapter Twelve discusses ways of so improving the Saharan peoples' lives that slavery can die out naturally, as it has already done among the Toubous and has been doing for many years among the Tuareg.) There seems little doubt that slavery has been in decline in this area. But it survives, particularly in Mauritania, where it takes a degrading form not found elsewhere and makes the crime of kidnapping all too easy. This should not be forgotten, but neither should the impossibility of abolishing slavery as an isolated action. When all Moors, Tuareg and Chaamba, slave and free, can live well without slavery, and without necessarily abandoning the rest of their traditional life, slavery will no doubt soon end.

*Notes*

1. Among many lives of de Foucauld are *The Sands of Tamanrasset* by Marion Mill Preminger, and *The Desert My Dwelling-Place* by Elizabeth Hamilton.
2. L. C. Briggs, *Tribes of the Sahara*, pp. 135 ff.
3. Claude Bataillon *et al.*, *Nomades et Nomadisme au Sahara* (UNESCO), p. 29.
4. E. W. Bovill, *The Golden Trade of the Moors*, p. 43.
5. Ibid., p. 47.
6. Bataillon *et al.*, op. cit., p. 31.
7. Briggs, op. cit., p. 138.
8. L. C. Briggs, *Living Races of the Sahara Desert*, p. 162.
9. Briggs, op. cit., pp. 135 ff.
10. Ibid., p. 135.

## 54 AFRICA'S SLAVES TODAY

11. Bataillon *et al.*, op. cit., pp. 171–2.
12. Ibid., p. 63.
13. Ibid.
14. Robin Maugham, *The Slaves of Timbuktu*, pp. 203 ff.
15. Johannes Nicolaisen, *L'Esclavage entre les Peuples Pastoraux Tuareg en Ahaggar et en Aïr* (paper presented to the 1962 Congress of Africanists), University of Ghana.
16. Ibid.
17. Briggs, *Tribes*, op. cit., p. 138.
18. Nicolaisen, op. cit.
19. Ibid.
20. Ibid.
21. Briggs, *Living Races*, op. cit., p. 97.
22. Maugham, op. cit., p. 150.
23. Ibid., p. 192.
24. Ibid., pp. 193 ff.
25. Ibid., pp. 197 ff.
26. Ibid., p. 205.
27. Ibid., pp. 234 ff.
28. Ibid., pp. 224–6.
29. Ibid., p. 189.
30. Briggs, *Tribes*, op. cit., p. 142.
31. Bataillon *et al.*, op. cit., p. 171.
32. Ibid., p. 64; Briggs, *Tribes*, op. cit., pp. 135 ff.
33. M. Pollaud-Dulian, *Aujourd'hui l'Esclavage*, Chapter Two.
34. H. Barth, *Travels and Discoveries in North and Central Africa* (1858).
35. A. Adu Boahen, *Britain, the Sahara and the Western Sudan*, p. 104.
36. Boahen, op. cit., pp. 112 ff.
37. Ibid., pp. 122 ff.
38. Bovill, op. cit., p. 246.
39. Boahen, op. cit., pp. 155–6.
40. *Anti-Slavery Reporter* (February 1957).
41. Briggs, *Tribes*, op. cit., p. 93.
42. Ibid.
43. N. Heseltine, *From Libyan Sands to Chad*, p. 18.
44. *Anti-Slavery Reporter* (October 1955).
45. V. Thompson and T. Adloff, *The Emerging States of French Equatorial Africa*, p. 473.
46. Bataillon *et al.*, op. cit., p. 83.
47. Briggs, *Tribes*, op. cit., p. 185.
48. Briggs, *Living Races*, op. cit., p. 108.
49. Heseltine, op. cit., p. 192.
50. Ibid.
51. Briggs, *Living Races*, op. cit., p. 106.
52. Briggs, *Tribes*, op. cit., Chapter Seven; Bataillon *et al.*, op. cit., pp. 143–54.
53. Briggs, *Living Races*, op. cit., p. 118.
54. Ibid.
55. Bataillon *et al.*, op. cit., pp. 113 ff.; Briggs, *Tribes*, op. cit., p. 95.

*Chapter Three*

# Savanna Slaves

South of the Sahara lies the great grasslands region of West Africa, called the savanna, or sometimes, in the past, the Sudan.* This region stretches from the Atlantic coast eastwards, in a belt hundreds of miles wide. On its northern side it merges with the desert but this frontier is always shifting or vague. Rainfall becomes more plentiful as one moves southwards across the broad grassy plains and low hills of the savanna belt, until one reaches, in the Western State of Nigeria and other regions at roughly the same latitude, the edge of the great forest.

The grasslands cover much of West Africa and support most of its population. A large part of it is watered, inadequately, by the great Niger River, its tributary the Benue, the Senegal and Gambia Rivers, the various branches of the Volta River, and some other rivers, and a fairly large area is in the basin of Lake Chad.[1] The Niger and Senegal Rivers rise in the Fouta Djalon mountains, now in the Republic of Guinea. The West African savanna includes one other major upland area, the Bauchi plateau of Nigeria and the adjoining hill and mountain regions covering part of Northern Cameroon. Otherwise, the grasslands are mainly low-lying. Besides grasses, there are many different trees, and some areas are even thickly wooded.

There are millions of cattle in the savanna, usually reared by the Fulani and other nomads, who travel large distances in search of pasture and water and eventually send the cattle to markets, which can be far to the south in the forest belt. The rearing and marketing of cattle are major occupations of the people of Northern Nigeria, Niger, Mali, Upper Volta and other savanna areas. Most

---

* This term is now used to denote only the Republic of the Sudan, and cannot be used in its old sense without confusion. The old application of the term survives in the names of two Protestant missions active in Northern Nigeria, the Sudan Interior Mission and the Sudan United Mission.

of the people, however, are farmers. For food they grow above all millet and sorghum, two hardy cereals suited to rainless regions, and maize and 'cowpeas', together with groundnuts, sheanuts, various types of beans, onions, tomatoes and sometimes rice. As cash crops, for local processing or export, they grow above all groundnuts and cotton (mostly in the Northern States of Nigeria).

*Hausaland and Bornu*

For over one thousand years this area has been settled by a group of people commonly called 'Hausa' by others and speaking the Hausa language.\* It has been the scene of many important local states (see the reports and chronicles of travellers), many of which still survive, in altered form, in the Northern States (formerly the Northern Region) of Nigeria.

Those states have a sorry prominence in the history of African slavery. They were among the more important states at the southern termini of the old trans-Sahara trade-routes, mentioned in the last chapter. By the nineteenth century Kano was a leading centre for the export of slaves and other 'goods'. Its ruler (called Emir or, in Hausa, *Sarki*), like the other rulers of Hausaland, used slaves to run the administration of his state. Slaves were also important, for example, for farm labour and domestic work.

Slavery was also important in the kingdom of Bornu, which lies to the east of Hausaland. The Kanuri and Kanembu peoples, related in language to the Toubous, ruled the state of Kanem, south-east of Lake Chad, and then, from the fifteenth century, the successor state of Bornu, south-west of the lake. Bornu was, in many ways, the most important of the traditional states incorporated in 1900 into the British Protectorate of Northern Nigeria. It had periods of great power, for example in the sixteenth century under Mai (King) Idris Alooma, and its capital, Kukawa, was for a time an important desert-trade terminus.

According to tradition, the first seven Hausa states were Kano, Rano, Katsina, Zaria, Gobir, Daura and Biram.[2] These and other states founded later constantly rose and fell in importance, fighting many wars among themselves and with Bornu, Songhay to the west, and the Jukuns of the Benue valley. Gobir was for some time the

---

\* Hausa is properly the name of the language, perhaps the most widely spoken of all African languages, and the people who speak this language are properly called Habe, but it is general usage now to call the people Hausas, and because the (originally very different) Fulani people are so intermingled with them, the term 'Hausa-Fulani' is commonly used in Nigeria.

leading Hausa state. Over the centuries, Islam gradually spread throughout these states and Bornu, but by the eighteenth century it was still only very incompletely established. The very Islamic character of the whole area today – the flowing robes of Muslims are worn everywhere, the teaching of the Koran in Arabic is still the most normal form of primary education – is due to events which took place in the early nineteenth century. Between 1804 and 1817 revolutionary forces, under the leadership of a devout Muslim Fulani scholar of Gobir, Uthman dan Fodio, conquered all the Hausa states in an Islamic *jihad* or 'holy war'. This was partly a rising of Fulanis, mostly still nomadic herdsmen and not generally Muslim, against the rule of the Hausa Emirs, and partly a true religious crusade against régimes which dan Fodio thought were corrupt and half-pagan. The old states were not destroyed by the *jihad*, but new rulers were installed, a new Hausa-Fulani upper class (*sarakuna* in Hausa) was created, and the reformation and extension of Islam started.

The new régime installed by the *jihad* has lasted until the present day, for the British Administration deliberately preserved it. Bornu was not conquered by the *jihad* forces but went through many changes of its own, including a change of dynasty, in the nineteenth century. All these changes did not alter the importance of slavery in Bornu and Hausaland. This was probably not much affected by the strength or weakness of Muslim belief, for slavery in the West African savanna region has always existed independently of the Muslim religion. It was important not only in Hausaland before the general conversion to Islam there, but also among the Nupe people (neighbours of the Hausa on the Niger) who were mainly non-Muslim until the present century, and in the two old states of the Moshi people further west in what is now Upper Volta. Islam provided a pretext for enslavement of pagans, but as Muslim laws on slavery were widely disregarded[3] one should not regard Sahelian slavery as a by-product of Islam. This is worth stressing in order to cast doubt on the belief that Christian Europeans, or Muslim Arabs formerly enslaved Africans *because* they were Christians or Muslims.

Certainly, slavery was not regarded generally as something too sacred for good Muslims to renounce, and the Emirate Administrations left in power by the British after 1900 were able to co-operate in the suppression of slave-raiding and the gradual ending of domestic slavery. These Administrations were characterised by flexibility and efficiency, rather than fanaticism. Thus they were very adaptable, and the story of Northern Nigeria under British rule is a story of clever adaptation which left the Hausa-Fulani ruling class with its power essentially intact. A recent study by Professor C. S. Whitaker has shown how British 'Indirect Rule' worked out in that way.[4] Northern Nigeria is a classic case of this variety of British colonial administration, whose essence was to rule through the traditional chiefs, leaving them with real power and authority locally but guiding them and, through them, their people towards the general aims laid down by the British. That, at any rate, was the original idea.

Sir Frederick Lugard, who led the campaign against Emirates in 1900-3 and was the first High Commissioner of Northern Nigeria, and later (1914-19) Governor-General of all Nigeria, was the outstanding theorist and practitioner of 'Indirect Rule'. He and his colleagues and successors applied the system because it seemed so obviously suitable: the British did not have enough money, staff or troops to effect day-to-day control of the people of the most populous part of the savanna, a people only recently conquered (and with difficulty) and likely to respond to calls for a new *jihad* against the infidel British. Moreover, the Hausa-Fulani administrative system headed by the Emirs, oppressive and corrupt as it often was, did seem to 'work'. To keep it going, under British supervision, seemed the obvious answer.

So the rulers – for example, the Emir of Kano, the Shehu of Bornu, the Emir of Zaria, the Etsu Nupe, the Emir of Gwandu, the Emir of Bauchi and others, with the Sultan of Sokoto, descendant and successor of dan Fodio, recognised as supreme – remained on their thrones. Much was retained of the centralised bureaucracies headed by them, with their courtiers, officials (including the district heads responsible for local government, with village heads below them), tax-collectors, market overseers and others. The Emir was called the Native Authority, and there were one or more NAs to each of the provinces established by the British. A British Resident lived at the capital of the Emirate, seeing the ruler regularly to pass on orders on some matters and to consult on others. There were consultations on taxation, censuses, road-building, cattle inoculation, crime prevention, well-digging and other everyday matters.

The Resident could insist on reforms, such as further measures to end slavery, and if it was felt that the Administration of any Emirate was too corrupt or otherwise unsatisfactory, the Emir could be dismissed. But generally, as far as the ordinary people were concerned, the old Administration remained in being. The British did modify it, but they also reinforced it, going so far as to carry out brutal punitive raids on villages which failed to pay the exorbitant taxes often demanded by the NAs. Lugard did not intend 'Indirect Rule' to be conservative; he hoped the NAs would be encouraged by it to become more humane and 'civilised' in their government and to accept the progress and change seen as necessary. But many sorts of corruption and misgovernment continued as before the conquest. This was partly because the British Government, like the French, at that time (before 1940) expected every colony to pay its own way, which meant that, if necessary, the 'natives' had to be forced to pay for it. The Emirs in Northern Nigeria were very good at collecting taxes, and the British, who needed the money, were more inclined to help them than to protect the peasants from extortion. Much, it seems, was forgiven if an Emir brought the tax in on time. There were some Residents who cared for the ordinary people and restrained oppressive NAs, but there were others who were truly conservative, interfering very little in the running of a system which they probably admired as other British people have admired other hierarchised Muslim societies.[5] Much depended on individual Emirs and Residents, but there was always the basic dilemma: the British wanted reform but depended for their administration on people who might be threatened by reform.[6]

When the British really tried to enforce reforms, the Hausa-Fulani rulers gave in and adapted themselves. So well did they do so that Northern Nigeria can be considered one of the least colonised parts of Africa; in few other parts of the continent, apart from Ethiopia, is Western influence less dominant. This does not make educated and nationalist-minded Africans proud of Northern Nigeria; rather the reverse. Southern Nigerians, who were used to less autocratic rule in pre-colonial times and would never accept in the British period anything like what the Hausa commoners (*talakawa*) had to accept, have tended typically to treat Northern Nigeria with contempt and anger, as 'feudal' and oppressive. They have also criticised the British for tolerating this state of affairs so gladly. There is some substance in these charges, but there is also a point missed by the critics: that Northern Nigeria has a built-in conservatism, affecting both *sarakuna* and *talakawa*, and the latter either accept their lot or use ways left open in the traditional order for improving it.[7] In this part of Africa, as in several others mentioned in this book, political and social conservatism does not need to be imposed by anyone. The built-in conservatism, and not any forcible British suppression of popular opposition (which has been negligible), is the reason for the slow acceptance in Northern Nigeria of changes which have gone much farther in other areas.

The 'backwardness' of Northern Nigeria is only relative; many changes have obviously taken place there. It already had important cities such as Kano, Zaria, Sokoto and Katsina before the conquest, but during the British period many more were built, for example, Kaduna and Maiduguri, and the existing cities generally expanded, with new towns built beside the old cities and immigrants coming in from all parts of Nigeria. Kano remained an important metropolis, but now it looked south, not north. Railways reached the north before 1914. The growing of cotton and groundnuts as cash crops spread between the wars, though cotton had been so grown for centuries. Christian missions and Western education came slowly to the north, from deliberate official policy, but they did come and had their effect.

*The British, Emirs and slaves*
How was slavery affected by the conflict in Northern Nigeria between conservatism and organised and spontaneous change?

It was bound to be affected from the very beginning. The British, as already mentioned, did not intend to change everything: Lugard said that local customs should be preserved 'in so far as they are not repugnant to natural justice'.[8] Slavery was always considered as one of the customs not to be tolerated, but it was also a very basic institution in the Hausa states and Bornu.

Barth estimated in the middle of the nineteenth century that half of the 400,000 people in Kano Emirate were slaves.[9] Slaves were born into slavery, or bought, or captured. The Pagan peoples of the plateau were continually raided for slaves by Bornu and the neighbouring states. Despite efforts at self-defence by the Birom, Jarawa and other non-Muslim tribes who retreated uphill and surrounded their villages with thorn bushes to stop the raiders' horses, slave-raids continued with devastating effect. They were rife in the period just before and during the British conquest, and reports from that time show that large areas were depopulated. If not sold to trans-Sahara merchants, those who were captured might be relatively well treated by their owners who could be quite humble free people as well as Emirs or nobles. Many of the slaves were farm labourers; they might be sent out to plant in outlying areas, with enough food to last until the first harvest, or else they might be made to work with the master's sons on a plot, or they might even be given their own plot.[10] Slaves could become concubines (a Muslim could not, strictly speaking, make a free woman a concubine) or officials. They could be, and were, assimilated into the aristocracy or *sarakuna*, and so ended up higher in the social scale than the commoners who had always been legally free.

SAVANNA SLAVES 61

The British, on taking over, were horrified more by the slave-raiding than by the state of the slaves after capture. As soon as they controlled an area they took action against the raiders, and the effects of their policy could be seen after a few years. Slave-trading, cut down by the prevention of raids on the plateau, was also outlawed immediately, and began to decline sharply. But its abolition was hindered by the terrible famine of 1904, which affected most of Northern Nigeria but was particularly bad in Bauchi and Yola Emirates, where many Pagans lived.* To avoid starvation, they sold themselves and their children – the children for as little as 1s 6d or 2s each.[11] Slaves could be got then without raids, and probably similar things happened in the next appalling famine, in 1914.

Despite these setbacks, it was easier to deal with slave-raiding and slave-dealing than with the large number of people already in slavery in the Northern Provinces. The anti-slavery Proclamation issued in 1900 (soon after the establishment of the Protectorate) abolished the legal status of slavery and laid down that all children born after 1st January, 1901 were free. It allowed those already in slavery to leave their masters and have the courts declare them free, and therefore deprived slave-owners of legally enforceable authority. But it did not prevent voluntary continuation of slavery. The British authorities felt that any action taken against voluntary slavery would be strongly resisted by the owners unless they received compensation, for which money was lacking, and that it would be bad for the slaves, who would be turned out into the streets with no work to do.[12]

The policy laid down at the outset was continued, even though only a few slaves – 38,000 by 1914[12] – were freed by court order and many others were probably forcibly prevented from seeking manumission, as the British could not make sure that every slave was really left free to seek it everywhere at all times. Even so, by the 1920s it was thought that slavery was disappearing in Hausaland. Some slaves were freed by the courts and others by their masters; those who died were, in so far as the law was obeyed, not replaced. The Government ran homes for freed slaves, which it later handed over to the missions.[13]

Kidnapping, always made easier when slavery still survives, was apparently common in Northern Nigeria in 1920. The Governor of Nigeria, Sir Hugh Clifford, said then that peasants must be protected against child-stealers, but added, in a fairly extreme expression of the doctrine of 'Indirect Rule', that the British Government should

* From this time, many non-Muslims of the plateau became Christian, but they have continued to be called collectively Pagans (with capital P).

not take the initiative in the matter.[14] He meant, no doubt, that the NAs should take the initiative. The NA courts did punish kidnapping and slave-dealing, but the effectiveness of British laws, even a generation after the conquest, seems limited when one reads[15] that in the 30s Pagans who had fled into the hills of Bida Emirate to escape slave-raids were still afraid to move back into the plains, despite efforts by British officials to persuade them that it was safe.

Even if slavery lasted for a long time and slave-trading continued to occur, on the whole time and changes due to colonial rule worked gradually against traditional slavery. Economic changes probably helped to end it, and the British authorities regularly forced action on reluctant Emirs; for example, they ordered the slave officials of many Emirates to be removed from office (these were removed in Kano after the accession of Emir Abdullahi Bayero in 1926, and in Sokoto a few years later).[16]

By the 1930s it was clear that Lugard's policy of gradual abolition of slavery was generally working. The old order seemed to survive quite well without real slavery, thus proving its adaptability. Margery Perham, who visited the Emirates in the 1930s, said that slavery there had 'ceased remarkably soon to be an important question, though it would be rash to assume that even now there are no cases of slavery, or even of slave-trading, in Northern Nigeria, for both occasionally come to light'. She added: 'There are still those who find it honourable and profitable to remain the slaves of rulers, and with these the law can hardly deal.'[17] This is inevitable when slavery is abolished gradually. There will always be some slaves who, being relatively well treated and knowing no other life, and often feeling the loyalty of an old family retainer, stay with their former owners, perhaps with only a vague awareness on both sides that there has been any change. Their situation may be the cause of some suspicions that slavery has not ended in Northern Nigeria.

*The slavers of Northern Cameroons*
In what is now Nigeria's North-Eastern State, slavery seems to have lasted longer than elsewhere. That state includes Bornu, whose people have retained traces of their old slave-system, and is the home of many of the Wodaabe Fulani cattle herders, who retain traces of an old slave-free class distinction. The same state also includes part of the former territory of British Northern Cameroons, home of a number of Pagan peoples among whom slavery survived well into the colonial era.

Northern Cameroons, originally part of the German colony of

Kamerun, was divided, in 1919, between Great Britain and France. While ruling this territory as a Mandated and later Trust Territory, the British administered it for practical purposes as a part of Nigeria, until it was formally added to Northern Nigeria in 1961. In that remote mountainous territory, the British Administration, appended to that of the Northern Provinces of Nigeria, seems to have been a relaxed affair. The number of British officials was very small, and for some time large areas of Adamawa Province, which included a part of Northern Cameroons, was 'closed' under the Unsettled Districts' Ordinance. This did not mean that the inhabitants were in open rebellion, but that the British were not really able to enforce their authority. In 1926 the hill tribes of the northern Mandated Territories, no doubt taking advantage of this lack of control, were reported to be still trading in slaves.[18] Many cases of slave-trading came to court every year and were duly reported to the League of Nations. But a considerable traffic in slaves went on well into the 1930s.

About 1930 a famine, perhaps due to locust swarms, occurred in Northern Cameroons, and another tragic mass sale of children followed. The Wulla or Matakam people, living in the hills of Northern Cameroons and the adjacent French-ruled territory, were so badly hit that they sold hundreds of their children, mainly to people of the nomadic Shuwa Arab tribe living between their homeland and Lake Chad. When they grew up the boys among them were free to return to their original homes, but they had been circumcised and brought up as Muslims. Shuwa Arab men were willing to marry Wulla girls who then became free, while the families in the hills reclaimed some daughters by paying the bride-price for them as wives for Wulla men, or else simply by carrying them off – though this caused disputes. If the children so enslaved really were able to return home eventually, the story ended less sadly than it might have done, and perhaps as well as it could have done in the absence of official relief measures, which a penniless *laissez-faire* administration could not carry out. A British official who described all this thought that the children had benefited by their forced move to the plains,[19] while Margery Perham said that the Pagans objected to the abolition of slavery because it meant that they could no longer sell themselves and their families to avoid death in times of famine (also because they could no longer sell undesirable members of their communities).[20]

The Pagans certainly cannot have felt this way about slave-raiding. A few years after the tragedy of the Wullas, other Pagans of British Northern Cameroons, in the Gwoza hill area of Dikwa Division, were terrorised by a mysterious 'man on a white horse' who kidnapped children. He also operated on the French side of the near-by border.[21] The border between the two Mandated Territories had not much physical reality; the Shuwa Arabs who purchased the Wulla children crossed the border without difficulty to do so, and slave-traders regularly took advantage of the easily crossed 'frontier'.

In 1934 the British Government told the League of Nations that the 'main recruiting area' for slavers was the Mandara hill country on the border, inhabited by the Matakams (Wullas). It described how the slavers worked: 'The buying or, in some cases, the abduction, of women and children of this tribe is carried out chiefly by Arabs, Kanembus and Mandaras, who sell to the inhabitants of the Lake Chad area and to dealers from Wadai, Kanembu and Tibesti. The route followed runs approximately north by north-east and traverses the south-eastern corner of Dikwa Division. It is said that up to the year 1918 the slave-route across Lake Chad from Wulgo to the north-western shore was cleared regularly for the traffic.'[22] This brief report suggests the existence of a very widespread slave-trading network, extending across Chad as far as the Tibesti mountains (and perhaps further, for would the Toubous have bought slaves after a 1,000-mile journey which must have made them very expensive?). The French Administration was thin on the ground all over the vast and unpopulated area concerned, and a good deal could have gone on unhindered. This might prove, on closer examination, to have been one of the main clandestine slaving operations in colonial Africa, and one wonders how long it lasted. The Second World War could have provided opportunities for its revival, and in British Northern Cameroons some districts were 'opened' to regular administration only in 1950 and a few areas even later.[23]

*Survivals in Northern Nigeria*
A rather different story is that of the survival of clear traces of the old slave-system among the Kanuri people of Bornu. In a study of this people in the late 1950s, the anthropologist Ronald Cohen, found that slavery still existed to a certain extent. There were slave concubines (*chir* in Kanuri), born to men slaves and brought up to a life of concubinage; and people referred to slave women and other women working on farms together. A man's children by a slave woman, however, were free, so that 'the slave population in Bornu is reproducing itself only through the efforts of functioning male slaves who are producing children'.[24]

SAVANNA SLAVES 65

Cohen did not make any reference to slavery as being of great economic importance. He described a system of clientage by which a labourer could place himself in the service of a Kanuri farmer in what was apparently more than a mere employer-employee relationship. This, however, is not slavery, and it may not even be serfdom if the 'client' workers are free to change masters. Slaves do not seem important as labourers, still less as pieces of property, except for slave girls used as concubines and for other women's work.

Slavery, as well as clientage, does seem to have survived in Bornu until the end of the colonial era. But it is not easy to be precise. It seems from Cohen's researches that people of the traditional slave class are clearly distinguishable from other Kanuris by special facial scars and shaved heads, and a consciousness of their social status survives, though without degrading treatment on the whole. Although 'slave' girls can no longer be sold, they can be given away; formerly (but almost never in recent years) they were given to upper-class boys on circumcision, for practical sex education. Some of the old status of slave concubines must therefore have survived, and the girls and their masters may be unaware of any change. Other Kanuris of the old slave community may be similarly unaware, and the position of many people may be ambiguous, with the law saying that they are not slaves and local opinion assuming that they are. If anti-slavery laws are respected enough to prevent people from exercising full property rights over others, but not enough to stop people referring to 'my slave' or 'my master' out of engrained custom, then does slavery still continue or not? It is not a simple question.

To a lesser extent, the descendants of slaves form a recognisable and distinct community in Hausaland too. There they can be distinguished by special facial marks, though not by shaven heads. One who bore these marks was Sir Abubakar Tafawa Balewa, Prime Minister of Nigeria from 1957 until his assassination in the *coup d'état* of 15 January 1966; he was of Gerawa (related to Hausa) slave origin, born in Bauchi Emirate; and some may have called him a slave.[25] This does not mean that the Prime Minister of Nigeria belonged to anyone, only that some of his countrymen did not distinguish slaves from ex-slaves. The anthropologist, M G. Smith, referring to Zaria in particular, said slave ancestry persists as a distinctive Hausa social classification, although slavery as a social institution does not.[26]

The general disappearance of real slavery is suggested in a close study recently made of one village, Batagarawa, in Katsina Province, near the Niger Republic border. There, as elsewhere in Hausaland, an old system of farm labour called *gandu* continues. In the nineteenth century this system meant that a man's slaves worked with his own sons on the farm; the slaves had to work a certain number of hours, but one of them could be a *sarkin gandu*, supervising the work and even giving orders to his master's sons. The sons of newly enslaved people could do craft work as well as farm labour; they could have their own plots and do much of their farm work on those, paying a part of their produce in lieu of their labour on the master's farm. *Gandu* slaves were inherited, and no doubt in time alien slaves became assimilated to the Hausa population in this way. Slave labour, according to the study of Batagarawa, 'was common in some areas until the mid-1920s', but after that the number of able-bodied slaves declined rapidly. This led to a change in the *gandu* system. At first, the farmers' wives may have done some of the slaves' work, but then the farmers began to hire paid labourers, and now, in Batagarawa, *gandu* simply means a system in which a married son works on his father's land, in return for benefits which include a share of the food grown, perhaps with the help of hired labourers. It no longer involves slaves, and clearly has not done so for a considerable time.[27]

If abolition became effective some time ago in rural areas like this, one can assume it did so in the towns as well, with their greater opportunities for escape and alternative employment, except perhaps for the slave retinues of the Emirs' courts, mentioned earlier. There remained, however, the social distinction of slaves' and free people's descendants, important in a society which pays a lot of attention to ancestry. This distinction, and the survival of a great deal of tradition in Northern Nigeria, may be responsible for the idea that slavery still goes on there outside the North-East State. Public ceremonies attended by Emirs are demonstrations of a great love of tradition, and the survival of class distinctions is far from ceremonial – the difference between *sarakuna* and *talakawa* really matters. Has a society which is so conservative really ended slavery, which was so important for it not very long ago? Did 'Indirect Rule', which preserved many elements in Hausa tradition, really end this one? Such questions are bound to arise, especially as the Emirs' retainers may look a bit like slaves, at least to critics of 'feudal' Northern Nigeria.

The Anti-Slavery Society has even accused one outstanding Northern Nigerian of being a slave-owner: the Sardauna of Sokoto, Sir Ahmadu Bello, Premier of the Northern Region from 1954 until the January 1966 *coup* when he, like Tafawa Balewa, was assassinated. The Anti-Slavery Society's view that the Sardauna was 'an un-

SAVANNA SLAVES 67

scrupulous autocrat' is widely accepted in Nigeria and elsewhere.[28] As head of the Northern Peoples Congress (NPC) which dominated the coalition government in Lagos led by Sir Abubakar, he was generally regarded as the most powerful man in Nigeria. Within the Northern Region his power was even greater; the NPC dominated the region and used all means to stifle local opposition – for example, in the Middle Belt south of Hausaland, opposed to the NPC, its rule involved suppression of uprisings by the Tivs. At the same time, Sir Ahmadu Bello, proud descendant of Uthman dan Fodio, personally headed Muslim missions in Pagan areas, so that older men in the Middle Belt must have wondered if old times were not returning. But all this is no reason for the Anti-Slavery Society to say that the Sardauna 'possessed many slaves'; and since it gives no evidence for this, there is no reason to believe it at all.

This report no doubt arose from the general survival of tradition and of old social distinctions in the six Northern States which in 1967 replaced the Northern Region. But this does not mean that real slavery survived, except perhaps in Bornu. There Cohen's research has shown that some people were in a social situation which was tantamount to slavery. But even these may be yet another group of people who look very like their slave ancestors but who are not treated fully as the slaves of individuals. Many gradations are possible between true slaves and people who are not in any way like slaves but whose slave ancestry still matters socially, and no doubt all the gradations are found in Bornu and Hausaland. There are also cases of small-scale kidnapping which may be linked to petty slave-dealing, but their frequency in Northern Nigeria may be due to its large population and widespread poverty, as much as to the tradition of slavery.

On 8th April, 1973, the *Sunday Times* published a startling photograph (see plates 6 and 7), apparently taken in Northern Nigeria, near the Niger border, of a group of Africans roped together, at a village of thatched conical huts typical of the savanna. The picture and others, showed what seemed to be a young white man examining some Africans, and the photographer, Mauro Colasanti, suggested that he was a slave-dealer. He said that he had traced a local traffic in slaves to its source, and had seen these slaves and photographed them as a sign that slavery still continued. Although it is a pity that no details were published with the picture, and the short caption showed limited knowledge of the area, one may accept the photographer's interpretation of what he saw (how, incidentally, was he able to get so close to such a scene?). Enough cases of petty slave-dealing do occur in Northern Nigeria to make it possible to imagine seven or eight men (the number in the picture) being rounded up and sold at once; in such a large area this could be done now and then. But the role of the European is mysterious. A European would scarcely need so many male slaves, and if he was taking them to sell, who would buy them? The Tuareg in Niger might be possible customers, but a recent drought has caused such famine or near-famine among them that they have been reduced to destitution – a fact which would prevent them from buying new slaves, especially if the price of a man at source was, as Colasanti said, £285. The same drought disaster, however, could make slave-trading possible, so that the report cannot be totally dismissed; but it is not wholly convincing either. One can only be fairly sure that some victims of the drought have been driven to sell others, perhaps children, to avoid starvation; such tragedies generally occur in famine conditions, and relief efforts after the West African drought (at its peak in 1972–4) have certainly not been great enough to make such things unnecessary for desperate people.

*Cases of tribal servitude*
The slavery which used to exist in Bornu and Hausaland was different in many ways from the slavery of Saharan and Sahelian nomadic tribes, for it prevailed among sedentary people who depended on slaves for the administration of their kingdoms. States of this sort existed all over the Sahel for centuries: for example, east of Bornu there were Wadai and Baguirmi, in what is now the Chad Republic, and in the modern Middle Belt of Nigeria there was Kororafa, the Pagan state of the Jukun people. More famous were a number of states west of Hausaland, around the upper Senegal River and the middle and upper Niger, and in the Fouta Djalon mountains. The most celebrated western savanna states were Ghana (nowhere near the modern state called after it, its capital being in what is now Mauritania), Mali (which existed further east and was powerful and flourishing in the fourteenth century), and Songhay (a powerful but short-lived – in the sixteenth century – state around the Niger bend). South of that bend, from Ouagadougou and Ouahigouya, the Moshi Kings called the Moro Naba and Yatenga Naba ruled important states for centuries and are of some importance to this day in Upper Volta.

The main savanna states declined and fell long before the arrival of the French; so did the state formed in the nineteenth century at Masina on the upper Niger by Seku Ahmadu, leader of another Fulani *jihad*, and one created further west by Al Hajj Umar, the Tukulor ruler. Slavery was important in all these states, as in

SAVANNA SLAVES 69

Hausaland, but a difference was that not many important states with slave-systems were intact at the time of European conquest in the areas which fell to the French. This accidental circumstance made the problem of slavery in the savanna slightly different in French and British territories. But the difference was slight, and colonial policies in fact differed little; in the Sahel the French practised something very like Lugard's 'Indirect Rule', and their approach to slavery – suppressing slave-raiding and slave-dealing, but proceeding gradually and cautiously in the ending of slavery itself – was like that of the British.

This colonial policy applied to peoples with well-developed state organisations as well as to smaller or less politically organised peoples, nomadic and settled. The distinction between slavery in the two cases is only a rough one and there are general similarities.

One of the mysteries of African history is that of the origin of the Fulani people, one of the most important groups in West Africa. It is known that they migrated to the Fouta Djalon mountains, to Hausaland and elsewhere from the Senegal River valley, but their history before then is a matter for speculation not because of their language – which is related to those of the Wolof and Serer tribes which have remained in modern Senegal – but because of the existence of two groups among them, called 'red' and 'black'. It seems that the Fulanis were all originally 'red' (in fact brown), but intermarriage with black peoples during their migrations produced the other group. The 'red' Fulanis may have been originally Berber, but other theories, often fantastic, have been put forward. Slavery probably did much to produce the present distinction. But the 'red' Fulanis are themselves divided, traditionally, into slave and free castes. These survive among the 'red' Fulani or Wodaabe of Nigeria's North-Eastern State, who are still mainly herders or, as Nigerians call them, 'Cattle Fulani'.

The Wodaabe are nomads, as Fulani herdsmen have been throughout their migrations, and have a hierarchised society like other nomads. A study made several years ago by D. J. Stenning noted that there were ranks among the free Wodaabe, while '... the Wodaabe exact from their communities of ex-slaves the kind of servility they give their superiors, and the slaves themselves seek to emulate their Wodaabe lords.'[29] The reference in one sentence to 'slaves' and 'ex-slaves' surely indicates the uncertain status of the people in question. It seems a familiar case of an age-old relationship no longer recognised by the civil authorities but hardly changed in practice among people who live largely independently of these authorities. But it also seems that there has been some change, with the result that the class distinction is partly concealed and implicit now. There are separate festivals for 'equals' (free men) and for 'inferiors', the latter's festival being called the 'slave dance' or *daddo*. This, says Stenning, is a 'wet season feast in which the slave communities of the Wodaabe dance for their masters who provide meat and kola-nuts for them'. The free Wodaabe are supposed to deride the slaves' antics and lampoon the slaves' praise-songs. 'The Wodaabe conduct of these feats, which are their only formal contact with the outside world on their own ground, exhibits quite clearly a sense of social separation, of status-consciousness, of competition, and of tacit antagonism.'[30] The fact that all this has to be suggested by elaborate games makes one think that slavery is no longer blatant and taken for granted among the Wodaabe.

The Nigerian Wodaabe customs are probably found among Fulani communities in other countries; for example, in Cameroon, Niger, Mali and Upper Volta. In Senegal, the Tukulor or Toucouleur tribe, neighbours of the Fulanis to whom they are closely related, have retained a social hierarchy which includes slavery. They have four castes of freemen allowed to own slaves, freedmen (*gallunkobe*, singular *gallunke*) and slaves proper (*matyube*, singular *matyodo*).[31] Usually a third-generation *matyodo* becomes a *gallunke*, and before this he lives independently, with his own family, within his master's compound.

Here, then, is a case of slavery persisting among a non-nomadic Sahel people, and as a well-established part of the social order. It has no doubt lasted partly because it is not too oppressive; if slaves have usually become free after two generations their number must now be greatly reduced. It is interesting that tradition has lasted so well in Senegal, which is more subject to French influence and modernisation than the inland states. The Wolofs, the majority tribe of Senegal, have retained something of their well-developed old social hierarchy, in which there are nobles, other free men (*geer*), low-caste men (*nyenyoo*), and then slaves (*dyaam*).[32] There are said to be some semi-servile groups still among the Wolofs, and in 1962 a Senegalese said that in his country the distinction between people of free and slave descent was still made.[33] This is paralleled in Nigeria, and shows that the French were no more successful in eradicating old social distinctions than the British.

*Cameroon: belated freedom for Lamido's slaves*
The Fouta Djalon region of Guinea and the northern areas of ex-French Cameroon are two widely separated regions of West Africa where the Fulanis established states and enslaved Pagans

SAVANNA SLAVES 71

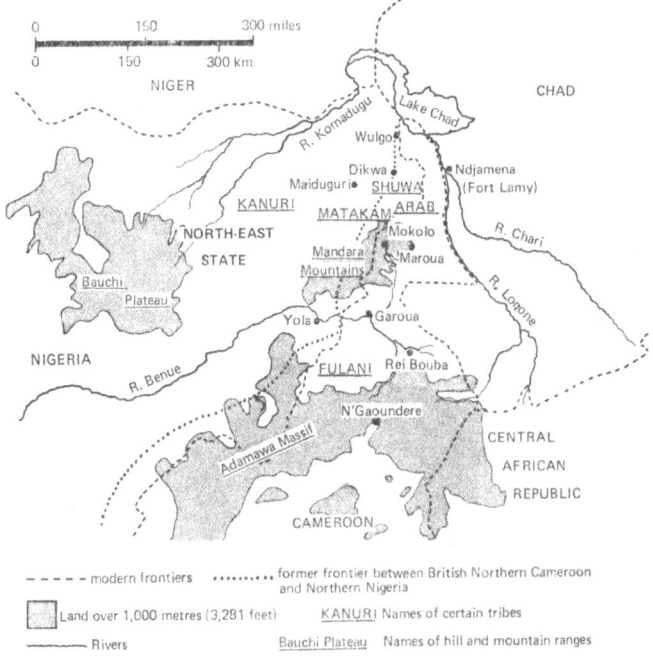

The Lake Chad and Upper Benue Basins

before colonial (mainly French rule). The Cameroon is exceptional in that one ruler, the Lamido of Rei Bouba, was allowed to go on owning thousands of slaves, treating them as his personal property and making them work on his farms, until well after independence. His slaves were freed only about five years ago. Until then, they were perhaps the only large group of slaves living regularly in chattel slavery in modern Africa.

This ruler was originally only one of many *lamibe* (Fulani plural of *lamido*) owning slaves in the northern area of what became Cameroon: the Adamaoua uplands, the valley of the Benue, the mountains further north, and the plains of the Logone River and Lake Chad. The Germans who conquered this area at the turn of the century started to free the slaves, but apparently they had an easy-going attitude about it and left the Fulani aristocrats with much of their old power, which included general domination over the Pagans (collectively called 'Kirdi', but of many diverse tribes). After the First World War, most of the Fulani and Kirdi areas of German 'Kamerun' were ruled by France, the rest being turned into British Northern Cameroons. In the general process of ending slavery which then began, the Lamido of Rei Bouba seems to have been left out. This was not because his region was the most inaccessible to the Administration – it is a low-lying, though admittedly arid, region between the upper Benue and the Chad border – but because, it is said, he helped the Allies against the Germans in the 1914–16 campaign and was allowed in return to keep his slaves.[34] But it is difficult to imagine that the French, ruling under a League of Nations' Mandate and then a United Nations' Trusteeship and therefore under some international supervision, felt bound by such a promise until independence in 1960 (was it normal for colonial powers to feel bound by promises to African rulers who helped them establish their rule?). The French clearly decided to 'let well alone', but it is not easy to tell why.

The process of ending slavery elsewhere was slow and difficult. Like the Germans but (in their view) with more determination, the French aimed first to stop the raids for slaves on Kirdi villages – and this limited aim was achieved, except for the continued smaller-scale kidnapping already mentioned in connection with the British Mandated Territory. But the traditional inferior status of the Kirdi remained, and the position of the Fulani rulers confirmed, for despite their protestations that they rejected the British 'Indirect Rule' policy the French in fact practised it to a great extent in Northern Cameroons. The rulers co-operated in suppressing the slave-trade, and several cases of it were brought to court: for example twenty in 1930 and three in 1932 in the Circonscription (roughly equivalent to a Division in Nigeria) of Maroua.[35] The traffic across the frontier (mentioned by the British Government in 1934 and also noted by the French Government) was rather harder to deal with.[36]

About 1930 it was said that servants, descendants of the house slaves of the settled Fulanis, knew that they were now free and often regarded their former owners merely as employers, but many stayed with them, for they provided them with food and housing and paid their head-tax. Some left, however, not for their 'often distant' homes but for urban centres.[37] The problem of ex-slaves abandoning the fields which they traditionally farmed during the nomads' absence was already noticeable in Ngaoundere Circonscription (in the Adamaoua uplands), as it has been for Saharans more recently.[38]

Once more, however, famine intervened. In 1932 Kirdi parents were reported to be abandoning their children, who were cared for by Fulanis. The French representative at the Permanent Mandates

Commission in Geneva (which watched over the Mandated Territories of the League of Nations) was asked by Lord Lugard, a member of the commission, whether this situation would not encourage a revival of slavery. The French representative said it was being closely watched.[39] Lugard took a considerable interest in slavery, no doubt because of his work as High Commissioner of Northern Nigeria and later Governor-General of Nigeria. But he was faced with the lack of money available for famine relief and the absence of rural development in the colonies (among other obstacles). This lack of money was not felt only in the depression years like 1932. Both Great Britain and France felt that their colonies should pay their own way as much as possible – a policy which did not help to prevent repeated tragedies caused by famine.

In spite of such setbacks, slavery no doubt declined generally over the years. The Kirdis, who had lived in the mountains, began to move down to the plains (though many remain in the mountains today, arousing the justified admiration of all by their skilled terraced farming). They began to work as labourers and servants for wages, while their general situation was improved by their acceptance of Christian missions and schools. In the late 1950s they were trading successfully and growing richer. They were also multiplying in numbers, thus improving their situation relatively to their traditional overlords. While on a visit to the north, Mongo Beti, Cameroon's best-known novelist and one of her most militant political writers, said that despite this in many ways the Kirdis remained still subject to their overlords. Writing with his usual strong feelings and, it seems, with the disdain felt by many southerners in Cameroon and in Nigeria for the 'North' in those countries, Mongo Beti called the Fulanis 'Muslim conquerors, feudal rulers straight out of the *Thousand and One Nights*, intractable masters of a multitude of slaves, horsemen with escorts and innumerable praise-singers (*griots*), the lords of the North'.[40] Even if they did not all merit this highly coloured description, the Fulani aristocrats probably retained then, and still retain, some of their traditional status, for the example of Northern Nigeria shows that old class and caste divisions outlast slavery. And slavery itself – even if there were no 'masters of a multitude of slaves' elsewhere in Northern Cameroons in the late 1950s – lasted in Rei Bouba until the late 1960s.

The slavery which, for some reason, had been allowed to continue in Rei Bouba was of a particularly cruel sort. About 50,000 people were thought to be the ruler's slaves. He arranged their marriages, and separated wives from their husbands if no children were born; so it was breeding rather than marriage that was important, as among the Moors[41] and as in ancient Rome. Children were separated from their mothers, no doubt so that they would remain loyal only to their master. This was all seen by a European film-making team, and when that team was in the area – when, therefore, the Lamido knew that foreigners were watching! – the slave farm labourers were working all through the daylight hours with only a fifteen-minute break. This was one of the worst cases of slavery surviving in Africa.

The film team which visited Rei Bouba in 1966 was a Norwegian team, and its visit was the result of efforts by the Revd Halfdan Endresen, a pastor of the Norwegian Lutheran Mission which has worked in Northern Cameroon for over forty years. In 1964, after working for thirty years in Ngaoundere, he gave evidence about slavery which was passed on to the UN and to the Cameroon Government for comment. The latter must have known something about the situation, especially as its President (Ahmadou Ahidjo) and other leading members are northerners (the same area of Rei Bouba has a prison camp for political prisoners). But, to its credit, the Ahidjo Government did not reply to Endresen's testimony with resentful denials and hostility as other governments in such situations have done. It allowed him to return to Ngaoundere when he retired in 1966, and it also allowed the Norwegian film team to go to Rei Bouba and see all.[42] Earlier, Endresen had said that he and his wife had often helped fugitive slaves, commenting that the French Government had not even tried to enforce its abolition of slavery in that area. He thanked the independent government for arranging for the release of some slaves, but added that this was not enough.[43]

Then, in 1969, action was taken – quietly. The release of the slaves in this bastion of the past was ordered. Early in 1970 Endresen returned to the area on behalf of the Anti-Slavery Society and reported that the 50,000 people whom the Lamido of Rei Bouba had considered as his personal property were free. Equally important, he reported that land reform and other measures were ensuring their true emancipation. The following year he returned again, and reported that he was satisfied that there was no more chattel slavery; ex-slaves were being re-settled on the land.[44]

This, then, is something of a success story. It shows how informed foreign protests can influence governments in matters on which these do not have a firm conviction of their rightness. Where slavery of the Rei Bouba sort is concerned, this is easier because such things are considered 'backward' as well as oppressive. The fact that real slavery on a large scale went on in that part of Cameroon until well after independence is fantastic, even grotesque, and one wonders what would have happened if Pastor Endresen had not taken action. But action was eventually taken, 'better late then never'.

Endresen, however, said that he had had no reply to another matter about which he had protested, namely the harems of the Northern Cameroon *Lamibe*. He assumed that the Lamido of Rei Bouba still kept his harem, and he claimed that that ruler and another, the Lamido of Ngaoundere, treated their harem women as slaves.[45] He paid particular attention to the harem kept by the traditional ruler of Ngaoundere. In 1932 there were about 300 or 400 women in it, obtained by marriage, purchase or kidnapping. By 14th November, 1961, when the reigning Lamido was dismissed, the number had fallen, but was still considerable. In the eight days that lapsed between that ruler's dismissal and the installation of his successor, Ibrahim Tafada, seventy of the harem concubines escaped. The ruler sent the police to find them and most were recaptured, but then they escaped, one by one, to the Norwegian Lutheran Mission. The mission told the local *sous-préfet* (Cameroon's local administration is based on France's, without the elective element) about the fugitives and generally secured his approval for their liberation, to the anger of the Lamido. But later, when eight more fugitives from the harem arrived at the mission and were taken by Endresen to the *sous-préfet* the official sent them back to the Lamido, who was ordered to free them one by one himself. One of the eight, named Atadjumba, escaped again later; the mission asked the *sous-préfet* to free her, and on receiving no reply arranged for her marriage to a new husband to make her free; then the Lamido freed the other seven.[46]

So some of the women detained in the harem against their will were eventually freed, but what about the others? The problem raised by Endresen was a serious one. The Cameroon Government said that he was confusing slavery with polygamy, which could not be abolished. In Africa, Christian missions have always opposed polygamy, mainly on the grounds that it involves degrading, even virtual enslavement, of the wives, or of all but the principal wife. For Muslims, slavery traditionally went together with harems, for although a man was allowed to have four free wives the mistresses whom he was also allowed were supposed to be slaves.[47] This provision of Muslim law was no doubt re-interpreted when slavery was generally abolished, as leading Muslims have for long opposed slavery. But the large harems of Muslim rulers are a relic of slavery, and this is probably evident to all concerned. The same may be true in some non-Muslim areas of Africa, where the number of wives is not always limited as it is in Muslim law.

But independent African governments are no more faced with an obvious solution than colonial governments were. Enforcing legal monogamy would be difficult enough; enforcing fidelity would be impossible. As long as the possession of many wives remains socially acceptable, it will go on even if only one wife can legally be called a wife. As polygamy is still widely accepted socially in Africa, it is not surprising that black African governments have not tried to abolish it. While it goes on, the maintenance of slave harems in some areas may be easy, but it is hard to see where the line could be practically drawn. Without 1984-style spying into all private households it is almost impossible to tell whether all the wives of a ruler like a Lamido have consented freely to live in his harem, and whether any of them are being intolerably ill-treated. To order all of them – or all of them beyond a certain number – to leave would be hard on those who genuinely do not mind staying. There could be many of these, for the position of a 3rd or 4th wife, or even of a 283rd concubine, is not always regarded as shameful. Educated African women are often ready to accept polygamy, even if they do not really like the thought of it. Not all women consider it as slavery and want to be liberated.

When all this is conceded, however, it remains that in modern Africa a chief who tries to recapture a runaway member of his harem needs to prove his right to do so – to put it mildly. Even a monogamous husband has, of course, no absolute right to reclaim a fugitive wife, neither legally nor in practice. In Africa wives are not always treated as prisoners, any more than they are in Europe. In fact, even in polygamous households they do not necessarily seem like abject slaves. This may be because they can, in the last resort, leave, though not always easily. All that seems necessary is that a woman in a northern chief's harem should be free to leave if she wants to; a chief is bound to have more effective power than an ordinary husband but he need not be allowed to reclaim any runaway harem girl. Still less, should he be allowed to kidnap or buy a new one. If these minimal preventive steps are taken, harems in various parts of Africa will no doubt before long lose their quasi-slave character.

### Revolution and slavery in Guinea

In the Fouta Djalon mountains slavery was even more widespread in the 1950s than in Northern Cameroon, 1,500 miles further east. But it also ended more swiftly and spectacularly, as a result of a social and political revolution in which slaves partook.

As in Nigeria and Cameroon, the Fulanis in Guinea have always

West Africa

been partly nomadic and partly settled (few are nomads in Guinea now). The settled ones became Muslim first and, in the Fouta Djalon, established the state ruled by 'Almamys' in the eighteenth century. The half-converted Fulani nomads, cattle-herders there as elsewhere, were treated as vassals but not as slaves. Some of the slaves were descendants of earlier peoples, for example the Dialonke and Baga, who were conquered by the Fulanis in the seventeenth century and later; others were taken in raids, or bought. Other tribes in the area (which, at the end of the nineteenth century, became French Guinea) also had slaves, including the Diakhanke *marabouts* or Muslim 'holy men' in the north. All these were subject to early French regulations against the slave-trade and slavery itself. But the regulations were enforced very incompletely, as a recent study by the French geographer and historian, Jean Suret-Canale, shows.[48]

In other parts of Guinea, according to this study, 'since the years 1900–14, all those who have really wished to emancipate themselves (if necessary by flight) have managed to do so'. But in Fouta Djalon slavery continued. Chiefs who opposed the colonial Administration might be punished by the release of their slaves, but loyal chiefs were allowed to keep their *'captifs'* (other Fulanis also had these). Generally, the slaves had their own hamlets, *roundé*, situated next to the free people's hamlets (*foulasso*), but some stayed in the latter to do domestic work. In hilly areas the *roundé* were built on slopes or on dry terraces, among the fields.[49] This sort of farm slavery was more like that found in Rei Bouba than among the Wodaabe of Bornu. It was tolerated by the Administration, which could have runaways recaptured as 'vagrants'.[50] Sale of slaves became rarer, and prices for them also fell; by 1936 a slave could be bought for a cow or for 150 francs, compared with three cows (or eight for a blacksmith) earlier. With trading in slaves now unimportant, the number in captivity fell, even though famine in the 1930s had the same effect here as in many other parts of West Africa.[51] In 1904 half of the population of the Fouta Djalon was thought to be servile; in 1955 less than one-quarter of the population were considered as 'servants'.

The end of slavery came suddenly soon after this. After the introduction of party politics into French Africa, first for the African deputies in the National Assembly and then for local assemblies, the *Parti Démocratique de la Guinée* led by Ahmed Sekou Touré became the dominant party in French Guinea in the mid-50s. It was a radical party which won popularity and power, not exactly by democratic means (rather the reverse at times) but certainly by appealing to popular desire for reform, particularly in rural areas. There the French ruled through chiefs who were tools of the Administration rather than traditional rulers, and who had to enforce demands for taxes, food deliveries, forced labourers and army recruits (when men had to be provided, slaves were often the ones picked: a combination of traditional and modern oppression).[52] In the Fouta Djalon it also involved toleration of slavery. So in 1956–7, when there was a general popular resistance to the Administration in rural French Guinea, chiefs were deposed, and slaves were freed. The abolition of chieftaincy was decreed by the PDG Government already in effective power in Conakry; it was part of a general imposition of the party's rule in the countryside.[53]

Several slaves took part in this mass movement, which was less an actual revolt than a simple general rejection of the administrative set-up. It is the only case in Africa where slavery has been ended by revolutionary action. This may have been possible only in Guinea, because of the special circumstances there. But there it seems to have worked, and one of the last bastions of traditional slavery fell, and many slaves were freed.[54] Sekou Touré, who in 1958 took Guinea into independence against the wish of de Gaulle and who established an iron-handed régime during the difficulties which followed, has continued to have some Fulani opposition. This makes it all the more probable that the emancipation of Fulani slaves has gone on. And Touré's government, though a complete dictatorship which has recently distinguished itself by horrifying 'purges', could be said to be egalitarian – at least relatively. It has even tried to curb private traders and to discourage polygamy, in the name of ending 'exploitation', and it is not likely to tolerate any vestiges of the slavery which was supposed to have ended in the 1950s.

*Kurteys and others*
Mali, Guinea's vast neighbour, has had her share of slavery, as her government admitted in reply to the UN questionnaire. As mentioned earlier, the Tuareg enslaved the peoples collectively called Bela, there and further east in Niger. It was in Niger, at Tillabery on the Niger River, that a British visitor in 1963 saw a market where one could buy cattle, fish and ... slaves. Or so he thought, after having some girls offered to him for sale. It is possible that they were prostitutes and that it was their ponces who were offering their services for sale; but they may have had so little say in the matter that the transaction was true slave-dealing, 'white slavery' being quite often an accurate expression. This was especially likely in that area, the home of the Bela.

Not far from Tillabery live the Kurtey people, a small tribe which traditionally raided for slaves, and whose slave caste is still distinct if not actually still enslaved. The Kurtey number about 15,000, and live between Dessa, upriver from Tillabery, and Say, below the capital city of Niamey. Some of them, along with the neighbouring Wogo people, have emigrated to Nigeria. Others have emigrated for months or years to Ghana, which is a much richer country, but the migration of Kurteys is said to be due partly to frustration on the part of the ex-slave caste at denial of rights and duties and consequent boredom.[55]

The Kurtey are of Fulani descent, and like Fulanis they keep cattle, although some grow rice by the river. A number live on islands in the river, and it was from there that they carried out their slave-raids by canoe in the old days, capturing slaves for their own use or for sale, ransom or exchange. The Tuareg also raided along the river, but they let the other peoples there keep their own slaves, and the Kurteys, fleeing to the river islands, seized Tuareg slaves among others. Their own slaves sometimes lived in slave villages, and to this day such villages remain dependent on freemen, paying them heavy dues in work or in kind. This is one aspect of the continued subordination of the old slave caste, which formerly made up nearly two-thirds of a Kurtey community. Slaves were then minors for life, as among the Moors, and hut slaves were tied to one family for three generations, although they could become integrated into the free family.

The inferior position of ex-slaves seems to be unusually well maintained among the Kurteys. A few years ago a study of them noted: 'Officially freed by the coloniser, the former captives kept their dependent status and their state of economic subjection'; and that, 'contempt for the captive is, still today, more deeply rooted than elsewhere'.[56] If this social distinction is still important enough to encourage men to emigrate, it seems that only in a limited sense can one say that slavery has ended among the Kurteys. Generally, Niger may be a stronghold of slavery or related institutions.

The abolition of slavery by the French seems to have been a slow and partial process in another poor, landlocked territory – Ubangi-Shari, now the Central African Republic. A Catholic missionary reported in 1955 that he had been told that slavery still existed there; some slaves had been passed off as their masters' sons after 1930–2, he said, and there were still young children who were in fact bought slaves, though passed off as brothers and sisters of the children they were employed to care for. He heard of an alleged 'son', really a slave, re-sold by his 'father' at Bondoko, and of employees of firms who paid over their wages to an owner.[57] Some of these reports may have related to 'pawning' of children (of which more will be said in Chapter Eleven) rather than to actual slavery, and others to petty rather than to large-scale slave-dealing. But generally, there is no reason to doubt this report; the poverty of what is now the CAR makes it possible that such things have not ended. As this missionary said, regulations could not end them.

The number of people involved in all these cases of slavery, in Northern Nigeria, Niger, Northern Cameroon and elsewhere, is probably very small in relation to the population of the Sahelian belt. The survival of some sort of slavery is no greater, perhaps less, than what one would expect in an area where slavery was a normal part of life for centuries, until two or three generations ago. Bearing this in mind, one is impressed by the changes which have taken place in these old slave societies; such slavery as still goes on is isolated and exceptional, and is only a small part of the problems of one of the world's poorest areas.

## Notes

1. S. Sikes, *Lake Chad*.
2. S. J. Hogben and A. H. M. Kirk-Greene, *The Emirates of Northern Nigeria*.
3. A. G. B. Fisher and H. Fisher, *Slavery and Muslim Society in Africa* (1970), pp. 17 ff.
4. Whitaker, *The Politics of Tradition* (Princeton University Press, 1970).
5. R. Heussler, *The British in Northern Nigeria*, p. 66.
6. Whitaker, op. cit., pp. 40 ff.
7. Ibid., pp. 412–13.
8. Ibid., p. 41.
9. H. Barth, *Travels and Discoveries in North and Central Africa*, Ch. XXIV.
10. Polly Hill, *Rural Hausa: A Village and A Setting*, p. 40.
11. Sir Alan Burns, *History of Nigeria*, p. 205.
12. Ibid., pp. 204–5.
13. Ibid.
14. Heussler, op. cit., p. 61.
15. Ibid., pp. 153–4.
16. Ibid., pp. 128, 134.
17. M. Perham, *Native Administration in Nigeria*, pp. 49–50.
18. A. H. M. Kirk-Greene, *Adamawa Past and Present*, p. 180.
19. Stanhope White. *Dan Bana*, pp. 108–9.
20. Perham, op. cit., p. 50.
21. White, op. cit., 44–5.
22. Report on the Administration of Cameroons under British Mandate for the Year 1934, p. 188.
23. Kirk-Greene, op. cit., p. 4.
24. R. Cohen, *The Structure of Kanuri Society* (unpublished thesis), p. 129.
25. Whitaker, op. cit. p. 339.
26. M. G. Smith, *Government in Zazzau*, pp. 253ff.
27. Hill, op. cit., pp. 38–47.
28. *The Anti-Slavery Society: Its Task Today*.
29. D. J. Stenning in *Islam in Tropical Africa*, ed. I. M. Lewis, pp. 387 ff.
30. Ibid., p. 395.
31. A. Gerteiny, *Mauritania*, pp. 95–6.
32. V. Monteil, Lewis (ed.), op. cit., pp. 342 ff.
33. Mbaye Gueye, quoted in V. Monteil, *l'Islam Noir* (1971), p. 284.
34. *The Anti-Slavery Society: Its Task Today*.
35. Report for Maroua, in Cameroon Archives, Yaounde, file APA 11751.
36. Permanent Mandates Commission, report of 24th session (1933), p. 42.
37. Report for Ngaoundere, in Cameroon Archives, file APA 11751.
38. See Chapter Two.
39. Permanent Mandates Commission, report of 24th session, p. 41.
40. Mongo Beti in *Preuves* (Paris, 1959), No. 104, p. 35.
41. See Chapter One.
42. *The Anti-Slavery Society: Its Task Today*, pp. 12–13.
43. Anti-Slavery Society Annual Report 1969–70, pp. 9–10.
44. Anti-Slavery Society Annual Report 1970–1, p. 9.
45. Ibid.
46. M. Pollaud-Dulian, *Aujourd'hui l'Esclavage*, p. 46.
47. Fisher and Fisher, op. cit., p. 100.

48. J. Suret-Canale, *La République de Guinée* (1970), pp. 104, 136 ff.
49. Ibid., p. 134.
50. Ibid., p. 136.
51. Ibid., p. 104.
52. Ibid., pp. 97, 136.
53. Ibid., pp. 164–7.
54. Ibid., p. 136.
55. J.-P. Olivier de Sardan, 'Les Voleurs d'Hommes', in *Études Nigériennes* (Niamey, 1969), No. 25.
56. Ibid.
57. R. P. Charles Tisserant, quoted in *Anti-Slavery Reporter* (June 1960).

*Chapter Four*

# Black African Slaves and Serfs

Black Africa can be defined roughly as the region south of the Sahara and of the Ethiopian highlands. The great majority of its population is made up of several hundred tribes of Negro African peoples, perhaps half of them speaking Bantu languages. The forest belt, which extends up to 200 miles inland in West Africa from Liberia to Cameroon and covers considerable areas of former French Equatorial Africa and Zaire (the former Belgian Congo), is the home of some tens of millions. In the eastern part of the continent, the rain forest is much smaller and less important. However, considerable parts of black Africa are covered with other woodlands, besides savanna and other sorts of vegetation. One large region, the West African Sahel, has already been described. Parts of East, Central and South Africa resemble it, but are more hilly, even mountainous.

There is a wide variety of peoples in black Africa, ranging from tribes of several millions, such as the Yoruba, Ibo, Ashanti, 'Hausa-Fulani' and Kanuri peoples of West Africa, the Bakongo around the Zaire (Congo) River estuary and the Baganda of Uganda, to groups of a few thousand, such as the Embu of Kenya and the Batanga of Cameroon. The fame of some, for example the Zulu of South Africa and the Ashanti of Ghana, has spread to Europe; others, for example the Bemba of Zambia, the Shilluk of the southern Sudan and the Mende of Sierra Leone have been minutely studied by specialists. Mostly farmers, often herders, sometimes fishermen, the black African peoples have been affected by many economic changes, particularly in the south where white settlement and other aspects of colonisation have been the most pronounced.

So far as slavery is concerned, one part of black Africa has already been discussed in the last chapter. In the rest of the southern two-thirds of Africa there are all the variations one would expect. Slavery had its place in great numbers of tribes. In the old days of the European slave-trade much was written about it, often with the intention of showing that African slavery was traditional and had nothing to do with the Europeans and their trade. These writings are often not reliable, just as those of the nineteenth-century anti-slavery writers are not always accurate, but it is clear that slavery was traditional in much of black Africa. This chapter looks at the ways in which it survived, or did not survive, among various peoples during the colonial period.

The Ashanti of Ghana are one of the leading tribes of West Africa. For two centuries before the establishment of British rule in 1900 they had a powerful confederacy, ruled by a King called the Asantehene, with many tributary and vassal states. The power of successive Asantehenes varied, the Ashanti wars of conquest and rebellion providing supplies for countless slave-ships calling at Accra, Anomabo and other ports on the 'Gold Coast'. The Ashantis also had domestic slaves. Some of these were destined for a use which contemporary British writers often mentioned in connection with this and other African peoples: human sacrifice, for example at the funeral of chiefs. Some reports of human sacrifices at Kumasi, the Asantehene's capital, were clearly exaggerated, but nevertheless this was certainly one possible destiny for a slave. Most slaves, however, were used for domestic and farm work.

In a detailed study made a quarter of a century after the establishment of British rule following the Ashanti wars (the last being in 1900), Captain R. S. Rattray noted that all Ashantis were considered to be slaves of a sort: '... a condition of voluntary servitude was, in a very literal sense, the heritage of every Ashanti; it formed indeed the essential basis of his social system.'[1] But there were people who were subject to a more particular sort of servitude. A non-Ashanti bought for slavery was called an *odonko*; many such slaves came from areas to the north, whose people were once generally called *odonko* by Ashantis.[2] The big market for slaves and other goods in the area in pre-colonial times was at Salaga. A prisoner-of-war could become a slave; he was called a *domum* but could be an *odonko* too, as could slaves paid as tribute (a common custom in many old states in Africa). An Ashanti could become a slave like an *odonko*, but was always distinguished from a foreign slave. He might be enslaved because of an unpaid debt of his master.[3]

Ashanti slaves had rights. 'A slave might marry; own property; himself own a slave; swear an "oath"; be a competent witness; and ultimately might become heir to his master.'[4] However, although a slave girl could marry her master or another free Ashanti, her children by him became her master's slaves.[4] In many cases, possibly nine out of ten, a slave could become an adoptive member of his master's family and his origin could be forgotten. But *odonko* status could never be lost, and in pre-colonial times it made one liable for selection for human sacrifice; some villages were considered as human reservoirs for this purpose.[5]

A slave could become free, sometimes becoming a pawn (*awowa*) as an intermediate stage. As a pawn he was handed over to a creditor pending payment of a debt; he could be the slave of the debtor, but was often one of his free relatives. However a slave progressed to freedom, his slave origin was remembered. The same remained true even after the colonial government abolished slavery. Thirty years after Rattray's study, another was to say: 'Slavery was legally abolished by the British, though the memory lingers on.'[6] This seems to have been the normal pattern. Class societies in pre-colonial times were certainly not confined to the savanna states; class distinctions were very important among the Ashantis, and such things do not change overnight. The main change among the Ashantis has been that modern developments have created new sorts of distinction among people. Now education and money can be as important as birth, and chiefs and nobles must send their children to school in order to keep up their position.[6] This is true of many of the coastal regions of West Africa where Christianity and Western education have spread and come to be generally respected. A slave's son can have a better education and a better job and earn more money than a nobleman's son. But even so, he may not be considered as his equal. Ashantis for long regarded it as important if a man's ancestors were slaves, and some still do so.

In the Gold Coast the British authorities took hastier action against slavery than usual. Their normal custom was to outlaw slave-dealing immediately, but to leave the abolition of slavery itself until a little later. While they wanted to end slavery, both out of conviction and because of pressure from missionaries, the Anti-Slavery Society and others, they knew how important slavery could be in a society and wanted its abolition to be done with the minimum of fuss and trouble. Sometimes domestic slavery was tolerated for a considerable period. This happened in Sierra Leone, and obvious ironic comments were made on the persistence of legal domestic slavery in a colony originally based on a settlement for freed slaves. These comments missed the point, however. The people in this ex-slaves' settlement at Freetown, with its small extensions in other areas, were very different from the people of the interior, which in the nineteenth century was no more under British rule and Western influence than most other parts of West Africa. The members of the coastal community ('Creoles') were mainly of Christian belief and European culture, though most were Africans freed from slave-ships in the nineteenth century, or descendants of people so freed, and therefore kept many African traditions. They were businessmen, lawyers and officials who had been educated at home or in England. Not much of their special way of life penetrated to the interior tribes, of whom the Mende were the most important. So when those tribes were brought under the Sierra Leone Protectorate in 1896 they retained traditions and customs, including slavery, which were unknown to the Creoles of Sierra Leone Colony.

This helps explain the apparent irony of a court judgement delivered in Freetown, the home of freed ex-slaves founded in 1792, in favour of the legality of slave-holding in the Sierra Leone Protectorate in 1926. The judgement was given on 1 July 1926 by the Sierra Leone Supreme Court and quashed the conviction of two Protectorate men on a charge of recapturing runaway slaves. By it those traditional slave-owners, and all others, were recognised as having a right not only to own slaves but to recapture them if they left.[7] In this respect, the law was far behind that of Northern Nigeria, where efforts to recapture runaway slaves had been illegal since 1900. This was no doubt due to simple inefficiency; in March 1926, just before the case, an Ordinance had been passed to 'remove the last vestige of recognition by the local law of the status of slavery in Sierra Leone, but the loop-hole found by the Supreme Court had been left. This was closed by a new Ordinance in 1927.[8]

The Mende waged many wars in pre-colonial times, and slavery was partly connected with these wars. Kenneth Little considers that: 'Though predatory warfare ... was carried on partly for the purpose of enhancing prestige, the main incentive was slaves. Slaves constituted the principal form of wealth, and were bartered and exchanged for goods, notably for salt from the coast. They also served as currency in a large variety of transactions. They provided the basis, in fact, of the social system, and upon their labours as domestics depended, very largely, whatever agriculture the Mende possessed.'[9] They felled trees, prepared the ground for rice, collected and cracked palm kernels and extracted palm oil. In the interior, the Fulani cattle herders would sell three to six cows for a slave.

The Mende slaves who worked on the land were usually members of their master's household and had a number of rights. They were not usually sold, except for serious offences like adultery with a free man's wife. They had their own plots of land and kept what they grew there; later, in the British period, their descendants obtained secure possession of land, but even earlier it was felt wrong to separate a slave from the land where he was born and bred. Traditionally, a slave could own a slave.[10] In all these respects, slavery among the Mende was similar to that among the Ashanti and other African peoples. It is clear that the idea put out in the days of the Atlantic slave-trade – that the victims of that trade were only being taken away from slavery equal to West Indies plantation slavery or worse – was generally false.

Mende slaves could also become free, and it seems that when British rule was established fourth-generation slaves were hardly distinguishable from free men; at that time, however, ex-slaves were used by the British to enforce their rule over the Mende, a fact which provoked the great rising of 1898.[11] One important difference between Mende and Ashanti traditions was that a freeman's child by his slave girl was free. All over the world one vital difference among slave-systems has been the treatment of such offspring, who have always been numerous.

It is not surprising that slavery lasted so long among the Mende, for they have preserved other traditions well, such as the system of control over the people by secret societies – the Poro society for men, the Bundu society for women – which are also for initiation and social education. They have resisted both Christianity and Islam more than many other African peoples. However, like the other peoples of the former Protectorate they have for long had Western education which has put them on a cultural level with the Creoles, and this must have changed the old society as in other countries. Probably the usual pattern prevails: only a few people actually belong to others but many of slave origin are felt to be still slaves in a sense (Little says that the Mende call the Creoles 'sons of slaves'.[12]) And Sierra Leone is one place where kidnapping and slave-dealing occurs quite often. Sometimes it is for ritual purposes such as cannibalism – outlawed and severely punished, of course, but still occurring from time to time. As elsewhere, vestiges of domestic slavery may make such crimes easier.[13]

Nigeria contains some of Africa's largest 'tribes'. In the southern and partly forested districts are found the Yoruba, Ibo and Ibibio-Efik peoples. The Yorubas form most of the population (perhaps about 10 million) of the Western State and are more numerous than the populations of most African states. There are great variations among the Yorubas, who were not given that collective name until the nineteenth century and were traditionally better known by the names of their various sub-groups – Egbas, Ekitis, Oyos, Ibadans, etc. Even today these distinctions remain important, and it is mainly other peoples who see 'the Yorubas' as one unit. But they

## 88 AFRICA'S SLAVES TODAY

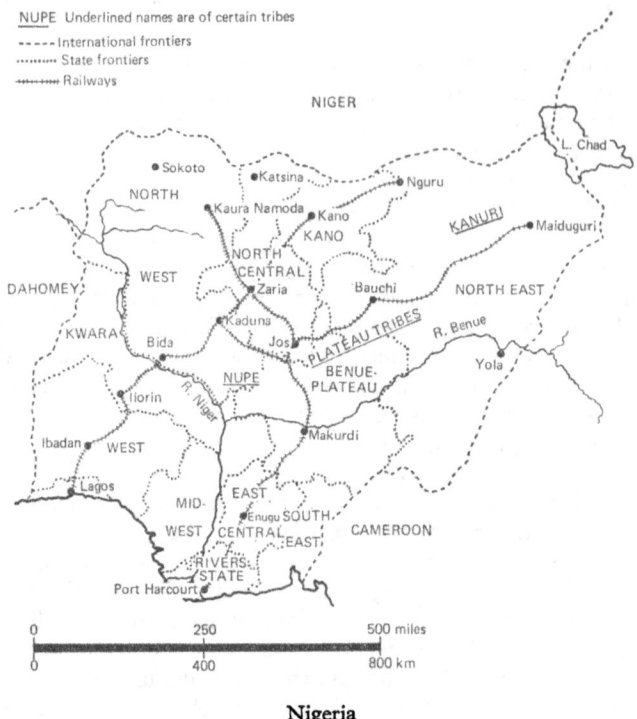

Nigeria

have a common language and a common culture and body of traditions, including the tradition of descent from Oduduwa, the legendary ancestor who lived at Ife, the historical Yoruba heartland. They have one of the most elaborate (and most elaborately studied) African religions. In the history of African slavery, the Yorubas figure prominently. Slavery was important in the old Empire of Oyo which ruled most of the Yorubas for a time, and the wars of that Empire and its subject states provided slaves for the slave-ships, especially during the early nineteenth century when there was an active slave-traffic (whose result is the persistence of large Yoruba communities in Brazil and Cuba).

In a sense, slavery brought Europeans to Yorubaland: slave-traders first, then the British Government acting against the slave-trade and missionaries who opposed the slave-trade and slavery itself and were aided by Yoruba ex-slaves or sons of ex-slaves. Among the Ebgas in western Yorubaland, where Christian missions were established as early as 1845, slavery was a problem before British annexation in the 1890s. One Yoruba clergyman born in Sierra Leone, James Johnson, was a fierce opponent of slave-holding by his fellow-countrymen. (Johnson was also a pioneer nationalist, who thought Africa could become Christian and be reformed without being conquered. Whether this could have happened, and whether slavery could have ended in such a way, is an intriguing academic question.)[14]

There were several sorts of Yoruba slavery. Many slaves were used for the usual domestic and farm work; it was their labour, as among the Mende, which extended the area of agriculture. But as there were powerful states, another sort of slavery existed – administrative and court slavery, as in Hausaland. The *Obas* or Kings, such as the Alafin of Oyo and the Oni of Ife, had slave-officials who could be very powerful, dreaded by all except the ruler who, in the last resort, remained the master. In one Yoruba state, Ijebu, the Oba (there entitled the Awujale), had about twenty specialised groups of court slaves: messengers, drummers, etc.[15] Palace slaves were called *odi* and, at Ijebu at least, could make use of some of the ruler's land, although they did not actually own it. Generally, a slave could not own land but could have his own farm on his master's land and might be allowed to stay on it if passed together with the land to the master's successor on his death.[16] A slave could buy his freedom and become the owner of his farm. The possibility of self-redemption is found in many old African slave-systems; it also existed, at least sometimes, in the New World. Such old systems should on no account be idealised; slaves could be used as currency by the Yorubas and other peoples.

In the twentieth century, the usual processes of abolition and economic change affected slavery in Yorubaland. As early as 1903 chiefs were protesting against the loss of their slaves.[17] Education and money-making, both likely to affect the old social order though not to destroy it, advanced rapidly in Yorubaland (the Yorubas are renowned as traders and businessmen) and politics provided new social values and hierarchies. But many of the social distinctions based on past institutions remained. About the time of Nigeria's independence (1960), P. C. Lloyd wrote of the Yorubas: 'The stigma of slave origin still prevents the full absorption of many nineteenth-century captives into the communities to which they formerly belonged and in which they now live as free men.'[18]

The same writer mentions legal problems which resulted from the old free slave distinction. As a slave could not own property, though a freed ex-slave could, problems over succession to property arose, which the colonial abolition of slavery could not prevent, it seems. In one case heard in 1935 a woman who owned several farms bequeathed a third of her land to a former slave who had, on being emancipated, remained with her as her adoptive son, planting cocoa (the main cash crop of the Yorubas) for no pay; her daughter contested this but without success.[19] Such cases no doubt are much rarer now, since the number of ex-slaves and their children has declined (half the population is under twenty in much of Africa today). But the law has a long memory and slavery may for long leave traces legally as well as socially.

The Obas, like the Asantehene and Hausa Emirs, also have retainers and courtiers whose predecessors were slaves and who may not always seem very different themselves to public opinion. But that does not imply any real survival of slavery.

*The Ibos: oru and osu*
The Ibos, second only to the Yorubas among the peoples of Southern Nigeria, not only retained traces of domestic slavery for decades after abolition (in the usual way), but also maintained until the present day a caste distinction based on a particular sort of old slavery connected with the traditional religion.

The Ibos are the largest ethnic group in the former Eastern Region of Nigeria, which was known for a terrible two-and-a-half-year period as the 'Republic of Biafra' (1967–70). They number perhaps 7 or 8 million. In Nigeria they have for long been noted not only for their numbers but also for the way Christianity and modern education have progressed among them, and for their migration over the country to do jobs for which their advance in education has qualified them. The Ibo homeland, the East Central State, is one of the most Christian parts of Africa, and the Ibos are more 'Western', for example in family life and clothing, than most other Nigerians. But tradition is very strong in Iboland, although this may not be noticed by the traveller who sees the bustling modern market-town of Onitsha, the un-traditional local capital of Enugu, and the Christian churches in every village. The old religion survives well, and so does the maintenance as a separate caste of the descendants of former 'ritual slaves' of that religion, called *osu* in the Ibo language.

Before the British occupation at the beginning of the twentieth century (which was resisted strongly), the Ibos lived mainly in self-contained village units, ruled by popular assemblies. Except for those who were ruled by the Kingdom of Benin to the west (one of the major West African states for several centuries), the Ibos governed themselves in a democratic way, equalled in few parts of the world. But that did not prevent them from having domestic or farm slaves. These do not seem to have been seriously oppressed; they could own property and, although they had to ask for permission to marry from their masters, they usually received it. Runaways, however, were cruelly punished if caught.[20]

If the treatment of slaves in the home was usually mild, the way in which they were caught or bought was not. Kidnapping was a normal feature of life in old Iboland; children were often kidnapped in their sleep and sold as slaves. Others were made slaves for committing some crime. Large numbers of Ibos were taken south as slaves. Their coastal neighbours, the Ijaws of the Niger delta and the Ibibio-Efiks further east, bought many of them for export or local use. As ports in this area were very prominent in the slave-trade – namely the Efik port of Calabar (Old Calabar) and the Ijaw port of Bonny – the number of Ibos sent as slaves to the New World was large. Slaves were brought from many parts of the interior to these ports, often by the Aros, a branch of the Ibos who specialised in long-distance trade. The Aros had a shrine, the so-called 'Long Juju' of Arochuku, which was supposed to be an oracle; human beings were paid as fees for consulting the oracle or given as sacrifices to appease the deity, and then enslaved and taken to the coast. Many Ibo slaves remained in the hands of the Ijaws, Efiks and Ibibios. Some worked as farm labourers, but many became part of a local institution called the 'House'. This was a business firm run as an enlarged family concern, and comprised the master, his family and others, including slaves.[21] The 'House' system, the basis of the trading states in the nineteenth century, was tolerated by the British early in the twentieth century, despite the fact that it involved slavery. It was declared legal in 1901, but abolished in 1914.[22]

The Ibos had no similar system, and slavery among them was a small-scale institution. But it was so important socially that prejudice against ex-slaves, normal in Africa for some time after emancipation, was still surviving among the Ibos in the late 1930s. Then G. T. Basden, who had spent thirty-five years in Iboland, wrote that: 'Slavery is not, of course, tolerated or recognised by the British Constitution, whereas the native adheres rigidly to the division in social affairs',[23] and '... the accident of being of slave-descent is still a powerful element in the lives of the people ... In normal daily life, free- and slave-born mingle together unconcernedly, and little difference is observable on the surface; in actual fact, the superiority of freedom is constant and always effective in operation.'[24] There was some segregation in schools and in cemeteries, and the

Christian missions, Basden thought, had 'done little' to end inequality.[25]

The ordinary Ibo slave, called an *oru*, was distinguished from the ritual slave or *osu*, who was 'a living sacrifice' offered to a deity of the old religion. Ibo towns had statues and mounds in honour of such deities, and priests handling the worship of them; when a boy or girl was sacrificed as an *osu* he or she remained for life attached to the shrine, as a special type of slave. Children born under *osu* conditions became *osu*, and a free man having sexual relations with an *osu* girl was obliged to become an *osu* himself. Children were bought or kidnapped for this sort of sacrifice.[26] They and their descendants could not be redeemed, and they formed a separate caste.

Kidnapping and purchase of human beings for this purpose, as for others, were banned by the British. But Basden reported that many chiefs and others still found 'means to retain, or increase, a retinue of slaves by clever manipulation of the "osu" and "pawning" systems.'[27] Pawning was then very common in Iboland and people placed in pawn for debt were in practice hardly ever redeemed; some better-off people, Basden said, secured by this custom 'a considerable number of wageless workers; in plain language, slaves'.[28] Continued recruitment of new *osu* slaves was no doubt less easy, though kidnapping was still common. But the number of *osu* was always increased naturally anyway, and the main problem was that they and their children were still regarded as inferior and different. Many of them went to school and obtained good jobs, but they remained a distinct and despised caste.[29]

This residue of slavery has lasted longer than others in Iboland, and is far from dead today. Twenty years ago a work by two anthropologists, G. T. Jones and the late Daryll Forde, could state that among the Ibos: 'There is no open domestic or chattel slavery today, nor, save in a few exceptional areas (e.g. Nara, among the Northern Ibo), does slave origin (*ohu*) connote extreme social inferiority.'[30] Later, there were isolated cases of kidnapping and slave-dealing, and even of a revival of a custom to which Forde referred, namely the killing of men to accompany the funeral of a leading person. This particular reversion to tradition, however, was punishable by hanging, and was no more typical of general practice than the murderous 'leopard-men' cult in Eastern Iboland in the 1950s, similarly punishable by death. Such crimes, officially banned and severely punished, are not in the same category as traditions openly tolerated and approved in defiance of 'modern' ideas. One such tradition was, and is, that of contempt for the *osu*. However numerous and well-educated and prosperous they might be, *osu* people are still regarded as inferior and subject to discrimination.

This discrimination lasted into the days when Eastern Nigerians were among the leaders of nationalism and party politics. After the attainment of internal self-government in the Eastern Region, the contradiction between the political ideals professed at the time and the *osu* system was acknowledged. In 1956 an Act was passed in the Region's House of Assembly to abolish all discrimination against *osu* people. It was made an offence to deny equal rights and privileges to people on account of their origin, and to call someone either *osu* or *oru*. During the debate, the *osu* were compared to the 'untouchables' of India and the American Negroes.[31] The comparison was not altogether accurate because the *osu* system does not seem to imply *economic* relegation. An *osu* may suffer discrimination in access to schools and jobs, but there has for long been no serious effort to maintain him in menial occupations. The main discrimination is social. Another Ibo may treat an *osu* on terms of equality in the office but rebuff him socially in the evening. And it is this sort of prejudice (not comparable in degree to what happens in India, of course) that laws are least able to abolish.

The law of 1956 could not, in fact, have abolished prejudice against the *osu* caste, and it has not done so. To this day, Ibos know who is an *osu* and who is not, and the difference still matters. This is one of the most extreme cases of a survival of prejudice dating from the days of slavery.

*Central African examples*
Those who divide Africa into geographical regions commonly make Nigeria's eastern frontier the eastern end of 'West Africa'. This arbitrary division makes some sense because it happens that Cameroon, and in particular the ex-British part of that country bordering on Nigeria, is at the north-western edge of Bantu Africa. Bantu-speaking peoples are found in Southern Cameroon and due east of there in other countries, and further south, as far as South Africa. How much the 'Bantu' peoples, who have occupied this vast area of Africa for centuries, have in common, seems to be in dispute, but their languages link them all; the Duala and Bakweri languages spoken on the coast of Cameroon are recognisably related to Sesotho and other Bantu languages of Southern Africa.

Slavery is traditional in much of Bantu Africa, as in West Africa. The overseas slave-trade has had the same effects on the coast as it has had all over the continent. Some peoples such as the Vais of what is now Liberia, the Efiks of Calabar, and the Dualas, near neighbours of the Efiks and living like them on an estuary which became an important port for Europeans, were specialists for centuries in the export of other Africans. The Dualas' domestic slavery may have been powerfully influenced by their trading in slaves with white men. Among the slaves they kept for themselves, the Dualas distinguished between the prisoner-of-war (*mukoma*), the slave purchased as an adult (*mukaki*) or as a child (*etumbe*), the slave presented as a gift (*mujabedi*), and the half-free son of a slave (*muyabedi*).³² The Germans, after establishing their colony of Kamerun, decided that the existing custom of making a slave's son a muyabedi was a good way of gradually ending domestic slavery, and in 1902 ordered that it should be adopted by all other tribes.³³ This can hardly have been easy to apply everywhere (the limited abolition in the Fulani areas has already been noted).

Among the Dualas slavery gradually declined but, at the same time, many Dualas were encouraged by the German and later French Administrations to develop plantations for cocoa and palms and the labourers employed in these plantations were the same interior people who had formerly been enslaved. The difference between the labourers and former slaves was not at first clear to everyone and may have been slight. In the town of Douala itself, after it began to be developed as the main commercial centre of the territory, many immigrants from the interior came to work, and for long they used to live among the Dualas as clients performing services in return for houses or food, and sometimes becoming absorbed into the Duala community. So the old relationship between the former slave-dealers and the former slaves was not wholly changed. The Bamileke people may now dominate Douala's population and its small businesses, but a Duala may still call a Bamileke, as a term of abuse, a *mukom'a grafi* – a 'Bamileke slave'; for many of the slaves sold by Dualas (and by Efiks) to Europeans in the past were Bamilekes.

The Bamileke people are the most numerous group in Cameroon, numbering some hundreds of thousands. Their homeland (from which many have emigrated) is in the mountains separating ex-French and ex-British Cameroon. There they have, or had, an elaborate social system in which the chiefs had power over the land but traditionally used it for the benefit of all; a fairly democratic system, in fact, where there was only a limited role for slavery. A man's children could be seized for his debts (debt-pawning was abolished by both the Germans and the French, the French taking care to specify that gambling debts were also covered, but it went on); however, a study of Bamileke society notes that: 'Slavery did exist in Bamileke country, but it never constituted, as it did in the Fulani lamidates of Northern Cameroon, the basis of social life. It disappeared rapidly when the Europeans established their administration in the country, leaving only feeble traces.' Only the leading chiefs still had traditional servants by the late 1950s, and their position was honorary.[34]

In the southern part of what is now Cameroon large states and large-scale slavery were not common in pre-colonial times. In other parts of the great Congo River basin, particularly in what is now Zaire, there were large pre-colonial states with considerable slave-systems, comparable to old Ashanti and Benin.

The Kongo (Bakongo) people, who live around the Congo estuary in the modern territories of Zaire, the Congo and Angola, were an important tribe in the days of the first European visits to the area. In their state a man could become a slave by capture, purchase, birth to a slave mother or insolvency; he could be freed or redeemed.[35] The 'Kingdom of the Congo' had collapsed long before the imposition of colonial rule, so that slavery among the Bakongo was no doubt of the smaller, more local variety when it was officially abolished.

In much of Africa the colonial powers, while abolishing local slavery, introduced new labour impositions which often turned out to be more burdensome for ordinary people than the old slavery (see Chapter Eight). While common enough in West Africa, this extreme sort of exploitation by colonial régimes seems to have been worst in the Congo basin – in Angola, in the French Congo and Ubangi-Shari (now the Congo and Central African Republics), and above all in the Belgian Congo. For the Bakongo and other peoples, the abolition of domestic servitude did not give a man a passage from slavery to freedom; for many Congolese, it did the reverse.

Slavery was important in pre-colonial days among many peoples in the interior of the Congo basin, for example, among the Bapende between the Kwango and Kasai Rivers,[34] and among the Baluba, who live further south and are one of the leading peoples of the former Belgian Congo. Luba slaves were traditionally called *bapika*; they were at the lowest level in a social order which also included superior and vassal free men. Some slaves were fugitives from other tribes accepting enslavement in return for protection. Slaves could marry free people.[36]

As elsewhere, a slave's life in the traditional set-up was not idyllic. Among the Baluba, as among other peoples, slaves were often killed to be buried with their masters.[37] No one, of course, can dispute the fact that the abolition of such practices by the colonial powers was a good thing. Domestic slavery, however, was in most ways preferable to the long-distance slave-trade. In this, the Lunda people, southern neighbours of the Luba in Katanga (now called Shaba), were prominent. Their powerful state, ruled by a King called the Mwaat Yamv, dealt in slaves with the Portuguese on the Atlantic Ocean coast and the Arabs on the Indian Ocean coast. The combined efforts of these slavers ravaged large areas of the Congo basin, particularly the eastern part where the Arabs were active in the nineteenth century. But the country was similarly ravaged by the régime of Leopold II's Congo Free State, which prided itself on defeating the Arab slavers in the 1890s but itself killed or ruined a great many Congolese people through forced labour, forcible rubber collection, and other crude exploitation. These efforts, combined with the disruption caused by the recruiting and dragooning of workers for decades afterwards, no doubt helped to disrupt traditional society and hence traditional slavery, but the net gain to the people was hard to see.

*Pygmies, Hutus and Tutsis*
Among the Bantu peoples of Zaire and in some countries further west, in the rain forest regions, live the Pygmy people, among the most remarkable in a continent of which they may well have been the first inhabitants. They may number little more than 100,000, living mainly in Zaire.

Besides their well-known short stature, the Pygmies are distinguished by their light skin and by their concentration on hunting and food-gathering, though nowadays more are turning to settled farming, like the Bantu peoples around them. They live in a close relationship with the Bantu peoples and speak their languages, their own being extinct; for example in the Ituri forest of North-East Zaire, the Mbuti Pygmies speak three Bantu languages.[38] Pygmies retain their own religion, a monotheistic one, and their own customs (which do not include polygamy and witchcraft as practised by their neighbours). But many have ceased to live an independent life in the forest. Pygmies seem to be increasingly tied to the Bantu farming peoples in a relationship rather like that of serf (rather than slave) and master.

Pygmies, who in some areas west of the Congo River are called simply 'hunters' (*Babinga*), hunt a variety of game – antelope, okapi, pangolin, flying squirrel, sometimes buffalo and elephant. They gather wild honey and caterpillars, snakes and termites.[39] They do all this partly for their neighbours, who value them for their skill in hunting. Pygmies exchange game for salt, bananas, groundnuts and

1. Traditional Moorish nomad society outside modern Nouakchott: a servant (slave?) pours the tea.

2. One of the last part-slave tribes: Tuaregs, some black and probably slaves or of slave parentage, at a well in Niger.

3. The Sahara – the sea of sand where security comes before other considerations in life . . .

other goods. They are also employed by their neighbours as singers, dancers and entertainers, Pygmies being renowned for accomplishments of this sort, and I saw a 'healer' in Douala who employed Pygmies for their knowledge of forest herbs.

Sometimes Pygmies are employed for farm work in a servile way. On the Ubangi River they have to grow cassava for the Bantus,[40] but they are able to insist on being paid in maize and cassava on the same day, and can escape back into the forest if dissatisfied.[41] This must ease the burden of their serf condition. The Pygmies' life in the forest is simple; they move camp every fortnight or so and bury the dead where they die in the forest.[42] But they can be relatively healthy, often living to about seventy and, probably, quite often dying of hypertension due to excessive eating of meat.[43] However, many Pygmies now live as farmers and not as hunters in the forest, and these may be more effectively subject to the Bantu headmen. And the area of forest is declining all the time, with persistent and reckless felling of trees for timber, and this will affect many Pygmies.

Some Pygmies have intermarried with other peoples to form 'Pygmoid' groups such as the Batwa (Twa) of Eastern Zaire. These extend into Rwanda and Burundi, where they form the lowest element in a social-tribal hierarchy in which the Tutsi and Hutu peoples are more important. The Twa are few in numbers and their position in those countries and others further west does not seem to be a matter for great concern. The relationship of the Hutus and Tutsis, however, is a very different matter. It is a traditional master/serf relationship, which has continued into modern times with bloody consequences.

Rwanda and Burundi were important pre-colonial states which, after being part of German East Africa, were ruled by Belgium as Mandated and later Trust Territories until 1962. They are very similar, both being small and mountainous but densely populated. In both, the Hutu form the great majority, over 80 per cent, but for centuries they were ruled by the Tutsi people. These arrived four or five centuries ago, apparently from the north-east, and conquered the Hutus. The Tutsis were, and are, distinguished by their very tall stature (6 feet 6 inches is common) and by the herds of long-horned cattle which they brought with them.

The usual term in the Kinyarwanda language (a Bantu language which both the Hutus and Tutsis speak in Rwanda) to describe the relationship between the two peoples is *buhake*. This involves offering services to someone in exchange for protection and the use of his cattle. This no doubt began because the Tutsis were both the conquerors and the owners of the cattle which are the basis of the system. But the client (*garagu*) of a Tutsi lord (*shebuja*) could be a Tutsi also. A client, either Hutu or Tutsi, could be obliged to travel with his lord, or build or repair a part of his house, and give him presents like beer, or give him cattle and milk if he lost his herds, for he, the lord, remained owner of the herds, the *garagu* having only the right of usage. Some services were demanded only of Hutu clients, such as working on the lord's farm or helping to guard his enclosure at night.[44]

Generally, the Tutsis were the master tribe and the Hutus the client or serf tribe. Hutus were not only conquered as a whole, but were subject as individuals to Tutsis in a special relationship roughly like a serf/master relationship, which one entered freely in theory but not in practice. Everyone had to have a lord, even a Tutsi noble, whose lord was the Mwami (King) of Rwanda or Burundi. Nearly all the Hutus had Tutsis as lords. They could marry Tutsis, but these marriages, it seems, were 'neither favoured nor frequent', and very few Hutus could reach wealth and power like the Tutsis.[45] Tutsis, Hutus and Twas were, it has been concluded, 'in a hierarchic order ... from the standpoint of social power, both collective and individual', and any Tutsi could 'exert strong pressure on any Hutu or Twa irrespective of their personal qualities and possessions.'[46]

It is hard to understand how this system was maintained for so long. It was not challenged, it seems, until the growth of nationalism and politics. Then, in Rwanda, the Hutus formed a party of their own and started a revolution in 1959, leading to the overthrow of the Tutsi monarchy and of the entire Tutsi overlordship in 1961. This revolution was accompanied by terrible massacres of the Tutsis and the flight of thousands across the borders. Independence was granted in 1962 to a Rwanda ruled by the Hutus. It is not clear, however, whether the old social order had been completely destroyed. Certainly, many Tutsis remained, despite the massacres which resumed briefly in January 1964. It seems that in spite of the killings, Tutsis are still prominent in Rwanda, for recently efforts have been made to give Hutus more school-places and office jobs. More killings have been reported, but on a smaller scale. Recently, the tribal killings in Rwanda, where the Hutus have seized power, have been exceeded in Burundi, where they have failed to do so.

Burundi no longer has a monarchy, the last Mwami being deposed in 1966, and it is possible that some of the old social system has changed in spite of continued Tutsi domination. That domination is still total, however, despite the disproportion in numbers and the encouragement the Hutus must derive from the success of their brothers in Rwanda. In 1972 the Burundi Hutus tried to imitate the Rwandan success; they killed many Tutsis but failed to take power, and the Tutsis then took a hideous revenge. A general massacre began in which educated Hutus were singled out for murder (just as the Nazis concentrated on killing the best-educated Poles). People were murdered in their homes, in their schools and everywhere. Perhaps 100,000 people were killed in the first wave, and the slaughter has since continued. Protests in many parts of the world at this slaughter were matched by a scandalous silence on the part of African governments. Perhaps there were private approaches which helped to stop or at least slow down the killing; perhaps Colonel Micombero's government simply realised that it could not kill all the Hutus. But it seems that killing has continued unchecked, and one would scarcely expect there to be any real peace if it ended. Nobody could endure what the Hutus have endured from a minority without seeking revenge; this will surely come, and will be unspeakable, beyond anything seen in the area so far. One can only be thankful that relationships like that of the Hutus and Tutsis are not common in Africa.

*Examples from Eastern and Southern Africa*
The peoples of East Africa included the Bantu peoples such as the Baganda and Banyoro of Uganda; the Kikuyu of Kenya; the Nyamwezi, Hehe, Ngoni, Makonde and Nyakyusa of Tanzania; and the coastal people sometimes called 'Swahili' – though this term (meaning simply 'coastal') is more commonly applied to their language, an Arabic-influenced but Bantu language which is widely spoken all over East Africa, including eastern Zaire, and is Tanzania's national language.

Further to the south and south-west, Bantu peoples include the Yao of Malawi and Mozambique, the Bemba, Lozi, Ila and Tonga of Zambia; the Shona (Mashona) and Ndebele (Matabele) of Rhodesia; the Ovimbundu and Kimbundu groups of peoples in Angola; the Makau, Thonga and other peoples of Mozambique; the many tribes of the largely desert areas of Botswana and Namibia (South-West Africa), such as the Bamangwato and Herero; and the many peoples of South Africa and Lesotho, notably the Zulu, Xhosa, Sotho and Pondo peoples.

Apart from South Africa's aboriginal Bushmen and Hottentots (possibly related to the tropical Pygmies), almost all the peoples of East, Central and South Africa are classed as Bantu, except for a considerable number in Uganda and Kenya: the Luos of Kenya and the related Alurs of Uganda and Nuer and Shilluk of the Southern

Sudan, the famous Masai nomadic herdsmen in Kenya and Tanzania, the Lango and Madi in Uganda. (Then there are all the various peoples of Ethiopia; see Chapter Seven).

Besides being conquered and sometimes enslaved by the Amharas, other peoples in Ethiopia have known their own local serfdom and slavery, as have Bantu peoples further south. The Gurage of South-Western Ethiopia, who were conquered intermittently and often raided for slaves in the nineteenth and twentieth centuries, have subject peoples who are clearly different from the Gurage nobles, who are of the same Semitic family as the Amharas. These subject people, called Fuga, resemble Bantu Africans and are apparently descended from earlier inhabitants of Ethiopia who were conquered by the Gurage. They have a serf-like relationship with the upper-class Gurage, being hunters (like the Pygmies) and craftsmen and specialists in religious rituals (like some subject groups in Saharan tribes). Formerly there were also true slaves, who were distinguished by having few or no clothes. Slaves used to be bought from other tribes; those captured were often sold.[47]

More numerous and more famous among the tribes of the 'Horn of Africa' and neighbouring areas are the Somalis. They are found in the Somali Republic and in the neighbouring regions of Kenya, Ethiopia and French Somaliland (now called the Territory of the Afars and Issas), and they live partly by farming but mainly by herding. The Somalis are well known as a proud and free people with, traditionally, no government apart from the clan system – except on rare occasions when a leader like Mohammed Abdullah Hassan, known as 'the Mad Mullah' to the British whom he fought for twenty years until his death in 1920, united them. Inter-clan feuds were a common and important feature of Somali nomad life before and throughout the colonial period. The Somalis' warlike tradition has given force to their movement to attain unity by thorough resistance to their domination by Kenya, Ethiopia and France.

As among the Moors, some Somalis can place themselves in a state of clientage or dependence on others in return for protection; this was once important for the protection of caravans over the semi-desert Somali country.[48] There were also groups called Midgaan, Tumaal and Yibir, serfs of the herdsmen, practising, it is recalled, 'various skilled but despised trades such as shoe-making, leather-work, iron-work, and hairdressing'.[49] Again, there are parallels in the western Sahara. Formerly, many Somali families and lineages had bondsmen called *sab*, and although few have many of them now, this sort of bondage was still important about a dozen years ago. The *sab* remained distinct, could seldom marry freeborn Somalis, and showed their dependent status by accepting the protection of the Somalis and supporting them in their feuds. Probably this group of serfs still continues in the traditional way in some areas, but for some time now *sab* have often become emancipated, some going to towns to exercise crafts independently.[50]

While Somalis are therefore typical of African nomads in having a subject class or caste, it is not nearly so important as the slaves and *haratin* of the Sahara, and the contempt of nomads for farm work, common to both regions, does not always mean in Somalia that farm work is done by slaves or even serfs. In northern areas, farmers are simply herdsmen who have turned to farming, not a subject class.[51] But in some parts of the south, 'much of the labour of cultivation is performed by serfs (*boon*)'.[52]

Class distinctions are likely to prove as lasting among the Somalis as among other African nomads. The particular features of nomadic life which preserve slavery among the Tuareg probably account for the survival of *boon* and *sab* serfdom among the Somalis. Social contempt for the *sab* and for the particular groups already mentioned, such as the Yibir, is deeply engrained and will probably outlast the end of the traditional division of labour. Yibir people are especially despised and feared, being thought to have magical powers and to be able to curse those who do not give them customary presents in return for their blessing.[53] The unusual conservatism of nomads will no doubt ensure that such discrimination goes on for some time; such things, after all, go on in much more 'modernised' and settled parts of the continent.

The Amharas were for centuries enslavers of East Africans. More important than them, however, were the Arabs, operating from the Sudan or from the Indian Ocean coast, and, further south, the Portuguese. The combined slaving efforts of these peoples affected the lives of many other tribes between the Red Sea and the Mozambique Channel for several centuries (see Chapter Five). For this reason slavery had a two-fold character among many East African peoples; they had slaves for their own use but sold many others, while other people were captured in slaving expeditions. Arab-Swahili traders raided for slaves in areas around the upper Congo, while they traded in them in other areas where powerful states existed before colonisation.

Buganda was typical of a number of those major pre-colonial states in having plenty of local slavery, important in administration, but at the same time selling slaves to coastal traders in the latter part of the nineteenth century. Further south, in Tanganyika, the Nyamwezi were important slave-traders, while also having their own slaves. The German rulers of Tanganyika, like the British in Kenya and Uganda, followed the normal colonial policy of attacking the slave-trade first while proceeding more slowly with slaveholding. The Germans proceeded particularly slowly; in 1901 they made it possible for household slaves to buy their freedom, in 1907 they declared that all slaves' children born after 1906 were free, but it was left to the British to abolish slavery after conquering Tanganyika (then called German East Africa) in the First World War and receiving a League of Nations Mandate over it. So it was only in 1922 that domestic slavery was outlawed among the many tribes of Tanganyika.

The Nyamwezi, one of the largest tribes (about half a million people living around Tabora, south of Lake Victoria Nyanza), used to have several slaves, called *basese* (singular *nsese*). The chiefs owned many slaves, and the children of these slaves were considered to be the property of the chiefs, with the result that the descendants of such slaves often claim to be full members of a chiefly family. Some slaves were prisoners-of-war, others were people who sought the protection of a chief on fleeing from another one or on becoming unable to support themselves. Slaves acted as ritual officials at a chief's court, and some of them had the particular task of strangling a chief who became too ill to rule.[54] Generally, domestic and royal slaves among the Nyamwezi seem to have been much better treated than victims of the Arab-Swahili slave-trade (they could not, however, have been much worse treated). Abolition of slavery came in 1922, but well into the British period a Nyamwezi chief was found to be keeping slaves.[55] In Africa there were probably many such cases of chiefs whose desire to maintain their traditional standing, generally approved by the British, led them to continue to hold slaves, which was not approved; and other cases where the position of court officials remained for long ambiguous.

The Chagga, an industrious people who live, traditionally divided into dozens of different chiefdoms, on the lower slopes of Mount Kilimanjaro, traded in ivory and slaves with the coastal traders and also had their own slaves, who were often prisoners-of-war.[56] But it is recorded that the Kamba, another Bantu people like the Nyamwezi and Chagga and today one of the leading peoples of Kenya, had no domestic slavery traditionally, though they too sold prisoners to coastal traders.[57]

The Ngoni people came to south-west Tanzania, Malawi and Zambia in one of the most dramatic migrations in pre-colonial

Africa. In the 1820s they fled northwards from the conquests of the Zulus under Shaka, enslaving on the way large numbers of men and women of other tribes. After many campaigns and wars they began to settle in their present home about the 1850s, and to some extent the people of other tribes whom they had subjected broke away from them.[58] This was one example of the way in which slavery could move populations over large areas. One early result of colonial rule with its ending of tribal wars and its abolition of slavery was the return of many enslaved people to their former homes. In West Africa many Yorubas held captive in Ibadan, the military centre of Yorubaland in the nineteenth century, were able to return home after the wars in which Ibadan had emerged prominent had been ended in the 1890s. In East Africa the colonial rulers aided former slaves in the Chagga country to return to their old homes.[59] But in many areas people did not know where their old homes were or did not wish to return to them. Many of the slaves who remained with their tribes after emancipation were from other tribes originally, and people like the Ngoni are of varied descent.

In colonial times the Ngoni had no slaves or serfs to work on their farms and had a problem in finding labourers at all.[60] Another important people, however, the Lozi of Northern Rhodesia, now Zambia, had serfs for some time after colonisation. Their ruler, the King of Barotseland, had a special position in the colony, ruling most of its western area as a 'protected' monarch. Lozi serfs or *batanga* were originally prisoners-of-war; they were bound to their masters but could not be sold as slaves, and could marry free Lozis. In pre-colonial days children could also be kidnapped and brought up by the Lozis, ending up as Lozis like the rest. For some time, the serfs, despite the fact that their numbers were not replenished and their status was in theory ended by an agreement in 1906 between the King and the British, remained important because they were needed to help in the Lozis' regular migration between the Zambesi flood-plain and outlying woodlands. In time it became necessary to employ people and pay them for this work.[61]

*Buying a wife*
One institution which is common to much of black Africa and which has sometimes been considered similar to slave-dealing is that of the 'bride-price', a payment made by the bridegroom to the bride's father at the marriage or afterwards. The Church has been foremost in denouncing such payments, saying that they amount to the buying of a wife. But neither its criticisms nor government efforts have succeeded in changing this old tradition, which has indeed changed

in other ways and for other reasons but still remains very important. It is one tradition which the most educated and 'modern-minded' Africans frequently see no cause to abandon.

Does a payment of so many cows or so many hundreds of pounds to the bride's father at the time of a man's marriage really constitute the buying of a wife? Traditionally, it did not.

Marriage was traditionally regarded in Africa, and not only there, as a contract between families, or clans, or lineages, rather than a contract simply between individuals. The bride-price was then part of a contract of this larger sort, and helped to set the seal on an allegiance of two groups of kin. Payment was quite often regarded as being made for the husband's, and his family's, right over the children of the union; it was very widely held that it was the bride-price that made children legitimate. The payment was also seen as compensation to the girl's family for their loss of her productive power, which was to swell the numbers of another family or clan; or as an expression of thanks for bringing her up so that she could fulfil this function.[62] The payment was often made in cattle, which if they lived long enough might well come back to the bridegroom's family when paid as bride-price for his sister. Formal exchanges of wives for brothers and sisters occurred, among the Tivs of Nigeria for example, but they were banned by colonial authorities.

The anthropologist Lucy Mair concludes: 'The marriage payment, then, legalises a marriage, determines the legal paternity of children, and creates the relationship of affinity between the kin of the spouses.'[63] The transfer of cattle helps to stabilise a marriage, because if the marriage breaks down the wife's family have to repay the cattle; this, of course, stabilises marriage by keeping the wife in submission, because it is her family who will have to pay if there is a divorce, and they have every reason to persuade her to put up with all that goes wrong. But matrilineal societies, i.e. those where descent is reckoned through the mother, also have the bride-price; it is quite important, for example, among the Ashantis. It is less important in these societies, and serves less to keep the wife in subjection, and divorce is more common, but the ideal is still a stable married life.

Bride-price traditions vary greatly. An Ibibio bridegroom in Nigeria might (after the introduction of payments in cash rather than in kind) pay £10–£12 usually, but sometimes up to £40, together with gifts such as dyes, kola nuts (the bitter nuts of West Africa widely used as stimulants), fruit, fish, and a headpad for the load-carrying which women learn from a young age.[64] Among the pastoral peoples of Southern and South-Eastern Africa the bride-price was traditionally paid in cattle and called *lobola*. But among the Bemba the main payment was in work; a man had to work for his prospective father-in-law, and although he gave presents too – bark clothes, a bangle for betrothal, etc. – these were not important, and no repayment was expected if the marriage failed.[65] In colonial times cash payments came to replace the work done by the prospective husband.

The general introduction of cash payments instead of the original bride-price paid in kind has certainly meant some changes. In traditional society there was probably no idea of purchase of the wife; the Ashanti view – that payment was for 'a sexual prerogative, coupled with the benefit of the bride's services and later those of her children, the last two within strictly defined limits'[66] – was probably typical. But when the old ties of lineage and clan became less important, in so far as they did, while the bride-price remained and was made a cash payment, the whole elaborate traditional business of negotiating and paying the 'bridewealth' was in danger of becoming a commercial transaction.

Churchmen believed from an early date that this was in fact happening, and that it was a sign of women's degraded status, especially when there was polygamy. They were also concerned about the many young men who could not marry because they could not afford the ever-rising bride-price. Numerous Africans came to agree with them. In Cameroon, the the bride-price can be considerable (over £300 in one case known to me), there has always been some opposition to the system as it has developed recently. Twenty years ago a Cameroonian wrote of 'shameful speculations' in which a woman is 'simply a stake in a true commercial transaction'.[67] But opposition to the bride-price by the Church, and efforts to limit it by the Government, have been ineffective in that country and others. The official limit has been quite unenforceable because there is nothing to stop the two families from meeting privately at any time to agree on an extra, unrecorded payment.

In Eastern Nigeria a commission of inquiry into the bride-price ordered by the Regional Government in 1955 said it was too early to recommend its abolition, though it hoped that the institution would eventually die away.[68] There seems little chance of this, even though hundreds of women demonstrated against it in the same region, at Enugu, in 1959, saying that they were forced to remain spinsters because the bride-price was impossibly high.[69] But the Cameroonian quoted above also said that women were commonly willing parties to the 'transactions' involving the bride-price, being proud to boast of the amount paid for them. This is probably one of the reasons why the bride-price continues in many countries. For those who feel differently, elopement is a traditional sort of rebellion. It was common in the past for a boy and girl who could not marry to run away together and force their families' hand; their marriage was commonly recognised then after payment of the bride-price plus, in some cases, a seduction fine. Opportunities for this have been greatly increased in the twentieth century by improved communications, the growth of towns, and the emancipation of the young. So, in practice, the high bride-price may not always be an obstacle.

In Flora Nwapa's novel *Efuru*, set in her Ibo homeland, a couple agreed to marry, the man had no money for the bride-price or 'dowry'. But, 'When the woman saw that he was unable to pay anything, she told him not to bother about the dowry. They were going to proclaim themselves married and that was that.' Later he did pay, and then for the first time 'the two felt really married'.[70]

The institution of the bride-price does not exclude consent by both parties, even though it started in the days of frequent arranged marriages. Educated people in modern times who marry partners of their own choice still pay, or agree that there should be payment of, the bride-price. And in many traditional societies the consent of both parties was required before the bride-price could even be discussed.

Describing the marriage customs of his Ibo people, Rems Nna Umeasiegbu says that after the suitor and his father have eaten a meal with the girl and her father 'the man calls his daughter. She appears, putting on an air of indifference. All eyes are now focused on her. A glass is filled with wine and handed to her. She has two alternatives, either to give it to her father or to her husband-to-be, after sipping it. If she gives it to the suitor, it means she has accepted him. If she does otherwise, then the matter ends there.'[71]

In many other parts of Africa, women have always had the right to refuse a husband. Among the Lozi of Zambia and the Kamba of Kenya the bride's consent was commonly required, if not always.[72]

However, there have been many peoples who accepted betrothal of children, and when their daughters were disposed of when too young to know anything about it the bride-price took on a slightly different aspect. Their own interests could be completely subordinate to others', including a father's financial interests. In fact, this probably was not a common occurrence, and traditionally there were safeguards for the bride's interests. But the possibility of trading in marriageable daughters was there. There was a celebrated case in

Gabon in 1964 when a schoolgirl, Colette Mekui, objected to her betrothal to an old man who already had three wives, and wrote a letter of protest to the President, Léon Mba, who then outlawed betrothals of children.[73]

One decree is hardly likely to change old customs which, of course, had their parallels in Europe until very recently – the idea that one can marry whomever one likes is, in terms of time and space, relatively rare in the world as a whole. Betrothals of children such as are traditional among the Ibibios and other tribes in Africa have occurred continually in the royal families of Europe. But in Africa the trend is almost certainly towards free consent by adults. The educated people, whose number is constantly growing, may sometimes be willing to accept arranged marriages, but great numbers will insist on choosing their own partners for life. If betrothals of children become less common the disadvantages for women of the bride-price will be reduced, and the phrase 'buying a wife', though quite often used, will become more generally inaccurate. African wives are not typically subservient like the traditional Arab or Spanish wife, and Women's Lib will not arouse much interest in Africa. The bride-price is a serious financial burden, for many people, but it is not, typically, a mark of enslavement of the female sex.

*Notes*

1. R. S. Rattray, *Ashanti Law and Constitution*, p. 33.
2. Ibid., p. 35.
3. Ibid., p. 37.
4. Ibid., p. 38.
5. Ibid., p. 42.
6. R. A. Lystad, *The Ashanti: A Proud People*, pp. 124–5.
7. *Anti-Slavery Reporter and Aborigines' Friend* (July 1927), pp. 104–5.
8. Ibid.
9. K. Little, *The Mende of Sierra Leone*, p. 37.
10. Ibid., pp. 38–9.
11. Ibid., pp. 56–7.
12. Ibid., p. 73.
13. See Chapter Eleven.
14. See A. Ayandele, *Holy Johnson*.
15. P. C. Lloyd, *Yoruba Land Law*, pp. 148, 154–6.
16. R. Dennett, *Nigerian Studies*, p. 205.
17. M. Perham, *Native Administration in Nigeria*, p. 17.
18. Lloyd, op. cit., p. 88.
19. Ibid., p. 256.
20. G. T. Basden, *Niger Ibos*, p. 257.

21. Sir Alan Burns, *History of Nigeria*, pp. 214–15.
22. Ibid.
23. Basden, op. cit., p. 143.
24. Ibid., p. 192.
25. Ibid., pp. 243–4.
26. Ibid., pp. 246 ff.
27. Ibid., p. 255.
28. Ibid.
29. Ibid., p. 253.
30. D. Forde and G. I. Jones, *The Ibo and Ibibio-Speaking Peoples of South-Eastern Nigeria*, pp. 21 ff.
31. *Anti-Slavery Reporter* (June 1956), p. 97.
32. R. Bureau, 'Ethno-Sociologie Religieuse des Duala et Apparentés', in *Recherches et Études Camerounaises* (1962), p. 57.
33. Ibid., p. 167 n.
34. J. Hurault, *La Structure Sociale des Bamileke*, p. 81.
35. J. Vansina, *Introduction à l'Ethnographie du Congo*, p. 123.
36. Ibid., p. 152.
37. W. F. P. Burton, *Luba Religion and Magic*, pp. 40, 63.
38. Vansina, op. cit., chapter on Pygmies.
39. Ibid., L. Demesse, *Quest for the Babingas*.
40. Demesse, op. cit.; N. Ballif, *Dancers of God*, pp. 143–4.
41. Ballif, op. cit.
42. Vansina, op. cit.; Ballif, op. cit.
43. Ballif, op. cit.
44. J. Maquet, *The Promise of Inequality in Ruanda*, pp. 129–30.
45. Ibid., pp. 136, 150–1.
46. Ibid., p. 136.
47. W. Shack, *The Gurage*, pp. 8–9, 121.
48. I. M. Lewis, *A Pastoral Democracy*, p. 187.
49. Ibid., p. 188.
50. Ibid.
51. Ibid., p. 104.
52. Ibid.
53. Ibid., pp. 263 ff.
54. R. G. Abrahams, *The Political Organisation of Unyamwezi*, pp. 75, 147.
55. Ibid.
56. K. M. Stahl, *History of the Chagga People of Kilimanjaro*, pp. 106, 166.
57. G. Lindblom, *The Akamba of Western Kenya*, p. 160.
58. J. G. Pike, *Malawi*, pp. 53 ff.
59. Stahl, op. cit., p. 115.
60. E. Colson and M. Gluckman, *Seven Tribes of British Central Africa*, pp. 246 ff.
61. Ibid., pp. 4–6, 13, 56.
62. Lucy Mair, *New Nations*, pp. 69–75.
63. Ibid.
64. Forde and Jones, op. cit., p. 77.
65. Colson and Gluckman, op. cit., p. 180.
66. Rattray, op. cit., p. 24.
67. J.-R. Owona Ndoukou in *Études Camerounaises* (Douala, March–July 1953), p. 46.
68. *Anti-Slavery Reporter* (May 1958 and April 1961).

69. Ibid.
70. F. Nwapa, *Efuru*.
71. R. N. Umeasiegbu, *The Way We Lived*, p. 14.
72. Colson and Gluckman, op. cit., pp. 79–81; Lindblom, op. cit., p. 72.
73. *The Anti-Slavery Society: Its Task Today.*

*Chapter Five*

# The Old Slave-Trade

Into black African societies which already had slavery of one sort or another there intruded, over the centuries, foreign slave-traders who greatly changed the meaning of the word 'slave' for Africans. How far local slavery was transformed – or even, in some cases, introduced – by the overseas slave-trade is an open question, probably unanswerable for some parts of Africa. But there is no doubt, whatever may have been said to the contrary at the time, that the European and Arab slave-trades greatly affected African society, and, as far as all but a few Africans were concerned, decidedly for the worse.

The abduction of a large part of Africa's population had such a great effect on the continent that, even though it is now (not very ancient) history, something about that large-scale crime needs to be recalled. Nobody will ever know just how many millions of Africans suffered. If one includes the slaves taken to the Americas, and those taken across the Sahara, down the Nile or by sea to North Africa and the Middle East, the number must run into tens of millions. There have seldom been such great forced migrations of people in history, until the recent age of Hitler and Stalin.

Today there are perhaps between 70 million and 100 million people of mainly black African descent outside black Africa. An accurate estimate is impossible because there has been so much mingling with other peoples; many people in North America, Europe and Asia must have African ancestry of which they are unaware, while Americans known to have seven white great-grandparents and one black one are called 'Negroes' in the USA (but other such people are not so called in other countries). In the 1970 Census, about 22 million Americans were classed as Negroes, a tenth of the US population. But the largest overseas African community is in Brazil, where it may number between 30 million and 50 million, depending on how many people of 'mixed' ancestry are included. Many coastal areas of Brazil, especially in the north-east and around Bahia, are very African in population and culture, and the world knows to some extent how Brazilian life has been profoundly influenced by Africa. So Brazil is in every way the first homeland of expatriate Africans.

About 20 million people of African descent live in the West Indies and on the Caribbean mainland, including 5 million in Haiti, the main stronghold of African culture in the New World after Brazil. The 'Afro-Americans' have moved on from the USA and the Caribbean to make second new homes in Great Britain, France and the outlying possessions and 'spheres of influence' of the USA (there are many Vietnamese and Korean children who, as a result of the passage of the US Army, are of African descent on their fathers' side).

The black African element in the populations of Morocco, Algeria, Tunisia, Egypt, Saudi Arabia, South Yemen and other Middle Eastern countries has never been accurately assessed, but it is certainly large. Some Turks, Persians and Indians have African ancestors too. Slavery also accounts for the large, West-Indian-style black African communities in Mauritius, Réunion and the Seychelles in the Indian Ocean.

When one remembers that many enslaved African men were probably unable to have children by African women in slavery, and that huge numbers of those sold into slavery died before reaching their destinations, it is clear that the number of people enslaved was far greater than the present number of their descendants would suggest, if a normal rate of natural increase were assumed. No such rate can be assumed, for slave-owners in the West Indies for long took little care to 'breed' slaves, relying rather on new shipments to replace slaves lost, and even after emancipation living conditions remained poor for most of the slaves' descendants.

The transatlantic slave-trade began early in the sixteenth century, when the Spanish and Portuguese conquerers had succeeded in killing much of the indigenous population of the West Indies and Brazil. Although Bishop de las Casas, the courageous defender of the Indians, approved the importation of African labourers for a time as a measure to spare the Indians, it is incorrect to allege that the importation of Africans was begun on his suggestion. It began considerably earlier, and the ground for it had been laid by the taking of many Africans into slavery in Portugal. This apparently began almost as soon as the Portuguese had begun to travel in their caravels beyond Morocco along the West African coast. Africans were kidnapped and taken as slaves to Portugal, perhaps for the first time, in 1444 from the coast of what is now Mauritania. A British slave-trader writing two centuries later recorded: 'In 1444 a company was erected in Portugal, paying an acknowledgement to the prince,* and fitting out six caravels, which setting men ashore on the isles of Arguim, brought away about two hundred of the inhabitants, whom they sold for slaves.'[1]

As the Portuguese and other Europeans travelled further along the coast, slave-trading began at many points. For centuries the 'Guinea Coast' was known to Europeans mainly as a source of slaves. Through their infamous business the traders came to know the coast and its rulers well, and they recorded in detail the way their business was conducted; few criminals have ever bothered less to conceal their crimes. The slave-trade was an essential part of an elaborate trade which grew up between Europe and Africa, in which European goods were exchanged for African exports which included ivory, pepper, and African food for the slave-ships, but mainly human beings. The European goods included cloth, all sorts of clothing, pewter and metal household goods, guns and gunpowder, and rum, brandy and other strong liquor in large quantities. The 'triangular trade' brought these goods to Africa, slaves to the New World, and back to Europe the sugar and sugar by-products which the slaves produced on the plantations.

The 'Guinea Coast', and the various sections of it called the Slave Coast, the Gold Coast, etc., had a variety of rulers. At that time no effort was made to displace them. Colonisation was to come later; during the time of the slave-trade the Europeans were content to establish trading posts or 'factories' and a few forts – the only sign of an important, permanent 'presence' on their part. The African peoples whose rulers retained control of the coast were, on the whole, the same ones who live in the area now. On the Gold Coast there were rulers such as those of Komenda and Anomabu, of the Fanti tribe. Further east, on the Slave Coast, the kingdom of Dahomey, created by the Fons living slightly inland, ruled for long periods in the eighteenth and nineteenth centuries a section of the coast important for slave-trading. The famous slave-port of Whydah (Ouidah) was there. The Yoruba people had contact with the Europeans at Ijebu, but some of them were subject in coastal regions, for example Lagos, to the big empire of Benin. In the fifteenth and sixteenth centuries, when the Portuguese began their trade, Benin's main outlet to the sea was at Gwato. Further east, the Ijaw peoples of the Niger delta and the Efiks of Calabar were among the most important of all the slave-dealing peoples. Bandy (Bonny) and New Calabar (Opobo) were Ijaw towns whose slave-traffic made them two of the

* Prince Henry 'the Navigator'.

4. A ruler with his harem – slave girls? – in Niger.

5. Kano market, once famous for slaves, now for these pots and other wares.

6 and 7. These photographs, circulated in 1973, seem to show a white man buying slaves somewhere in the Sahel and the 'slaves' then being led off to captivity. They are puzzling in some respects (where would a European want to employ male slaves and why?) but they may well show that slave-trading is not dead yet.

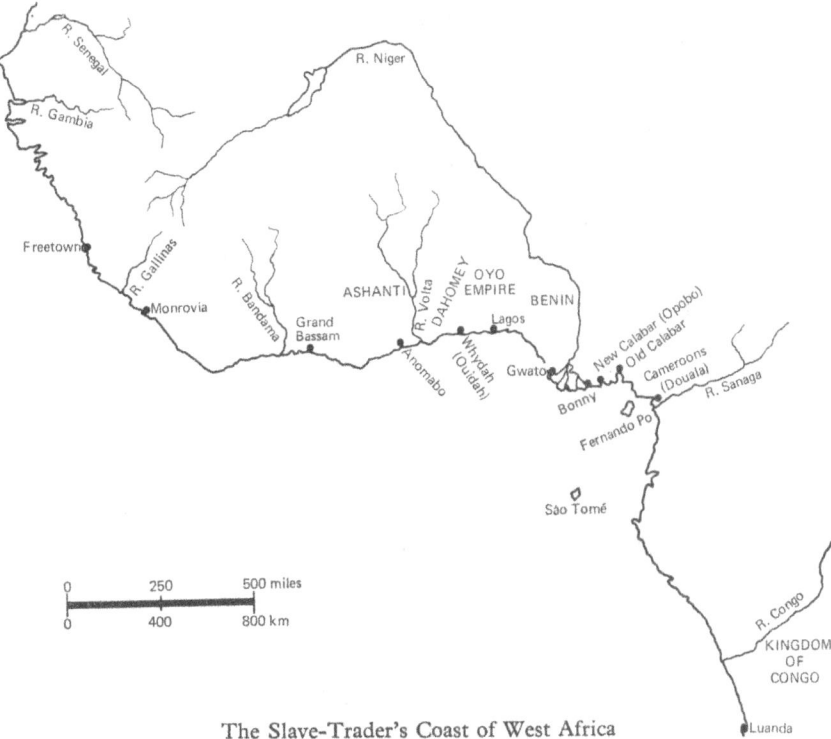

The Slave-Trader's Coast of West Africa

leading ports of the West African coast. They are relatively insignificant now; fittingly, the old slave-ports have often been superseded by others for other trade: for example, Whydah and Anomabu are mere relics of ports now.

John Barbot, a British slave-trader, described a slaving voyage he made in 1699, in a supplement to his massive and informative book published in 1746 with the title *A Description of the Coasts of North and South Guinea and of Ethiopia Inferior, vulgarly Angola*. He described the negotiations with the African ruler at Bonny, the haggling over prices, and the eventual exchange of imported goods for slaves. Coins were not used in the slave-trade; there were various other sorts of currency, including metal rods called 'manillas' and, in this case, iron bars. The price eventually agreed was thirteen iron bars for a man and nine for a woman, with prices of boys and girls fixed proportionately to age. Besides providing their imports, the slave-traders had to pay heavy duties and provide gifts which included slaves that they had to buy on the spot. Eventually, Barbot set sail with 648 slaves, including sixty-five loaded earlier on the Gold Coast.[2]

Barbot and other slave-traders often complained with righteous indignation at the hard bargaining of the African trader-rulers. It is always extraordinary to hear indignant mutual accusations by partners-in-crime. One fact revealed by the slave-traders' accusations is that they and their African trading partners dealt on reasonably equal terms. The Europeans were not much stronger, if at all, than the Africans, and had to submit to them in many ways. Africans were not, in general, forced at gunpoint to sell other Africans.

There was, it seems, mutual toleration and respect of a squalid sort between the European and African slave-traders in the long period when Europeans came to trade rather than to conquer and dominate. The Portuguese were the only Europeans who tried to bring their religion and culture to Africa at that time, and their efforts in this direction were probably undermined by their greed for slaves. Portuguese missionaries scored a spectacular success among the Bakongo; between the late fifteenth century and the late seventeenth century many kings of the 'kingdom of the Congo' were Catholics and, for a time, the kingdom was nominally Catholic. But slave-traders from São Tomé visited the kingdom for slaves despite the repeated protests of the Catholic kings. The fact that the same Portuguese came as slave-traders and as missionaries probably helped to cause the gradual disintegration of Catholicism in the Congo. The same cause could explain why the early missions in Benin (where some converts were made at an early stage), in Warri (where one Olu or King was a Portuguese-cultured Catholic in the seventeenth century), and in what is now Sierra Leone were so unsuccessful. African perhaps saw the incompatibility of slavery and Christianity better than most Europeans at the time.

However, the Portuguese efforts to combine purchasing of bodies with saving of souls was not typical. The slave-traders were generally hard-headed businessmen who concentrated on the lucrative trade and did not bother overmuch about spreading Christianity or 'civilisation'. Barbot could say that the possibility of conversion to Christianity was one of the blessings made available to Africans taken to the Americas, but he also reproached Protestant slave-owners there for not making that blessing available in reality. Traders cared even less than planters for Christian missionary work. The devout slave-trader, John Newton, was not typical; if Christians, including churchmen, generally accepted slavery and the slave-trade, the Europeans actually involved were apparently far from being keen Christians. Barbot said that the ordinary soldiers and workers sent from Europe to West Africa were 'generally men of no education or principles, void of foresight, careless, prodigal, addicted to strong liquors . . .' and often 'over fond of the black women'.[3] The seamier aspects of the traditional religions of the coastal peoples were mentioned to justify the 'rescue' of the slaves from West Africa rather than to promote missions.

This point is worth stressing because it shows that, however often and however shamefully Christians and Muslims have defended slavery and the slave-trade, it is wrong to suggest that people have owned or bought slaves *because* they were Christians or Muslims. The history of the European slave-trade suggests that people did not need (or wait for) approval by churchmen before trading in slaves. The attitude of Muslim slave-traders was probably the same, so that the suggestion that they traded in slaves *because* they were Muslims seems unjustified.

It is also worth noting that because Europeans in the slave-trade era were not interested, with rare exceptions, in spreading Christianity or Western culture, or in anything except their trade, the damage they did to Africa was not cultural. African peoples retained their own languages and cultures entirely. However, there was some Europeanised life on the coast. Portuguese Creole became the general trade language all along the coast of Africa, in South Africa and in the Far East (in Africa it has now died out except in Portuguese Guinea, the part of Senegal adjoining that Portuguese colony, and in some islands – the Cape Verdes and São Tomé and Principe). By the eighteenth century Pidgin or other dialects based on English had become the West African coastal trade languages. One Efik slave-trader, Antera Duke, wrote a journal in Pidgin in the eighteenth century. The Efiks and other coastal peoples enriched by the slave-trade adopted some aspects of Western culture; for example, English names like Duke were introduced, half-Europeans became 'merchant princes' in what is now the territory of Sierra Leone, African rulers sent their sons to be educated in Europe, European goods became widely used (and widely drunk, in particular), and European clothes and styles of architecture were introduced. But there was little or no conscious effort to change African culture.

African rulers retained their independence too, except on the Portuguese-ruled coast of Angola. They could take advantage of the rivalry between European slave-traders, and could refuse to sell slaves at all. The Europeans did not always find the slave-business easy. Although Barbot wrote that 'The road at Anamaboe is generally full of English ships, or those of other nations, anchoring there to trade, or else for corn or other necessaries; but more especially for slaves, which are sometimes to be had in considerable numbers',[4] he also said that sometimes hardly any slaves were to be had, anywhere along the coast. In such a case, what was to stop the slave-traders from raiding the first village to which they came? Clearly respect for the African rulers. Those rulers may have been bribed to sell fellow-Africans, but not forced. What would have happened if all had refused to sell slaves all the time, however, is a matter of conjecture.

If the conclusion seems inescapable that West African rulers sold slaves without being actually forced to do so, it is impossible to believe that the overseas slave-trade was therefore merely incidental and did not add to the effects of local slavery. This argument, which defenders of the slave-trade used (and extended to show that slavery in the West Indies was actually *preferable* for slaves to their likely fate in Africa), is incredible mainly because of the large numbers of slaves involved. What would have been done with such large numbers if they had not been bought by Europeans? Those taken as prisoners-of-war might have been killed, perhaps; but many were killed during the slave-trade era. Similarly, one cannot assume that all slaves exported to the Americas would have been used either for local domestic slavery or for the human sacrifices which European visitors often described at that time; for while selling slaves overseas, the Africans kept those they needed at home, and human sacrifices went on at the height of the slave-trade, which may have stimulated such ritual practices. For these reasons, it seems that the European slave-traders encouraged efforts to find slaves which would not otherwise have been made.

How far this was so in any place or at any time is hard to say. Barbot said that some slaves were offenders, sentenced to sale as slaves, others sold themselves in times of famine, others were victims of small-scale kidnapping, but 'those sold by the Blacks are for the most part prisoners-of-war, taken either in fight, or pursuit, or in the incursions they make into their enemies' territories'.[5] This was said of the Senegambia area, and confirmed for areas farther down the coast. In 1682, Barbot said: 'I could get but eight from one end of the coast to the other; not only because we were a great number of trading ships on the coast at the same time, but by reason the natives were everywhere at peace.'[6] Peace, of course, was fatal for that business – as for some others. That there could be peace so widely shows that the slave-traders' demands were not always the overriding consideration for Africans. Perhaps they were sometimes, however. How many of the wars which supplied the slave-ships were fought for that purpose? Slave-traders probably neither knew nor cared But, while the kingdoms of Ashanti and Dahomey, which were powerful in the eighteenth century, would have had to be fighting in any case for much of the time to maintain their rule, smaller states might have fought wars mainly to get slaves to sell. The great numbers involved suggest that this happened. It was affirmed categorically in 1627 by Alonso de Sandoval, a Spanish Jesuit who was among the first great anti-slavery writers, and at later dates by other writers.

There is, in fact, little reason to doubt this, and so one can be sure that the effects of the slave-trade were felt far inland. The slave-traders themselves knew only the coast, and such small European 'cultural impact' as there was took place also on the coast. But the abduction of millions of Africans for work across the Atlantic had effects far into the interior. There wars and raids led to enslavement, which could often be enslavement by Europeans. Barbot said that slaves sold at New Calabar came from Biafra, a kingdom which seems to have been in the territory of modern Cameroon, and 'other countries farther inland', and those were said to acquire some slaves from even farther off.[7] In the nineteenth century it was recorded that Kanuri and Nupe slaves were among those sold to Europeans. Over large areas, then, slaves could end up by being taken either across the Sahara or across the Atlantic. In either case, huge numbers died on the way. Because the horrors of the actual capture of slaves inland and their transport overland to the coast were so closely observed by European travellers in East Africa in the nineteenth century, it has been naïvely thought that, since no similar accounts existed for West Africa, such horrors did not accompany the delivery of slaves to the coast there. The few accounts which survive suggest that they did.

Not all the contemporary accounts of the slave-trade are by slave-traders. In 1789 a former slave, an Ibo named Olaudah Equiano, alias Gustavus Vasa, wrote a particularly valuable account. He recalled that there was some slavery at his home in Iboland, though of a sort not at all comparable to the West Indies' plantation slavery, and that his people had sold some criminals and prisoners-of-war to African dealers in exchange for European goods (these included dried fish, an important European export to West Africa for centuries, which has become a staple food in Iboland). But he also recorded that the fear of kidnappers who would sell children into slavery was so great that some children were regularly posted as look-outs.[8] He himself, however, was kidnapped at the age of eleven, with his sister, in a small kidnapping operation, rather than a major raid. He was sold to other Ibos first, but in the course of changing hands many times he came to a country whose language he did not know (Ijaw or Ibibio, probably), and finally reached the sea and a slave-ship.⁹

The nightmarish conditions of the shipment of slaves emerge clearly enough from Europeans' accounts, but Equiano's 'inside story' is the most damning evidence of all. Stunned by the brutality of the white crew, he feared, like many other Africans taken on to slave-ships, that he would be eaten by the strange men. He was told that the slaves were in fact to be put to work, and this reassured him somewhat, 'but I still feared I should be put to death, the white people looked and acted, as I thought, in so savage a manner; for I had never seen among my people such instances of brutal cruelty, and this not only shewn towards us Blacks, but also to some of the Whites themselves.'¹⁰

As Equiano said, European sailors (including those on slave-ships as well as those in Nelson's navy) fared little better than slaves. But it seems that life in England and elsewhere in Europe was so brutal that people there were more prepared for a cruel life at sea than Africans were. Far from being glad to leave the horrors of Africa (which Europeans exaggerated to show how much better life on a Jamaican plantation was), the enslaved Africans were in fact appalled and overwhelmed by the exceptional brutality of colonising Western European man.

Slaves were crammed into holds which, in the case of Equiano's ship, became 'pestilential', with many people dying from the foul air and others being almost suffocated by the closeness and the heat. 'This wretched situation was again aggravated by the galling of the chains, now become insupportable, and the filth of the necessary tubs, into which the children often fell and were almost suffocated. The shrieks of the women and the groans of the dying rendered the whole a scene of horror almost inconceivable.' Equiano was flogged for refusing to eat.¹¹ Other slaves suffered flogging and other punishments, from pure sadism as well as from fear of rebellion or suicide. Rebellions did occur, but as every precaution was taken against them it was more common for slaves to try to starve themselves to death or to jump overboard. For hunger-strikers, a refined instrument for forcible feeding was devised.

The sufferings of the slaves were equally great before loading, when they were herded into 'barracoons' (the slavers' crude warehouses) and often branded like cattle. They could be terrible on landing, when buyers often made purchases by a 'scramble' (described by Equiano), each African going to the man who first touched him, regardless of ties of family or friendship. As for how they fared with their owners, this obviously varied, but it was usually brutal.

The mind reels today at the story of such atrocities, carried on *for four centuries* by the 'civilised' nations of Europe. All the major European nations were involved. The Portuguese were the worst offenders in the sixteenth century, supplying both their own colonies and Spain's,[12] but by the seventeenth century the French, British and particularly the Dutch had become more important.[13] During the wars among the European nations, the forts and barracoons on the 'Guinea Coast' were among the prizes; Goree, the island off the coast of Senegal which was an important base for the slave-trade, changed hands many times. Eventually, there were several British, Dutch, Danish and other trading establishments along the West African coast. In the eighteenth century Great Britain was the leading slave-trading nation. In 1713 the English Guinea Company received the *asiento* or contract for the supply of slaves to Spanish America.[14] Companies of this sort were responsible for some of the slave-trade, but not all; there was a variety of entrepreneurs supplying a variety of customers, not necessarily of the same nationality. The coast was sufficiently well 'covered' by the slave-trade to make competition keen at some points. Liverpool and Bristol were the leading European ports for the slave-trade; and in 1752 eighty-seven slavers were owned in Liverpool.[15] Between 1733 and 1766 it was estimated that 20,000 slaves had been shipped across the Atlantic every year in British ships; later, 100,000 slaves were thought to have been shipped in 1798[16] – in spite of war conditions, then. Between 1783 and 1793 it was calculated that slavers owned in Liverpool made 878 journeys with 303,737 slaves, with an estimated value of £15,186,850, to the West Indies.[17]

Slaves were sold in Brazil, the Guianas, Jamaica, the French and Spanish colonies on Hispaniola (Saint Domingue and Santo Domingo), Cuba, the British and French islands of the Leeward and Windward groups, the southern colonies of British North America, and other places. Much of the West African coast was scoured to supply these markets. Society in the New World depended on constant supplies of 'Mandingo', 'Eboe' (Ibo), 'Nago' (Yoruba), 'Congo' (often Angolan), and other African slaves. In the West Indies and Brazil they grew sugar-cane, cultivation of which is particularly hard and exhausting. In North America they often grew tobacco, but more usually cotton. Household slaves were very important. White children were brought up by black 'mammies' and, indeed, much of the day-to-day running of plantations and households was left to slaves, as it was to servants in Europe. Many female slaves became concubines of the white men, especially in Brazil.

If some slaves held responsible positions in the white people's lives (Scarlett O'Hara in *Gone With the Wind* was brought up to accept orders from the black 'Mammy'), few if any could rise to power as slaves could in Arab countries, Ottoman Turkey or pre-colonial black Africa. Nor were the freed black people in the New World of great importance, though they were not negligible in numbers. White owners retained ultimate control over the mass of the unwilling black immigrants. They enforced it with discipline and cruelty which revealed, undoubtedly, a constant fear of rebellion. Flogging was particularly used to terrorise the slaves; after buying his own freedom (this could be done), Equiano saw on a visit to Jamaica that there were professional hired floggers (black). Sadism and pathological ill-treatment did not always occur, but they were always possible because of the absolute power of the master. France's very wealthy colony of Saint Domingue had a brilliant and brutally corrupt aristocracy of planters in the eighteenth century, and this was paralleled in other places. Slave-rebellions were common in Jamaica, the Guianas and elsewhere. In Jamaica and on the mainland, slaves ran away to form 'Maroon' communities (these still survive in Dutch and French Guiana, their people being called 'Bush Negroes'). The greatest of all slave-risings was the ultimately successful one in Saint Domingue, which after a dozen years of great bloodshed became the independent state of Haiti in 1804.

*Abolition and the peak of the slave-trade*
On 23 March 1807, after a century in which it had played the leading role in the Atlantic slave-trade, Great Britain outlawed slave-trading by an Act of Parliament. Such a change has seldom been seen in history. It was brought about by forty years of campaigning by a small but determined band of Abolitionists, headed by William Wilberforce, Thomas Clarkson and Granville Sharp. Their campaign began in earnest in 1772 when they secured legal judgement in the case of the slave Somersett, brought to court by Sharp; this declared free all the slaves brought to Great Britain from the West Indies (there were a number of these as for some time the British had thought it fashionable to have black pages). By 1795 the campaign had gone far enough for Wilberforce to introduce to the House of Commons a Bill for the total abolition of the slave-trade. This was rejected by only nineteen votes.[18] Already the Commons had appointed a committee which had collected a mass of material (valuable today for the history of the whole sordid subject) and had

tried to regulate the slave-trade in ways annoying to the traders.

The story of the abolition movement and its ultimate success in the 'Act for the Abolition of the Slave-Trade' is a heartening one, for in it moral principle triumphs over self-interest.[19] It may be true, as has been argued, that abolition came when the slave-trade was becoming less important for Great Britain – because new industries needed West Africa's palm-oil (which in fact became its main export after effective abolition) more than its people. But the slave-trade was very profitable, even so; Liverpool lived off it, great numbers of other British people benefited by it, and the victories in the French wars gave Great Britain an opportunity to control an even greater share of the world's slave-trade. Opposition to the abolition movement was therefore fierce; but it failed in the end. In 1811 Englishmen who carried on what had been one of their country's main businesses a few years before became liable to transportation or hard labour (those transported would have had some idea of what African slaves endured). Abolition went with a widespread change of attitude by British Christians towards Africa. Under the influence of this change, there was a new missionary effort in Africa and a new concern for moral improvement, for more Christian behaviour by Europeans, and for more preaching of Chritianity to others.

This genuine concern inevitably became mixed up with others. The missionaries and other Christian campaigners against slavery believed, on moral grounds, in the promotion of 'legitimate' trade in Africa, that is trade other than that in slaves, in addition to the preaching of Protestant Christianity; as David Livingstone put it, in 'commerce and Christianity'. But there was less spiritual profit in this combination too, especially since the need for palm-oil which West Africa could provide was so great. 'Legitimate trade' in palm-oil did eventually flourish, particularly in the 'Oil Rivers' of the Niger delta, where the traders deserved their name of 'palm-oil ruffians', being similar characters to the old slave-traders. This combination of moral considerations and other motives seemed particularly disagreeable to the other Europeans whom the British tried to stop trading in slaves. Besides the moral considerations, there was the fact that the British abolition made it possible for other countries to take over the lion's share of the slave-trade formerly held by Liverpool and Bristol, while in trying to stop them the British aroused all the resentment incited by a major criminal who repents and then tries to stop the crimes of others.

For a century after the abolition of slavery, British foreign policy was preoccupied with suppressing the slave-trade. This excellent aim was inextricably bound up with Great Britain's growing desire to throw its weight about the world; imperialism went with abolition of the slave-trade, defence of national independence often went with defence of slave-trading. But 'gunboat diplomacy' was used without hesitation and with effect with the genuine aim of abolishing slave-trading. The Royal Navy patrolled the West African coasts to stop slaves being sent to the New World. The colony of Sierra Leone, established in 1792 for freed Africans (at first from England, North America and Jamaica), was taken over by the British Government and used as a base for anti-slavery action; at Freetown, captured slave-ships were legally confiscated and the slaves freed. Meanwhile, British diplomatic pressure on all rulers still involved in slave-trading, whether European of African, never abated; there was a special department in the Foreign Office dealing with slave-trade abolition. In spite of all this, it is amazing to record that the early nineteenth century was the busiest period of transatlantic slave-trading ever known.

British diplomatic efforts to stop slave-trading by other countries were strongly resisted. The USA had abolished slave-trading at the same time as Great Britain, and Denmark had done so earlier, but there remained the Netherlands, France, Spain, Portugal and, after its independence from Portugal, Brazil. The Dutch Government agreed fairly readily to the abolition of the trade, which was effected by a treaty with Great Britain in 1823. Other treaties were signed with other countries, but neither they nor local laws and proclamations were always successful. The British insistence on the right to search the ships of other countries was often resisted. France did not make slave-trading a criminal offence until 1827, and the French slave-trade did not come under serious attack until an Anglo-French Treaty of 1831. The British treaties made with Spain and Portugal in 1817 were useless; both countries resisted or evaded agreements to end the slave-trade, and even after Portugal outlawed the slave-trade completely in 1836 the sea, according to James Bandinel who recorded all these diplomatic efforts, 'was crowded with slave-ships under the flag of Portugal'.[20] From then on, the French having officially stopped their slave-trading, the main slave-trading countries were Spain, Portugal and Brazil.

Although Brazil was one of the main markets for slaves, pressure to secure the abolition of slavery there failed and was to continue to fail until 1888. Bahia was the main slave-port in Brazil, and the main African port for Brazilian slave embarkations was Wyhdah, ruled by the King of Dahomey. Cuba was the other main destination for slaves; it, along with Puerto Rico, remained under Spanish rule even when Spain had lost all the rest of her American possessions,

THE OLD SLAVE-TRADE 123

and continued slavery after the independent states had abolished it. Slavery remained legal in the British colonies until 1834 and in the French until 1848; smuggling of slaves was possible until then, and in the USA until 1863. But Brazil and Cuba were the main destinations for illegal slave-ships, whose numbers were great because the business was so profitable. The eighteenth-century peak of 100,000 slaves shipped in a year is thought to have been exceeded in the nineteenth century.

The Royal Navy's anti-slavery Preventive Squadron had only a few ships which could not be everywhere at once. Sometimes slave-traders would allow the Squadron's ships to search their vessels when these had innocent cargoes aboard, and then go and pick up slaves. Most terrible of all, the crew of a slave-ship, seeing one of the British anti-slavery patrol ships approaching, could throw the slaves into the sea and pretend that they had never had any slaves on board; this happened quite often in the days when only ships found with slaves actually aboard could be arrested. Later anti-slave-trade treaties had an 'equipment clause' whereby a ship equipped for slave-trading could be arrested.

There were a few American and other anti-slave-trade ships in action at times, but most of the patrolling was done by the Royal Navy. Besides its main base at Freetown, it had from 1827 a lesser base on Fernando Po. There the British Consul for the Bights of Benin and Biafra resided, with the abolition of the slave-trade as one of his main tasks. Successive Consuls there made repeated visits to Bonny, Calabar and Cameroons to stop the Ijaws, Efiks and Dualas from selling slaves. The local rulers, however, evaded the treaties they had signed and continued to sell slaves. Slaves for Bonny and Calabar were commonly Ibos, who had often been enslaved by the Aros after being offered as sacrifices to the oracle at Arochukwu. The use of this oracle for slave-trading came to be a well-organised activity; people were taken there for solution of family problems or village disputes, and then seized and sent down the Cross River to Calabar, or overland to Bonny.[21] Others, like Equiano, were enslaved by kidnapping or purchase.

A hideous description of a slave-ship's journey from Bonny to Guadeloupe has survived. It is by a boy of twelve who (typically of those times with their casual brutality) was sent by his parents, planters in Guadeloupe, to travel as a passenger on a slaver to the island, calling at Bonny on the way. He wrote to his mother about what he saw on the ship *Le Rodeur*. Several slaves jumped overboard, three were shot and three were hanged. Ophthalmia spread among the slaves, making them blind, with the result that by the time the ship reached the West Indies all the slaves, and all the crew but one, were blind. Then, as the ship approached the French island, thirty-nine incurably blind slaves were thrown into the sea.[22]

The replacement of the slave-trade by the palm-oil trade in what is now Eastern Nigeria was a slow process, but it eventually took place because the region is rich in palms and the demand for palm-oil was often high. Ironically, this meant that the coastal peoples went on buying or capturing large numbers of slaves to run the palm-oil plantations, so that the internal slave-trade was actually encouraged by British efforts to introduce 'legitimate trade'. But the change was still a change for the better, for slaves who remained in Africa did not suffer the horrors just mentioned in the passage to the New World. They could rise to important positions in local society, like the Ibo-born Jaja, King of Opobo. Illegal shipments of slaves from this area may have gone on until after 1860.

British efforts to persuade the powerful Kings of Dahomey at Abomey to stop selling slaves were a failure. They did sell palm-oil too, but saw no reason why they should not sell both. At Whydah, the leading slave-port, the king's official in charge of trade in slaves and other 'goods' was a Brazilian called Francisco Felix da Sousa, who until his death in 1849 (at a fairly old age, with great power and wealth) was famous all along the coast as an illicit slave-dealer.[23] Dahomey had regular wars which, at this time, may well have been fought with the express aim of taking prisoners to sell.[24]

The main source of supply of slaves for Whydah, however, lay in the Yoruba states east of Dahomey. These states were frequently at war, especially in the nineteenth century when the power of the central ruler, the Alafin of Oyo, had declined. Prisoners taken in these wars were regularly shipped across the Atlantic, often from Whydah but also from Porto Novo, Badagry and Lagos (which in fact began to develop as a slave-port about 1830).[25] Many of these slave-ships were seized by the Preventive Squadron and the slaves freed in Sierra Leone. As so many of the slaves were Yorubas, there is a large Yoruba element in the Sierra Leone Creole population, many of whose members returned at an early date to their homelands in what is now Nigeria. And the fact that African culture in Brazil and Cuba is generally Yoruba is due to the fact that many of the slaves shipped there were captured in the nineteenth-century Yoruba wars. Some Yoruba religion and art continues almost unchanged in Brazil.

Many of the slaves freed in Sierra Leone and Liberia (where there were not many) after the capture of slave-ships were called 'Congoes'. Probably they were Angolans shipped before the Portuguese abolition of the slave-trade in 1836 – and afterwards, for that abolition did not take effect for some time. Many illicit Portuguese slave-shipments, however, came not from Angola but round the Cape from Mozambique, an unusually terrible journey for the slaves.

Illicit slave-shipments took place at many points, with only a small number being detected by the patrols, but the main place for them, apart from the 'Slave Coast' between Whydah and Lagos, was between The Gambia and Liberia. Here two notorious slave-smugglers, Pedro Blanco, a Spaniard, and Theodore Canot, half-French by birth but eventually an American, operated. The Rio Pongo in Portuguese Guinea was an important place for shipments from some time, and Canot made his first slaving voyage from there to Havana in 1827.[26] Later, British and French patrols stopped the slaving there, but the slavers continued to work for years, with great success, from the Gallinas Lagoon and the Sulinas River, situated between Freetown and Monrovia, the two settlements for freed slaves. After working from there, Blanco retired in 1839 with a fortune estimated at £1 million and ended his days on the Italian Riviera.[27] In 1840 a British expedition destroyed the slavers' 'barracoons' at Gallinas and Canot made what he said in his memoirs was his last slaving trip, with no less than 749 slaves bound for Cuba.[28] In 1849 there was another expedition to destroy the slavers' establishments in Gallinas.

In 1852 the British Government helped a claimant to the throne of Lagos to take power and imposed on him a treaty binding him to stop the slave-trade. However, many years were to pass before the trade began to die away. It was considered a good reason for outright annexation of Lagos in 1861. Slaves were shipped from the Cameroons until about 1860. From Whydah they were being shipped even later, and some slaves were even taken to Cuba by steamship; for example, the steamer *Nordagny* shipped about 4,000 slaves between 1860 and 1863 from Whydah to Cuba.[29] This was a very busy period, but it seems that soon afterwards slave-trading fell away and stopped.

There was a curious revival of a special sort of slave-trading later in the century, when the European powers, which professed to be against slavery, bought some prisoners-of-war from Dahomey to use as soldiers in the colonisation of other parts of Africa. Between 1889 and 1891, 680 such Dahomean soldiers were shipped to Cameroon by the Germans, and 200 were sent to São Tomé, the Portuguese island which became famous soon afterwards for its forced labour; 485 were sent to the Congo Free State.[30] Although the Europeans did not treat these soldiers as slaves, they were slaves in the eyes of the Dahomeans who sold them, and they were not bought to be freed, for they were then used as soldiers. This dubious episode ended a few years later with the conquest of Dahomey by the French.

*Across the desert and down the Nile*

Abolition of the slave-trade was an aim of British policy towards Africa after 1807, not only on the western side. The Government's attention was soon drawn to the slave-trade across the Sahara; it was lobbied by public opinion and particularly by the British and Foreign Anti-Slavery Society, which, after its foundation in 1839, paid close attention to the trans-Sahara traffic (see Chapter Two). Murzuk and Ghadames were the main centres for the trade with countries south of the desert; at Murzuk in 1845 James Richardson, one of the many travellers who reported on this slave-traffic, saw about 1,000 slaves from Bornu and other Sahelian areas. He thought that about 10,000 slaves were taken across the desert every year, about 60 per cent of them women and 10 per cent young children.[31] British Consuls reported on the traffic and revealed its full horror; on one occasion it was estimated that 770 out of 1,795 slaves taken from Bornu had died on one desert-crossing.[32]

There was a Consul at Tripoli, capital of the province where many slaves from the south were sold, and between 1843 and 1860 there were Vice-Consuls at Murzuk and Ghadames. These tried, like the British on the West African coast, to promote 'legitimate trade' as an alternative to the slave-trade for the local people. The British Government put pressure on the Bey of Tunis to abolish the slave-trade and slavery itself, which he did at the remarkably early dates of 1842 and 1846 respectively. Efforts to end slavery in the Ottoman Empire were less successful for a long time. The British Government thought that the end of slavery would be a disaster to that Empire, which it was generally British policy to support, but they persuaded the Sultans to take various steps against the slave-trade, and slavery itself was abolished in 1889.[33] Traffic in slaves across the Sahara went on for considerable longer, as already mentioned.

East of the Wadai-Cyrenaica slave-route, controlled for much of the nineteenth century by the Senussi order, was a slave-route which went south from Darfur. Arans from that old kingdom (in the area of the modern Sudan) bought slaves from the Azande and Mangbetu, important peoples in the north-east of the Congo basin who had slavery as an important local institution. From Darfur, slaves were sent across the Sudan to Egypt or Arabia.[34] This traffic was for a long time much less known to Europeans than the traffic in slaves down the Nile, but it was far bigger than that traffic in the nineteenth century. The Nile traffic became notorious because many Europeans were involved in it.

Egypt had imported slaves from up the Nile for centuries, but a new impetus was given to slaving in the Upper Nile basin by the efforts of Egyptians and Europeans to open it up to trade with Khartoum, Egypt and Europe. The peoples of the Southern Sudan, mainly Nilotic peoples such as the Shilluk, Nuer and Dinka, were unable to withstand the ravages caused by Egyptian colonisation and European commercial exploitation. Traders soon met opposition from the people and beat it down. At first, slaves were captured to carry the ivory tusks, which were much in demand by the Europeans; but by the mid-nineteenth century, traders' agents were regularly seizing or buying slaves, who were sent to Darfur, to the Northern Sudan, and as far as Egypt.[35] After the accession of Muhammad Sa'id in 1854, Egypt took action against the slave-trade, but with little effect beyond the closing of the open slave-market at Khartoum. Slaves were needed for the slave-army (*Jihadiyya*) whose main function to maintain Egypt's rule in the Sudan. The appointment by Egypt of Sir Samuel Baker and then General Charles 'Chinese' Gordon (both in the 1870s) as British representatives in the Southern Sudan with special orders to end slave-trading, achieved little, because the anarchy in which slave-trading flourished was beyond them.

So slave-trading down the Nile went on, but in 1877 Khedive Isma'il of Egypt agreed to end it by 1880. This was one cause of an uprising in 1881 by the Mahdi, Muhammad Ahmad ibn Abdullah, who eventually conquered most of the Sudan. Although he had opposed the abolition of the slave-trade, it declined sharply under him and his successor the Khalifa, Abdullahi ibn Muhammad, who controlled few of the old slave-trade areas.[36] In 1898 the British conquered the Sudan, and ended slave-trading. A few years passed before this stopped completely, but the British did much to ensure that the southern Sudanese suffered no more oppression from the northerners. Indeed, they kept the northern, mainly Arabic-speaking and Muslim, part of the population almost totally separate from the Shilluk, Nuer and other southerners, who were allowed to live in a peace they had not known for some time and protected from Islamisation (many became Christians). This was certainly a blessing for the southerners, at least initially, but eventually it meant that the Sudan developed as two separate countries, one more Arab and one more African than the other. But, instead of following their policy to its logical conclusion and separating the two regions at independence, the British suddenly put them together. So the Republic of the Sudan was born in conflict in 1956, and this conflict continued for sixteen years.

The Sudan War was the longest and perhaps the most terrible in Africa's recent history. The northerners despised and wanted to dominate the southerners, and their general treatment of them stopped short only of the actual slave-raiding of the nineteenth century. Attitudes dating from those days had clearly survived the colonial period. While northern Sudanese are Arab only by language, and belong to several tribes of which some are very dark-skinned, the cultural differences between them and the southerners are enormous. For that reason it was particularly welcome news when the war at last ended, in February 1972, in a compromise under which the south now has a large amount of self-government in a united Sudan. This peace agreement seems to be working and the Sudanese may now put the nineteenth century behind them at last.

*The East African slave-trade*
In the area of the Great Lakes and the upper Congo basin the hunting grounds of slavers from the north met those of slavers from the east. The later operated from the East African coast, and their slaving activities, covering a vast area of East Africa, became well known to the British public in the nineteenth century, in fact better known than any other slaving operations in the interior of Africa. Europeans had seen the slave-trade mainly on the coast, now they saw what it meant to the people of the interior.

Trading in slaves from the East African coast began at least 2,000 years ago. For centuries the Arabs took black slaves from there to Arabia, the Persian Gulf area and India. They also settled on the East African coast where they formed the aristocracy of port cities such as Mombasa, Kilwa, Pate (in modern Kenya), Sofala and Zanzibar; these were chiefly African cities, however, and their language was and is the Bantu Swahili language. The Portuguese occupation and intervention in the sixteenth and seventeenth centuries had only a limited effect on the Arabs of the coast, and after their expulsion the Arab state of Muscat ruled much of the coast down to the River Rovuma, beyond which the Portuguese still had settlements.

Both the Arabs and the Portuguese extensively traded in slaves from East Africa. The Arabs of Kilwa sold many slaves in the eighteenth century to the French, who took them to Mauritius and Réunion (as they are now called), and even round the Cape to the West Indies. One French slave-trader, J. Crassons de Medeuil, said that in three years in the 1780s, he and other Frenchmen had shipped 4,193 slaves in a dozen ships from Kilwa. He thought that in fact more had been shipped from Kilwa, and said: 'From Cape Delgado to Kilwa the coast is inhabited only by Moors and Arabs who take from it a prodigious number of Blacks'.[37] Another Frenchman described in 1804 public auctions for slaves in Zanzibar, from which shipments were made to Muscat, the Red Sea and the Persian Gulf. The Arabs shipped many slaves themselves, besides selling some to the French and other Europeans.

In the late nineteenth century Zanzibar became the leading port for the trade in ivory and slaves along the East African coast. From 1832, when the Sultan of Muscat moved there, Zanzibar was the capital of an independent state with power or influence over a considerable part of the coast and some of the interior. Trading with inland peoples was carried out by Arabs and by Africans of the coastal peoples collectively called Swahili, with Indians in Zanzibar providing the finance.

The slave-trade flourished for much of the nineteenth century, but even at the beginning of that century it was under attack from London. In 1822 the Sultan of Muscat agreed to prohibit trading in slaves between his subjects and Christians, but this agreement achieved little. The French slave-trade in the Indian Ocean enjoyed a revival in the early nineteenth century. An agreement signed between Britain and Madagascar in 1828 for the ending of the slave-trade was of little effect.

On the Mozambique coast, the Portuguese went on trading in slaves well into the nineteenth century. The French, after they stopped buying slaves for Réunion, bought contract labourers for that island in very similar conditions until 1861, on the Mozambique coast. Slaves from there were also sent to the New World, and many made the shorter journey to Madagascar.[38]

Further north, the Arab-Swahili slave-traders began taking caravans into the interior from the second quarter of the nineteenth century. Eventually, they had important inland trading settlements, such as Tabora and Ujiji, and their raids, or raids made to supply them, ravaged large areas well into the upper Congo basin. Several European witnesses, including David Livingstone, reported the horrors of the collection of slaves in East Africa. That missionary's zeal for abolition of the slave-trade was increased by what he saw. Soldiers raided and destroyed villages on a large scale, killing some people and taking the rest to the coast, which might be a thousand miles away. It was estimated that only a fifth of all the slaves captured reached the coast alive. There these lucky ones were sold at

Zanzibar and shipped in dhows to Arabia or other places across the Indian Ocean. Livingstone wrote a horrific report of one massacre by slavers which he saw near the upper Congo during his last journey.

Bagamoyo, on the coast opposite Zanzibar, was the usual base for the trading expeditions which sought palm products, copal and ivory as well as slaves.[39] To some extent slave-trading began, there as in the Sudan, with the recruiting of slaves to carry elephants' tusks. Through these expeditions, the Sultan of Zanzibar established a vague sort of trading empire in East Africa, but his authority was, in fact, slight: though it was recognised by the famous trader Hamed bin Muhammad, 'Tippoo Tib', who ruled and traded in Maniema by the upper Lualaba for many years and later became the Congo Free State's governor of the Stanley Falls district.[40] The African peoples generally did not recognise the Sultan as effective ruler, but sold many prisoners to his traders – the Chagga and Kamba, for example, and later the state of Buganda, where the Arabs established trade and influence a little before the Europeans.

The East African slave-trade extended to areas now included in Malawi and Zambia, and there its effects were very destructive. The Portuguese were engaged in slaving south of Lake Malawi (Lake Nyasa) in the 1850s and 1860s, and where their slaving ended the Yao, one of the most important African peoples of the area, took over. They were trading with Kilwa on a large scale by the late eighteenth century, selling ivory, copper, iron and a few slaves. Later, in the latter part of the nineteenth century, the Yao controlled a large area and sold slaves from it to the Arabs on a considerable scale; caravans of up to 5,000 slaves bound for Kilwa were reported in 1881. Arabs as well as Yaos operated in the region of the lake until the 1890s, when the British fought hard battles against the slavers who had depopulated large areas.[41]

Arab slavers did not really conquer, though they did assert their presence more than most European slave-traders on the west coast. The Yaos remained as independent as Dahomey did in the west in the slave-trading days. Further north in East Africa, in what is now Tanzania, the Nyamwezi chief, Mirambo, having conquered a large area from the Arabs of Tabora, in the middle of territory under the Sultan's vague suzerainty, tried to control one of the slave and ivory trade-routes; he ruled quite a large state until his death in 1884. It is a sad fact that rulers in East Africa, like those of Calabar and Anomabo on the western side, did far more in the way of slave-trading than they were forced to do. This does not in any way alter the fact that the external slave-traders, European and Arab, were the main criminals involved.

In 1873 Sultan Barghash of Zanzibar yielded to British pressure and abolished the slave-trade. The slave-market at Zanzibar town was closed and a cathedral was later built on its site. Already British naval patrols had been seeking out slave-ships in the Indian Ocean for some time, as they had done in the Atlantic in earlier years. Already, too, settlements of freed slaves had begun to grow up, for example in India, Mauritius (once a destination for many East African slaves) and the Seychelles, and in East Africa several were founded by the Catholic White Fathers, one at Bagamoyo, and by the Church Missionary Society at Mombasa.[42] At Mombasa many descendents of ex-slaves later recalled their Chagga origin.[43]

But neither the Sultan's abolition nor the founding of slave-colonies could end the slave-trade in East Africa. The Sultan's rule was not even effective on the coast, much less inland, and the traffic in slaves from the region of Lake Nyasa flourished in the 1880s. Then European colonisation began, and gradually action was taken against the slave-trade which was largely destroyed in the 1890s when the British extended their rule over Kenya, Uganda and Nyasaland further south, and the Germans extended theirs over Tanganyika as far as the border of the Congo Free State. The Arab slave-traders resisted particularly strongly in Nyasaland and the Congo. Leopold II's régime, which existed partly for the purpose of ending the slave-trade (though it employed Tippoo Tib as a governor), fought the Arabs for some years in the north-east of its territory in the 1890s. In Nyasaland the last major battle between the British and the slave-traders, Africans in this case, took place in 1899.[44]

Slave-trading from the East African coast did not die out altogether when the worst days of the slave-caravans from the lake regions were over. In Mozambique some slaves were taken to Madagascar until the first few years of the twentieth century, after which the effects of the French occupation of the island were felt and the traffic (presumably) ceased. Further north, illicit slave-trading went on in the mainland possessions of the Sultan of Zanzibar, on the coast of Kenya, as long as slavery remained legal there (which it did until 1907, ten years after the legal status of slavery was abolished in Zanzibar and its sister island of Pemba). Illegal slave-ships continued to put into coastal creeks and mangrove swamps to pick up slaves to take, presumably, to Arabia, where slavery was to remain legal for decades to come.[45] Even the abolition of slavery in the Sultan's mainland territory in 1907 probably did not end this secret traffic at once, for after visiting the Kamba a Swedish scholar was to note: 'During my stay in East Ukamba in 1911 one could ... still

132  AFRICA'S SLAVES TODAY

say that slave-trading took place to a certain extent, as I knew at least one man, in a good position, who secretly sold women to harems at the coast';[46] and if slaves could be sold at the coast some could no doubt still be put on the dhows. But this sort of secret traffic must have become rarer and have died out completely before long – or almost completely.

*Notes*

1. John Barbot, *A Description of the Coasts of North and South Guinea* (1746), p. 11.
2. Ibid., pp. 459–60.
3. Ibid., p. 195 (Chapter Twelve, Book Three).
4. Ibid., p. 177 (Chapter Nine, Book Three).
5. Ibid., pp. 47–8.
6. Ibid., p. 271.
7. Ibid., pp. 181–2.
8. Olaudah Equiano, *The Interesting Narrative of the Life of Olaudah Equiano* (1789), re-edited as *Equiano's Travels* (1967), pp. 2 ff.
9. Ibid., pp. 16–25.
10. Ibid., p. 27.
11. Ibid., pp. 27–9.
12. J. H. Parry, *The Age of Reconnaissance*, pp. 182–3.
13. Ibid., pp. 186, 264–5; J. Bandinel, *Some Account of the Trade in Slaves from Africa* (1842), early chapters.
14. Bandinel, op. cit.
15. G. F. Dow, *Slave-Ships and Slaving*, p. 91.
16. Bandinel, op. cit., p. 105.
17. Dow, op. cit., p. 110.
18. Bandinel, op. cit., p. 104.
19. See Bandinel's account.
20. Bandinel, op. cit., p. 222.
21. B. Floyd, *Eastern Nigeria*, pp. 43–4.
22. Dow, op. cit., introduction by E. H. Pentecost, pp. xxviii–xxxv.
23. C. W. Newbury, *The Western Slave Coast and its Rulers*, pp. 37 ff.
24. Ibid.
25. Ibid., pp. 28–36.
26. T. Canot, *Adventures of an African Slaver*.
27. Dow, op. cit., pp. 15–16.
28. Canot, op. cit.
29. Newbury, op. cit., p. 69 n.
30. Ibid., p. 130 n.
31. A. Adu Boahen, *Britain, the Sahara and the Western Sudan*, pp. 111 ff., 137–58, 167 ff.
32. Ibid.
33. Ibid.
34. R. Gray, *A History of the Southern Sudan, 1839–1889*, pp. 36–52, 65–9.
35. Ibid.
36. P. M. Holt, *A Modern History of the Sudan*, p. 123.

37. Quoted in G. S. P. Freeman-Grenville (ed.), *The East African Coast*, Chapters Thirty-eight and Thirty-nine.
38. M. D. D. Newitt, 'Angoche, the Slave-Trade and the Portuguese, c. 1894–1910', in *Journal of African History* 1972, No. 4.
39. K. Ingham, *A History of East Africa*, p. 58.
40. Ibid.
41. J. G. Pike, *Malawi*, pp. 58–61, 90 ff.
42. Ingham, op. cit., pp. 106, 109–10.
43. K. Stahl, *History of the Chagga People of Kilimanjaro*, p. 132 n.
44. Pike, op. cit., pp. 91–2.
45. Ingham, op. cit., p. 201.
46. G. Lindblom, *The Akamba of Western Kenya*, p. 353.

*Chapter Six*

# One-Way Trips to Arabia

The last transatlantic slave-ship probably sailed some time before the abolition of slavery in Cuba (1880) and Brazil (1888). Strangely, a number of Africans went to the New World as non-slave labourers after the abolition of the slave-trade in their areas, and the conditions which they experienced – while cutting the Panama Canal, for example – were in practice sometimes reminiscent of the old days, though not really similar.

Slave-trading to Arabia, however, went on until recent times, and may still go on today. There are few parts of the world where slavery has lasted so persistently as in the countries of the Arabian Peninsula, for example, Saudi Arabia, Yemen, Muscat and Oman. And Africa may still be what geography destined it to be from the start: a source of slaves for Kings, Sheikhs, merchants and other property-owners in Arabia.

In the Red Sea, the Persian Gulf, the Arabian Sea and the main body of the Indian Ocean, the sailors of Arabia have for thousands of years used a variety of small sailing craft, including the dhow, a simple but handsome and seaworthy craft. These dhows have plied between the ports of Arabia – Aden, Hodeida, Jeddah, Mukalla, Sur, Muscat and many others – and all parts of the Indian Ocean shores: Zanzibar and all the East African coast, Port Sudan and Massawa, Madagascar and the Comoro Islands, India, Ceylon and Indonesia. Besides dates, cloth, timber, pearls, arms and other goods, they have often been laden with slaves.

The efforts of British naval patrols to curb this traffic may have had some effect in the nineteenth century, and certainly had some later, when the Royal Navy patrolled the Red Sea and all the seas around an Arabian peninsula dominated by British influence, and the colonisation of East Africa had ended the Arab-Swahili trading empire and largely cut off the source of the slave-trade there.

But experience shows that while slave-markets remain open, ways will be found of supplying them, and British dominance in

The Arabian Peninsula

Arabia did not end slave-trading there. Aden Protectorate was the only part of the peninsula under direct British rule, and almost the only place where modern changes, including wage employment, considerably altered the old Arab society. Elsewhere, the policy was not to alter it unduly, and slavery fitted into this society. Slave-troops, loyal to the rulers because they were cut off from their homes and their lives were wholly confined to their job, were used extensively in Arabia as in other countries. Other slaves did domestic work, and there was a continual demand for slave girls for the harems. Patriarchal society and the Islamic religion both admitted the institution of slavery in Arabia, and the desire of the British to abolish it was hampered by their desire to alter traditional structures as little as possible. While some officials favoured this policy for idealistic reasons, all would have had to admit that British power in the area was simply not strong enough to impose a sweeping revolution on an unwilling and proud people. British policy could not, and did not intend to, use much coercion against Arab states over which she had very limited legal powers.

British action against slave-holding (as opposed to slave-trading, which the navy tried to stop) consisted of advice and influence. This was the position in the Aden Protectorate, whose Sheikhs, Sultans and Emirs ruled a vast area, including the Hadhramaut (one of the areas least known to Europeans), almost without interference. It was also the position in Bahrain, Qatar and the seven Trucial States of the Persian Gulf shore, all protected states in which Great Britain's role was chiefly confined to foreign affairs and defence. British action to end or limit such very traditional institutions as slavery was therefore necessarily small in those areas; smaller still in Muscat and Oman, an independent state with a long-standing and close relationship with Great Britain but no subordination to her Empire (the Persian Gulf protected states were so independent that they cannot be compared to the 'protectorates' in Nigeria and Sierra Leone). And there was little or no British anti-slavery influence in the Kingdom of Yemen, and little or none in the Kingdom of Saudi Arabia formed by Ibn Saud in the 1920s from the Hejaz and the Nejd.

In Saudi Arabia slavery was undisguised; there slave-trading by sea, banned though not effectively in British-protected areas, was legal until it was outlawed, on paper, by Regulations published on 2nd October, 1936. The same Regulations recognised the institution of slavery, laying down rules for the good treatment of slaves.[1] Its legality thus confirmed, slavery continued, and slave-owners were helped by two pieces of good fortune (from their point of view). One was the discovery of oil, which brought in wealth that could be spent on more and better slaves (whose price went up as a result) as well as on Cadillacs and Riviera villas. Another was the inclusion in the new kingdom of the holy cities of Mecca and Medina, where the enormous concourse of pilgrims which arrived every year provided, as the Prophet cannot have intended, a cover for slave-trading.

Reports from the 1930s onwards suggested that Saudi Arabia was the destination of many slaves taken from Africa. The oil industry did not affect traditional society, in Saudi Arabia or in the less nomadic Arabian communities further south. The (often fascinating) reports of travellers to these places tell sad stories of disease, poverty, ignorance and petty oppression. Not only did slavery fit well into such places (because of their tradition of respect for hierarchy and social discipline) but also the lot of the slaves seemed less intolerable in the context of the general poverty of life. British visitors pointed out the sense of security and lack of stress in these societies, which they romanticised a great deal, and often spoke of slaves who were better off than free Arabs. What emerges from such accounts is that African slaves in Arabia were more integrated into life and society than those in the 'Old South.'

In a book based on a journey he made on a dhow in 1939, Alan Villiers mentioned slaves and ex-slaves at many South Arabian ports. The picture he gave was of slaves and ex-slaves, not easily distinguished from each other and not noticeably different from other Arabs, as part of everyday life; some were in positions of trust on ships. Both slaves and free men around the Arabian coasts showed signs of African descent.[2]

The African element in the Arabian population is often noted. In his book, *Arabia and the Isles*, a record of his colonial service during which he was Resident Adviser in the Hadhramaut in the late 1930s, Harold Ingrams says that the Sultan of Mukalla had in 1934 a force of 250 slaves, 'all of African origin', provided with wives and with milk for their families besides other rations and quarters and $1–3 pocket money per month. Speaking of two slaves involved in a case that he had to deal with at Seiyun in 1937, he records that: 'The male slave was the genuine African variety, but the woman was a tribeswoman of the Sei'ar and should never have been enslaved.'[3] Generally, Muslims could not enslave other Muslims among their own people, though they could hold them in a fairly tight debt-bondage or sometimes in a serf-like client status; this ban was no doubt one reason for the importing of African slaves. The normal African origin of slaves in the Aden Protectorate is further indicated by Ingrams when he notes that, after the freeing of the Mukalla slave-soldiers in 1945, they were 'now called Africans and no longer slaves'.[4]

Ingrams tried to persuade the local rulers to free their slaves in 1936, and with some success. But he was one of the writers who stressed the normal good treatment of slaves in Arabia. In the Hadhramaut, he said, there were 4,000–5,000 slaves in the technical sense, 'free to do anything they pleased'. But the situation was very different in some parts: '... amongst some of the Bedouin tribes such as the Ja'da, the Mahra and the Wahidi, there were appalling tales of oppression and cruelty'.[5] In Saudi Arabia the Wahhabi Muslim movement prevailing there may have restrained such things, for it preached strict observance of the Koran, which orders proper treatment of slaves and says that releasing them is a virtuous act.

'Slave' and 'African' have not always been synonymous in Arabia. In modern times many slaves there have come from Persia and the Indian sub-continent. Whatever their origin, slaves and ex-slaves have sometimes been able to attain power and wealth. Wilfred Thesiger, one of the most famous British travellers in Arabia, noted, in describing a journey in the later 1940s across the *Rub' al-Khali* (the 'empty quarter', a big stretch of desert inland from Muscat and Oman), that 'Arab rulers raise slaves to positions of great power, often trusting them more than they do their own relations'. At Sulaiyil he met the local Emir, 'who was a young slave'.[6] As many slaves were captured as children, or born into slavery, they were culturally Arabs. In the 1950s it was noted that most indigenous Negroes in Dhofar (Muscat and Oman) thought of themselves as Arabs, though they formed a separate community at Salalah and some retained African customs.[7]

Many slave concubines have become free (on the birth of children fathered by free Arabs) or powerful, or both, and these have formed a large number of the slave population. The attractions of black girls have been one element in both the Atlantic and the Indian Ocean slave-trades. Arabs are sometimes said to want them particularly because the operation of clitoridectomy or excision, performed regularly on Arab women, makes them frigid, so that the men seek sexual satisfaction elsewhere; Wendell Phillips said: 'The survival of slavery and existence of concubinage in parts of the Arabian Peninsula is to a large extent due to the specific need to cohabit with non-circumcised, sexually keen women, who echo the man's desire and derive pleasure from love-making.'[8] But this is doubtful because the operation of removing the clitoris, though very dangerous in the way it is often carried out and a menace for that reason, does not destroy sexual desire in women (it is also quite common in black Africa).

The cruelty which slave-catching involves, however well slaves may be treated after capture, is illustrated by the reports of castration of boy slaves sold in Arabia, and by the frequency with which children have been kidnapped for slavery.

Decades after measures were taken against the slave-trade, adults also were still ending up in slavery in Arabia. Methods have varied. Villiers noted that at Zanzibar the authorities required that 'no native can be engaged as a seaman without having previously been questioned by the port officer with a view to establishing that he has contracted a free engagement', while nobody could be shipped as either crew or passenger without supervision. These measures against enslavement of Africans recruited as seamen on the dhows seemed to be still necessary, as there were slave-markets in Oman; Villiers heard of a boat running down a fishing canoe and taking the two Africans in it to be sold as slaves in Arabia. On the other hand, the master of his dhow said he had been looking for years for a cargo of virgins but had not found one; but perhaps he had not looked hard enough.[9]

Referring to the Aden Protectorate in 1937, Ingrams said: 'New African importations are not unknown'. Many slaves came from Somalia and Ethiopia, and it might have been possible to take wholly involuntary slaves on such a short run. Tadjoura in French Somaliland was a port for Ethiopian slaves in the late nineteenth century, and this trade went on well into the twentieth, according to a Frenchman, Henri de Monfried, who went in for other rackets himself. Quoting him, a recent book says: 'Ethiopian chiefs, Afar tribesmen, and Arab merchants all took part in this trade in human beings. After the First World War the efforts made by the European powers and by Ethiopia to stamp it out were only partly successful, mainly (according to Monfried) because the slaves themselves were willing victims of the slavers.'[10] If that were really so, it was probably due to some sort of trickery, for voluntary submission to the slave-trade is historically rare, despite the theory uttered by defenders of the old Atlantic slave-trade – and repeated by an Arab to Alan Villiers in the East African context[11] – that many Africans were really better off as slaves. But in Ethiopia there were for long many people already enslaved at home and therefore easily available to slavers. At any rate, slaves went to Arabia from Ethiopia, and from Somalia.

The last sightings of slave-dhows reported by European vessels in the Red Sea seem to have been in 1933 and 1935,[12] but much later a Danish traveller in British and Italian Somaliland, John Buchholzer, met a captain who told him how he had dodged British anti-slavery patrols in the old days. Writing about 1958–9, this traveller said: 'Undoubtedly, slave-transports still cross to Arabia.'[13]

Writing of the same period (he visited Oman for archaeological excavations in 1958), Phillips said that at Salalah a Negro 'who has recent or obvious connections with East Africa' was called a *sambo*.[14] He did not say how recent the 'recent' connections were. In the context of Saudi Arabia he mentioned Ethiopia as still being a main source of supply for slaves in the 1950s.[15]

During the Second World War or soon afterwards, the special Royal Navy anti-slavery patrols were stopped, though ships' captains in the Red Sea still had general instructions to watch out for slave-boats. The end of the special patrols cannot have helped to stop efforts to meet what seems to have been, at that very time, a rising demand for slaves in Saudi Arabia, whose ban on the importing of slaves by sea was a dead letter. Some slaves for Saudi Arabia came via the Trucial States, which also had their own domestic slaves. In 1948 Thesiger noted sales at Hamasa of slaves brought from the Persian Gulf coast;[16] the usual price was 1,000 to 1,500 rupees for a Baluchi, Persian or Arab, more for a young Negro (those areas use the rupee, having traded with India for centuries). The Negroes in this case presumably came from East Africa. Although slaves were still being brought in from across the Persian Gulf at a much later date – Phillips gave a horrifying report of children kidnapped from the Makran coast of Persia and Pakistan, to end up as slaves in Saudi Arabia and never see their homes again,[17] while adult Persians suffering that fate were noted by a German reporter in the early 1960s[18] – African slaves also continued to be taken into Saudi Arabia from the eastern side. There the Buraimi oasis was an important centre for slave-trading in the 1950s, as at the time of Thesiger's journeys. But in 1956 a detailed report on the Saudi Arabian slave-trade by the Anti-Slavery Society spoke of African slaves being taken through Yemen, and added that these had generally been replaced by slaves from Iraq, Persia and the Gulf States.[19]

One hair-raising account, from the 1950s, is often quoted in connection with the slave-trade to Saudi Arabia. It is found in the first chapter of Robin Maugham's *The Slaves of Timbuktu*. A friend of Maugham, who was a British representative at Buraimi during the frontier dispute between the British-protected authorities and Saudi Arabia, saw people being brought in by caravan or lorry and taken away by air; he saw children being pushed into the aeroplane, and spoke about it to one of the pilots, who were mostly Americans. On being accused of flying children into slavery, the pilot replied: 'When I took on this job, I was told to keep my mouth shut and my eyes shut as to some of the things that go on around here. And that's the way it's going to be. Another seven years of flying for King Saud and I'll have made enough money to retire for life.'[20] One wonders how many other retired slave-traders there are in the USA, a century after Lincoln's abolition of slavery. This particular criminal's statement was passed on to the Foreign Office in London, but apparently no action was taken, perhaps because there was no law under which the pilot and his colleagues could be arrested.

Before this report, stories were spreading about another form of slave-trading to Saudi Arabia, connected with the Muslim pilgrimage. The importance of the Hajj to Muslims is well known. Poor people spend their lifetimes' earnings on a journey, sometimes overland, to Mecca and Medina. In the Sudan today there are over a million West Africans, mainly Nigerians, working to earn money for the journey to Arabia or back from there to their homes. Many others live as free people in Saudi Arabia, perhaps after being stranded there without the fare for the return journey. And others, it seems, have gone to Saudi Arabia as pilgrims and remained there as slaves.

A not very reliable early report on this method of obtaining slaves by fraud was written in 1947; a second-hand Reuter report based on ships' officers' stories and date-lined Durban, it spoke of West Africans from the Ivory Coast, Gold Coast (now Ghana) and Cameroon being assembled in the Sudan and taken to Arabia.[21] This report is suspect because it is far from being first-hand and because the countries mentioned are not very important for their Muslim populations in comparison with Nigeria, where more than half the Muslims of West Africa live. However, more substantial reports later came to the notice of the Anti-Slavery Society. In 1955 Mr G. Percival-Kaye, FRGS, wrote a book called *The Red Sea Slave-Trade*, describing several ways in which Africans – mainly West Africans, but also people from Ethiopia and the Southern Sudan – became slaves in Saudi Arabia. He mentioned the improbable story of the 'slave-farm' at Kufra in Libya, and the report of the Afrika Korps deserters trading in slaves, and spoke of Southern Morocco and Spanish Sahara as important sources for slaves (also improbable, as these are very sparsely populated areas where slaves are needed at home). He also reported what others were to report frequently in the following years: that the pilgrims shipped to Saudi Arabia included slaves. He said that the port of embarkation for these slaves was at Agig, on the Red Sea coast of the Sudan.[22]

In the same year, 1955, a specific case of a Mecca pilgrim selling a servant into slavery in Saudi Arabia became world news. A Tuareg of the French Sudan (Mali), a chief named Mohammed Ali ag Attaher from the Kel Antessar clan, told his servant, whom he had taken to the Holy Cities, that he must work for the son of the Governor of Jedda to earn money for his fare home. The servant, Awd el Joud, who was then sixteen, agreed, but then found that he was receiving no wages and had, in fact been bought by the son of the Governor of Jedda.

In view of his place of origin, it is likely that Awd el Joud had always been a slave at home, and a 'servant' only for the purposes of the French Administration there. No doubt this is why ag Attaher considered it his right to sell him if he, being the owner, thought fit. Anyway, Awd el Joud claimed that he did, in 1949. He also described the sale of some others of his party, in considerable detail. In 1953, he said, his master, Prince Abdulla Faisal, left for France, and the Prince's wife allowed Awd to go to the Holy Places. Taking advantage of this he went to Jedda, which is the great seaport and airport for the Hajj and the biggest city in Saudi Arabia. He tried to catch a boat there but was sent back. Then, when a Guinean pilgrim let him carry his luggage aboard a boat, he (Awd) hid there until he could land in the Sudan. He sold his clothes to pay for the train journey to Khartoum and then worked his way back home, where he told his story to a White Father, Fr David Traore. He spoke of the slave-markets in Saudi Arabia, saying they were in all the big towns, with sales about 5 p.m. daily.[23]

A Protestant pastor, M. la Gravière, spoke of this case when slavery was debated on 14th and 16th February, 1956, by the French Union Assembly. He presented a police report stating that Mohammed Ali ag Attaher was well known as a dealer in slaves. In spite of this, many doubted Awd el Joud's story, and the Assembly (which was merely a consultative body on the affairs of the French Empire and had almost no power anyway) voted almost unanimously to drop the matter. Yet Pastor la Gravière was able to quote, in support of the Sudanese slave's story, a report by none other than the French Ambassador to Saudi Arabia, who was responsible for the welfare of the countless French subjects who made the Hajj. In his report, dated 7th November, 1953, the Ambassador, M. Morillon, said: 'Merchants established at Jedda or Mecca send emissaries, naturalised Saudis but of Senegalese origin for the most part, whose job it is to bring back for them a certain number of individuals collected in the villages of the Sudan, Upper Volta or Niger: Timbuktu in particular seems to be a centre often visited by these wretched persons . . .' Probably hundreds of Africans from French West Africa and French Equatorial Africa ended up as slaves, he said, adding that French Africa provided the biggest contingent of slaves, the Ethiopian supply having apparently dwindled.[24]

Other reports confirmed the Ambassador's. The Anti-Slavery Society reported the sale of about ninety Muslim Africans in Mecca in 1956, and then said it was customary for some West Africans going to Mecca to sell members of their families to pay for the return journey. The 'human traveller's cheque' reports were persistent from then on. Another form of slave-trading connected with the Hajj was popularised in fiction, in a book in the popular Tintin series called *Coke en Stock* (in English *Red Sea Sharks*); this was probably based on press reports of what was really going on.

This was at the time when, after a United Nations Conference

ONE-WAY TRIPS TO ARABIA 143

at Geneva, a new Supplementary Convention on Slavery was concluded on 4th September, 1956. Intended to supplement the 1926 Convention, it provided for the total elimination of all slavery and all practices related to it. But the Convention was difficult, if not impossible, to enforce. In particular, the British Government's proposal for a clause to allow the seizing and search of ships suspected of carrying slaves, regardless of considerations of nationality, was strongly opposed, and eventually withdrawn when it became clear that most states would reject it.

This clause had been suggested with the Indian Ocean and the Arabian slave-trade in mind. Its rejection did not mean that no antislavery sea patrols were possible, for the 1890 Brussels Convention on the elimination of slavery provided for them, and it remained in force.[25] But a new treaty provision of the same sort would have helped, though only in cases where a ship was known to be carrying slaves; the right of search would not have benefited people like Awd el Joud and others who did not know that they would be sold by their owners or, worse still, their families.

In a talk ('The Road to Mecca') on the BBC on 15th March, 1958, Lionel Fleming said that of 21,000 people recorded as crossing from French territory into the Sudan, only 9,000 were recorded as going back, and there were strong indications that many of the others were enslaved in Saudi Arabia. Since it is unlikely that frontier posts in the Sudan really kept records detailed enough to make it possible to trace all pilgrims who crossed, especially as many crossed on the return journey many years later, Fleming's figures should be taken as very approximate. He said in the same talk that 'travel agencies' went deep into Africa to offer cheap trips to the Holy Cities, and brought the pilgrims to Saudi Arabia, where they were arrested for having no travel documents, and enslaved. Fleming added that there were crooked travel agencies in Northern Nigeria, but not like that.[26] About this time, that is soon after internal self-government in Nigeria, there was some concern over the crooked travel agents in the north, and steps were taken to control the operation of the pilgrimage. These have continued.

A few years later a Swedish reporter, Lars Holmberg, said, on the basis of what people had told him, that even children were sometimes sold by destitute pilgrims to pay for the return fare.[27] Such horrifying reports were greeted with angry reactions and demands for action. Some British MPs in 1956 and again in later years called for more British Government action. Ministers replied that, with the residual right of search by ships, the interception of slave-traders by the Trucial Oman Scouts, and the existing UN machinery, enough was being done without the Government's interference.[28] In the House of Lords in 1960, during a debate in which Lord Maugham (Robin Maugham) described what he had seen in the French Sudan, suggestions that the British Government was complacent about slavery were rejected, Lord Lansdowne pointing out that it had taken the initiative for the 1956 Supplementary Convention.[29]

But, in fact, little or nothing was done by Great Britain, even to find a reliable estimate of the size of the pilgrimage slave-trade, still less to try to stop it. The days when British forces could intervene to arrest slavers anywhere in the world were over, and the task of preventing this new sort of slave-traffic was left to local governments, particularly that of the Sudan. Fortunately, the Sudanese authorities were aware of the situation and their responsibilities. They insisted that pilgrims should fulfil their home countries' travel regulations; in 1962, they turned back from the Red Sea port of Suakin 8,000 pilgrims who had failed to do so.[30] In Nigeria, the most important country involved, the travel regulations insisted that pilgrims should take enough money with them. Thus the Sudanese, through whose territory most of the Mecca pilgrims from Nigeria pass, co-operated in avoiding one cause of enslavement in Saudi Arabia. The Nigerian *Morning Post* carried on 4th November, 1961, an article referring to destitute Nigerian children in Saudi Arabia, and asking, with allusions to Anti-Slavery Society reports, whether they were simply stranded or had become slaves.[31] But such expressions of concern, and the measures taken by governments in Africa, could not suffice, for pilgrims could go on travelling without papers across unmarked frontiers, vulnerable to sharp operators. The only real answer was the abolition of slavery in Saudi Arabia, and in 1962 this was proclaimed.

By about 1960, slave-markets had been gradually suppressed. Total abolition followed in 1962 when Prince Faisal was appointed Prime Minister by his brother, King Saud. On 6th November, 1962, a few days after his appointment, Faisal issued a Ten-Point Programme of reforms, the tenth point reading as follows:

'The attitude of the Shari'a towards slavery and its keen interest in liberating slaves is well known. It is also known that any slavery existing at present fails to fulfil many of the Shari'a conditions laid down by Islam to allow slavery. Ever since its foundation, Saudi Arabia has been faced with this problem of slaves and slavery and has striven by all gradual means to abolish slavery, first by prohibiting the importation of slaves and imposing penalties on the violation of this prohibition, and later by prohibiting the sale or purchase of slaves. The Government now finds a favourable opportunity to announce the absolute abolition of slavery and the manumission of all slaves. The Government will compensate those who prove to be deserving of compensation.'[32]

In the Saudi Arabian context, this abolition was fairly revolutionary. How effective has it been? Some early reports were encouraging. In the 1963 and 1964 budgets, estimates were included for compensation of slave-owners; although one report in 1964 spoke of compensation only for the release of 1,700 slaves – a trifling number if the total slave-population was correctly estimated at between 100,000 and 250,000 – two French authors, MM. Soulié and Champenois, were able to write not long afterwards. 'The compensation is fixed, in each locality, by an *ad hoc* administrative commission. As a result, slavery has practically ceased to exist in the kingdom. The abundance of the state's revenues has made it possible to satisfy some without upsetting others.'[32] Moreover, a very good testimonial came in 1963 from a slave-trader, from Sur in Oman; he said that business was bad because of the abolition of slavery in Saudi Arabia.[34]

On the other hand, in the 5th April, 1964, edition of *Der Stern* (Hamburg), Gordian Troeller said that the oil industry and the expansion of business in Saudi Arabia had raised the price of slaves there and made the risks involved in slave-trading worth taking. He said that slaves in Saudi Arabia originated from many countries: Nigeria, Mali, Mauritania, the Congo, Ethiopia and other African countries, and Persia, Iraq, Afghanistan and Pakistan. At Jizan he saw an Eritrean 'servant' of an Arab; he had sold himself because he had run into debt when going to Mecca, and now he said he was better off as a slave, as his master cared for him: 'We slaves live much longer than the poor: yes, much longer.'[35] Probably many slaves have stayed with their masters for this simple reason, and, as in other cases, one wonders how much really changes when such a person has his status redefined by law.

Faisal deposed his brother in 1964 and became King. It is reasonable to assume that at least some action on his 1942 Proclamation has continued to be taken. One sign that it probably has emerges from the study of MM. Soulié and Champenois, just quoted. It says there is a large floating population of pilgrims from all over Africa and Asia who 'haunt the poorer quarters of the big cities of the Hejaz'.[36] Such destitute people would be easy, and perhaps not always unwilling, targets for slave-dealers if these were still operating. It is true that there are, and have been for many years, many free Africans from Nigeria, Chad and other countries in Saudi Arabia, so that slavery was never the automatic fate of Africans there, but it would be a likely fate for the thousands of destitute pilgrims if abolition had been really ineffective. In fact, the Saudi Arabian Government collaborates with others in efforts to get stranded Mecca pilgrims back home; in late 1972 an agreement was reached between Nigeria and Saudi Arabia on the repatriation of 1,500 Nigerians.[37] The Saudi Arabian authorities also insist that pilgrims should have a minimum sum of money with them on arrival.

In view of the experience of other countries, it would be fantastic if all traces of Saudi Arabia's once widespread slavery had vanished in ten years, and all danger of clandestine slave-trading thereby removed; and the problem of 'white slavery' very probably remains serious. But it does seem that the situation which gave rise to such scandalous cases in the 1950s has changed. One problem, noted by a foreign observer in 1963, was that the slaves, especially the slave concubines, were mostly foreign. This meant that they had nowhere to go if they left their masters, unless they were helped to return to their homes (which apparently they were not), while slaves were often left ignorant of their rights and no efforts were made to rehabilitate them.[38] These flaws in the implementation of Faisal's abolition may well have continued, but a long overdue start has clearly been made in reforming what was, not so long ago, the world's leading slave state.

In Yemen the abolition of slavery was the result of the revolution of 27th September, 1962, which may also have led indirectly to the Saudi abolition a few weeks later. Before then, the relatively few Europeans who knew Yemen, an isolated mountainous country ruled by despotic Imams, had spoken of slavery accompanied by frequent cruelties. A French doctor, Claude Fayein, who was working in Yemen in the early 1950s was once asked to inspect a girl wanted as a slave for a son of King Saud, to see if she had venereal disease. By falsely saying that the girl had another illness she (the doctor) saved her from slavery. Later she stated that she did not believe slavery to be a real institution in Yemen, but an Algerian doctor said that all the people of Yemen were really slaves.[39] However, in the narrower sense of the word, there certainly were slaves until 1962, when the revolutionary government freed them; in the civil war that ensued between that government and the Imam the latter made promises, but rather vague ones, to abolish slavery after victory. In the end, this brutal civil war ended in a compromise in which Yemen remained a republic, the Yemen Arab Republic. One can assume that slavery is not tolerated legally there, but the recent bad drought may have led to its revival, as this can easily happen in times of danger of famine in countries which have only recently abolished slavery.

The Yemen Arab Republic is not to be confused with the People's Democratic Republic of Yemen, as the Federation of South Arabia (the former Aden Colony and Protectorate) was renamed a few years after it became independent in 1967. The placing of Aden Colony, a centre of nationalism and trade unionism, under the control of the interior rulers in the Federation was a decision of the British Government widely criticised at the time in Great Britain, where it was known that some slavery went on in the interior. The British Government's view on this was that its policy of encouraging the rulers to free slaves gradually had paid off; the Colonial Secretary, Iain Macleod, said in 1961 that 'slavery has almost ceased to exist in the Aden Protectorate', and any remaining slaves knew that they could apply for, and immediately get, manumission certificates. The Permanent Under-Secretary of State for the Colonies, Nigel Fisher, said that slavery had almost ended, and its vestiges 'take the form of a social class, not technical bondage'. The Anti-Slavery Society was not convinced, claiming that slavery was still not illegal and it was hard for applications for manumission to reach the British officials.[40]

In 1962 allegations of slavery in the Federation were made at the United Nations. On 2nd August, 1963, the Supreme Council for the Federation denied the allegations, saying that slavery and the slave-trade were 'utterly abhorrent' to it; but its statement went on to say that it 'urges all member states, which have not already done so, to take urgent action to legislate against the evil practice of slavery'. This was an admission that a fair amount of slavery still existed, and conveniently near the African coast.[41] Two Italians in 1963–4 were able to photograph sales of slave girls at Mukalla.[42]

But as a result of the guerrilla campaign against the British forces in Aden in 1966–7, the Adeni politicians obtained both independence and control over the Sheikhs, sultans and other rulers of the interior, who were supposed to rule them. The régime in Aden, with pro-Soviet Marxist sympathies, is hardly likely to condone slavery, but it may not control the Hadhramaut much more fully than the British did.

In the Trucial States along the Persian Gulf, the Trucial Oman Scouts did much to stamp out slave-trading in the early 1950s. The British Political Resident reported in late 1951 that there had been no cases of abduction into slavery in that year[43], and later action was taken against the slave-traffic through the Buraimi oasis, already mentioned. But domestic slavery persisted in those states and in Qatar, where the ruler was alleged to have included slaves in his retinue on visits to Great Britain in 1953 and 1958. The Trucial

States' Council discussed the abolition of domestic slavery, and in 1962 the Anti-Slavery Society reported that it went on in Fujairah only.[44] No doubt the general rule that slavery does not end overnight applies to these Arab states (now independent) and to Muscat and Oman, the Sultanate where slavery was abolished as recently as 1970, when the old Sultan Saiyid was overthrown. He had aroused opposition from other Arab states, and these had supported a rebellion against him in the interior of Oman, which he suppressed with British aid. A refugee Muscat Prince, Faisal ibn Ali, alleged that the Sultan, his cousin, had slaves in his personal bodyguard from Dhofar, and girl slaves, and that one man slave, who fled to the British Consulate, had been returned to his master. The British Government confirmed that it did not grant asylum to fugitive slaves.[45]

This complacent British attitude matters less now, in theory, since the new Sultan, Qabus ibn Saiyid, has begun to reform the fairly prison-like state of the country, and has started freeing the slaves. The country is now called simply the Sultanate of Oman.

Where slavery has been abolished very recently, secret slave-dealing may still occur, and reports of Africans still ending up as slaves in Arabia from time to time should not be dismissed out of hand. I have heard recent reports, not first-hand it is true, of people being taken across the Red Sea from Ethiopia into slavery, and of girls being embarked for Arabia near Kilwa, the old Arab-Swahili port in Tanzania. But, in the latter case, it is worth remembering that girls may be ready to lend themselves without coercion into prostitution in other countries, even if they are commonly led to do so under false pretences according to the traditions of the white slave-traffic. It is well known that foreign girls occasionally end up in Arab harems, even girls from well-policed West European cities, so it would be surprising if this did not happen in Africa, with degrees of fraud and coercion varying according to cases. And reports of occasional slave-trading from Ethiopia are made more plausible by the fact that slavery there was abolished so recently.

*Notes*

1. *Anti-Slavery Reporter* (June 1956).
2. Alan Villiers, *Sons of Sindbad*, for example pp. 2, 13, 56.
3. Harold Ingrams, *Arabia and the Isles*, p. 315.
4. Ibid., pp. 365–6.
5. Ibid., p. 292.
6. Wilfred Thesiger, *Arabian Sands*, p. 221.
7. Wendell Phillips, *Unknown Oman*, p. 203.

8. Ibid., p. 136.
9. Villiers, op. cit., pp. 96, 152–3.
10. V. Thompson and R. Adloff, *Djibouti and the Horn of Africa*, p. 9.
11. Villiers, op. cit., p. 96.
12. Margery Perham, *The Government of Ethiopia*, pp. 223–4; G. Percival-Kaye, *The Red Sea Slave-Trade*, quoted in *Anti-Slavery Reporter* (October 1955), p. 52.
13. John Buchholzer, *The Horn of Africa*, p. 12.
14. Phillips, op. cit., p. 203.
15. Ibid., pp. 91–2.
16. Thesiger, op. cit., pp. 263–4.
17. Phillips, op. cit., pp. 87–8.
18. Gordian Troeller, 'Mit Sklaven Unterwegs', in *Der Stern* (5th April 1964), quoted in *Anti-Slavery Reporter* (January 1966), pp. 23 ff.
19. *Anti-Slavery Reporter* (June 1956), p. 93.
20. Robin Maugham, *The Slaves of Timbuktu*, pp. 14–15.
21. *Anti-Slavery Reporter* (October 1947), p. 65.
22. G. Percival-Kaye, quoted in *Anti-Slavery Reporter* (October 1955), pp. 49 ff.
23. Marcel Pollaud-Durian, *Aujourd'hui l'Esclavage*, Chapter One.
24. Ibid.
25. Statements in House of Commons (9th July, 1956 and 21st December, 1956), quoted in *Anti-Slavery Reporter* (February 1957).
26. Quoted in *Anti-Slavery Reporter* (October 1958).
27. Quoted in *Anti-Slavery Reporter* (April 1961).
28. Statements in House of Commons; see note 25.
29. House of Lords, Official Report (14th July, 1960).
30. *Anti-Slavery Reporter* (January 1966), pp. 29–30.
31. Quoted in *Anti-Slavery Reporter* (March 1962).
32. Quoted in G. de Gaury, *Faisal*, p. 151.
33. G. J.-L. Soulié and L. Champenois, *Le Royaume d'Arabie Séoudite face à l'Islam Révolutionnaire*, pp. 83–4.
34. *Anti-Slavery Reporter* (January 1966), p. 28.
35. Gordian Troeller, quoted in *Anti-Slavery Reporter*; see note 18.
36. Soulié and Champenois, op. cit., p. 67.
37. *West Africa* 8th January, 1973.
38. Annual Report of the Anti-Slavery Society, 1962–3, pp. 4–5.
39. Pollaud-Durian, op. cit., Chapter One.
40. *Anti-Slavery Reporter* (January 1963).
41. Annual Report of the Anti-Slavery Society, 1962–3, p. 4.
42. Ibid.
43. Donald Hawley, *The Trucial States*, pp. 173 ff.
44. *Anti-Slavery Reporter* (March 1962), pp. 16–17.
45. *Anti-Slavery Reporter* (January 1963), pp. 51–2.

*Chapter Seven*

# Ethiopia's Modern Slaves

Ethiopia, once known as Abyssinia, has a recorded history of at least 2,000 years, including only five recent years (1936–41) of colonial rule. This ancient state has not always covered the area now ruled by Emperor Haile Selassie, nor has its centre always been the same, but the dominant peoples of the country, the Amharas and the closely related Tigreans, have been the nucleus of the Empire from the days when its capital was at Axum until the present day, when it is at Addis Ababa.

Descendants of immigrants from Arabia and of the earlier inhabitants of the high plateau in which the Blue Nile rises, the Amharas and Tigreans speak related Semitic languages. Since the fourth century, if not earlier, they have been Christians; they belong to the Coptic Church, and until the present Emperor's reign they were nominally dependent on the Coptic Patriarch of Alexandria in Church matters. The liturgical language of their Church, which they have kept as part of their ancient heritage for centuries in the midst of Muslim lands, is Geez, a language related to Tigrinya.

The Ethiopian plateau, covering the north-western part of the present state of Ethiopia, is covered with mountains, including some of the highest peaks in Africa. Although it is farther south than much hotter parts of Africa, it has a high enough altitude to be generally cold at night. Most of it is farmland. Their mountain fastness was strong enough to enable the Amharas and Tigreans to keep their independence until the twentieth century. The southern area of their homeland, covered by the province of Shoa in which Addis Ababa is situated, has been the political centre of those peoples since the reign of Menelik II (1889–1913).

Ethiopia's other main racial group are the Gallas, about half the country's population, speaking a language of the Cushitic group which also includes Somali. The number of them under Amharic rule has varied greatly during Ethiopia's turbulent history; most were conquered in the nineteenth century and remain Muslims –

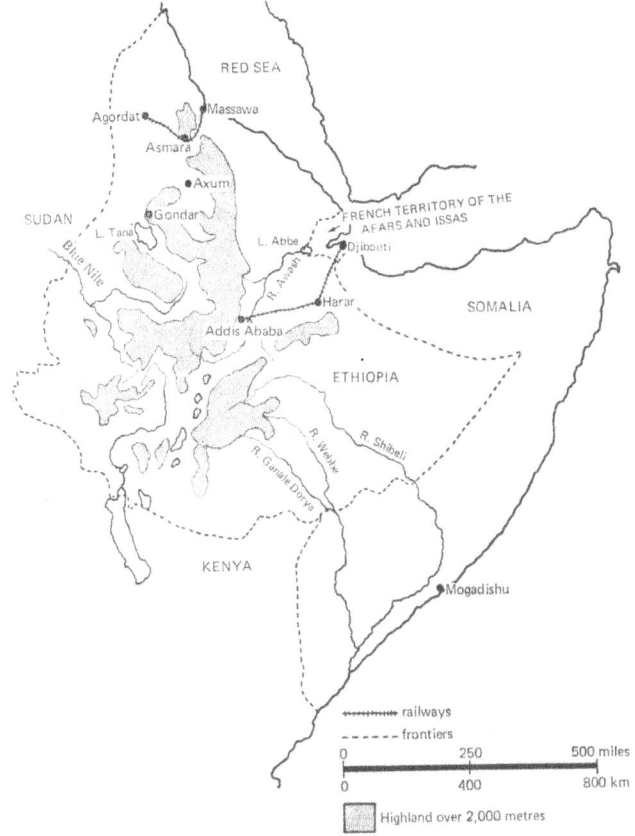

Ethiopia

as are about half of Ethiopia's present population. The actual number of Christians and Muslims, of Amharas and Gallas, is unknown; there has been no census, and estimates of the total population, usually between 20 million and 30 million, are very rough and contested.

The Gallas, like the Amharas, Tigreans, Somalis and Danakils, are different from Negro Africans; for example, they are dark brown in complexion rather than black. They have their similarities, and Amharic has spread among the Gallas. However, traditional rivalries are not dead, although it is the Somalis of the Ogaden and the Eritreans, many of them of the Danakil tribe, rather than the

Gallas who have a traditional feud with the Amharas. They are among the most recent subjects of the Ethiopian Empire. So are the peoples of Maji, Sidamo and other southern and south-western provinces, some of them Negro peoples for whom there is a traditional word of abuse, *shanqalla*, still current in Amharic.

Slavery was so normal in much of the world until recent times that there is no need to stress its importance throughout Ethiopia's earlier history. The medieval legal code, called the *Fetha Nagast*, said that enslvement of prisoners-of-war was right, and that Leviticus permitted the keeping of unbelievers as slaves; but it forbade the sale of Christians to Pagans. There were domestic slaves and slave soldiers, these being captured in childhood like the Turkish Janissaries. Slaves were also exported, probably including Christian ones. There were Ethiopian slaves at Mecca in Mohammed's time. Ethiopian girls were highly prized at Constantinople and elsewhere (with good reason; they are still advertised to foreigners, though not as slaves, by Ethiopian Airlines, who say that 'our girls had 3,000 years of tradition to call upon when we called upon them to staff our Boeings'). Ethiopian slaves were sent to India, where *Hapshi* (Abyssinian) Princes ruled for some time in Bengal; to Russia, where the Ethiopian-born Abraham Petrov was in charge of fortifications in the eighteenth century (and became the great-grandfather of Pushkin); and even to China.[1]

Slaves were the main export of Massawa in Eritrea in the eighteenth century, and Zeila was a big slave-port. So the Red Sea slave-traffic from Ethiopia is an ancient one. It has continued until recent times because there is still a market for slaves in Arabia and because slavery was abolished in Ethiopia as recently as 1942.

Many past Emperors had only limited control over the country, the Princes and nobles, some bearing the title of *Ras*, being very powerful, as also were the Governors of provinces. They either owned or were able to exploit much of the land, and the *gabar* system of serfdom was an important source of independent revenue for them. This was a system of fairly extortionate sharecropping, with the difference that the crops and other produce given to the landlord were considered as both rent and tribute.[2] The landlords, among whom the Church was very important, had sweeping powers over the ordinary people, and did not want to lose these powers and the independence derived from them. A measure like the abolition of slavery, which went against age-old traditions, could not easily be enforced throughout the country, especially as it benefited so many: especially the aristocracy, of course, but not only them, for even small farmers had slaves. So Menelik's abolition decrees were a failure and slave-trading became a major enterprise in the civil strife following his incapacity in 1907 and death in 1913.

In 1919, when Ras Tafari – the future Emperor Haile Selassie – was one of three regents of Ethiopia, its application to join the League of Nations failed because slavery was still legal within its borders. Since the effects of slavery extended beyond those borders, in slave-raids into Kenya and the Sudan, the British were particularly concerned about the matter. Ethiopia was eventually admitted to the League in 1923, and in the same year a law outlawing slave-raiding across the frontiers was passed. On 31st March, 1924, a law declared slaves born into slavery after that date to be free but said that they should remain in their masters' care until the age of fifteen. It also laid down that slaves should be freed on the death of their master, but must stay with his family for seven years. These measures, and other clauses ordering freedom for slaves cruelly treated or serving as priests, deacons or soldiers, were feeble in themselves and not, in all probability, enforced. Slave-trading, outlawed by the same law, went on, and the critics of Ethiopian slavery were not satisfied. It is incorrect to speak of Ethiopia abolishing slavery in 1924.

After becoming Emperor in 1930, Haile Selassie set about imposing central government control. He also took action against slavery, accepting a British adviser, Mr de Halpert, for anti-slavery measures in August 1930. A year later an edict ordered the registration of slaves and the release of all a man's slaves on his death, and looked forward to eventual abolition, which Haile Selassie promised in 1932 to bring about in fifteen or twenty years. But little was done until the eve of the Italian invasion, and Mr de Halpert resigned in protest in 1933. Not only slavery but slave-raiding remained rampant. As in Arabia, even though treatment of slaves in their owners' households might be good, the way in which they were captured was brutal. Both Amharas and Gallas took part in raiding and trading, the main source of supply being the south-western provinces, which were almost depopulated in parts as a result. In Beni-Shanqul on the Sudan border, slaves were used locally, on the coffee farms; but others were taken to different parts of Ethiopia or exported to Arabia. Many people fled into Kenya and the Sudan.[3]

The Italians made use of all this in their propaganda justifying their aggression in 1935–6. After conquering Ethiopia they proclaimed the liberation of all slaves. They said that they had freed 400,000 slaves in the Galla–Sidamo area alone, and done much to prepare slaves for a free life. The occupation also allowed many *gabar* tenants to escape what had often been a most oppressive serfdom. There is no need to recall the other side of Italian rule in Ethiopia, but even Ethiopians acknowledge that it did have some positive results. After the liberation of the country by the Allied Forces in 1941 and the restoration of the Emperor, it would probably have been impossible, if he had so wished, to re-impose the old slavery and serfdom systems undermined by Italian rule. It is generally accepted that Haile Selassie had always wanted their abolition anyway, and this followed soon after his return to Addis Ababa.

On 11th November, 1941, the Gabar form of tenancy was abolished. This was only a small step towards relieving Ethiopian peasants of their large burden of extortion, which could include a tithe to the Emperor, forced levies of grain or timber of firewood, porterage and other forced labour, as well as the actual rent in kind. But in view of the conservatism of the peasants themselves, this measure was, however limited and ill-enforced, a considerable step.

The Proclamation abolishing slavery in Ethiopia came on 27th August, 1942. Proclamation No. 22, 'to Provide for the Abolition of the Legal Status of Slavery and Certain Other Matters', adopted the 1926 Convention's definition of slavery; it repeated the two main pre-1935 measures against slavery, but went further, abolishing the legal status immediately and (in paragraph 4) making the death penalty possible for the transporting or trading in slaves – forty lashes, a $10,000 fine, or up to twenty years' imprisonment being alternative punishments.[4]

So it was only thirty years ago that slaves in Ehtiopia were definitively freed. There must be millions of people still living who remember slavery as a feature of everyday life, and many thousands who remember being slaves, even if the abolition was immediately effective in 1942.

But was it effective? Information is not easily obtained by non-Ethiopians, for since abolition the subject is officially ignored. What information there is, however, suggests that abolition took a long time to take effect.

In 1942 Haile Selassie was not fully master of the reconquered Empire, and it was only gradually that he enforced on it a degree of control not attained by any previous Emperor. Soon after the Emperor's restoration, came an important change, the introduction of a system of local administration dependent on the central government, by-passing the Rases and the Governors. The Central Government (which has developed partly on Western lines, with a Council of Ministers since 1943) and the Central Parliament (whose power, under the 1955 Constitution, is limited but not negligible), have extended their power at the expense of local potentates. The nobility has declined in power, and, as far as secular power is concerned, so has the Church. Taxation has been reformed, to make at least some of it more like taxation than tribute. Although the Imperial Government's power is challenged by rebels in Eritrea (since that province lost its Federal autonomy in 1962) and resented by Somalis in the Ogaden, on the whole it extends widely over Ethiopia. But this state of affairs has been achieved only gradually by a determined and skilful ruler, and so, one suspects, have reforms instituted by him.

Writers on Ethiopia, until the great revolution of 1974, stressed how much had *not* changed despite reform decrees. 'In the countryside', said Robert Hess, 'little has changed, and rural Ethiopia of the late twentieth century differs little in its social patterns and social attitudes from the Ethiopia of five hundred years ago. Religion still dominates the life cycle, and the peasants' life has a stability tinted with a fatalistic view of nature and the world. Land ownership is very important for the peasant,' Hess continues, 'but he also respects force, hierarchy and authority, whether of his elders, his landlord and local officials, or of his highly venerated Emperor.'[5] The way of life loosely, and not very accurately, called 'feudal' by its critics still prevails in Ethiopia. Resemblances to medieval Europe abound: in the power of the Church, the prevalence of crude and exemplary punishments designed to make fear do the work of an effective police force, and general poor health. Such conditions are all too common elsewhere, but their combination with a hierarchy, with the Emperor at the top and, historically, slaves at the bottom, is unique to Ethiopia and a few other countries.

Haile Selassie did not seriously alter this situation while he remained an absolute ruler, and the history of efforts at land reform shows how limited his reforming powers were. The abolition of the *gabar* system removed, in theory, one form of sharecropping, but otherwise sharecropping of an often oppressive sort continued. The Imperial family, the nobility and the Church continued to own much of the land, exacting a *three-quarters* share of many tenants' crops as well as tithes, and able to exact other services and evict at will, with little challenge until 1964, when land-reform efforts began in a serious way. They did not go far. In 1966 the Senate threw out a Bill to reduce the land-owner's share of crops from 75 to 50 per cent, to abolish forced labour for landlords, and to order four harvests' notice for evictions. Taxes on agriculture were reformed in 1967, but the Church, owner of 28 per cent of all the arable land, was excluded and landlords went on exacting the now outlawed tithes.[6] In 1972 new land-reform measures were announced. But only with the assumption of virtually full power by the armed forces in 1974 did action become probable.

In view of this, one would hardly expect the abolition of slavery to take effect quickly, especially as it has never done so anywhere. Slavery was no doubt less fundamental to society than the landlord's prerogatives, but it was traditionally important at the local level in Beni Shanqul and in the Gurage, and had been a part of life for centuries – the Amharic nobility seems to be equal to any other aristocracy in its view of certain work as servile. The surprising fact, therefore, is not that abolition was slow to take effect, but that so much was done immediately to put it into effect. It may have been the Italian occupation, as the British Minister suggested in 1946, that hastened the abolition re-decreed by Haile Selassie. Visitors in the years after 1942 saw little sign of overt slave-trading, and offenders against the abolition Proclamation were soon being gaoled.[7]

Before 1935 the south-west had been the main area for slave-raiding, and it was not surprising, therefore, that reports of continued activity of this sort in the 1950s came from there. In its Annual Report for 1954–5, the Anti-Slavery Society quoted a former British official in the Sudan as saying that people had recently been fleeing into that country from Wallega Province in Ethiopia claiming to be escaped slaves, and some owners had come to get them back – just as in earlier days. The society also heard about slave-boys inside Ethiopia, but no definite reports.

It must be stressed again how improbable it is that such a measure as the abolition of slavery could be really effected in a decade in a place like Ethiopia, even in places more accessible to Addis Ababa than the far south-west, which from the viewpoint of modern administration is one of the most remote areas of Africa.

But, allowing for the difficulties, it seems that the abolition of slavery in one of its last strongholds has had a great deal of effect. In the work just quoted, Richard Greenfield wrote: 'If in 1964 the status of some servants in certain houses, even in towns, is somewhat ambiguous, the days of the slave-trade and slave-markets may be generally regarded as over.'[8]

The question of the status of 'servants' is the one found all over Africa. In the late 1940s Margery Perham quoted with approval, as good for Ethiopia, Lord Lugard's view on the way to abolish slavery: to abolish the legal status and let slaves leave their masters if they want to or otherwise remain as 'servants', rather than force all masters to turn all slaves out of their houses at once.[9] This seems the only practicable method, but it is slow, and allows various sorts of evasion and pretence, for there are ways of preventing 'servants' from leaving one's household when they are legally able to do so; if they do not want to go, the number of people in an ambiguous-looking position may remain large for a long time. Reports of continued slave-holding in Ethiopia may amount to no more than this.

A relapse in this respect is unlikely, even if the death of Haile Selassie, now in his eighties, leads to some confusion and disruption; and that possibility, once feared, may have been reduced by the assumption of real power by radical army officers in Haile Selassie's lifetime, between February and August 1974. The educated younger men are fiercely critical of the state of their country, comparing it to that of other countries whose representatives regularly go to Addis Ababa for the meetings of the Organisation of African Unity. The old Emperor's image as a father-figure for independent Africa, and his frequent visits to Africa states whose régimes are often very different from his own (Guinea, for example), seem not to impress his educated Ethiopian and other critics, who point to their country's poor health services and low literacy rate (there has been improvement in these respects, but in both Ethiopia remains poor even by African standards), they have even alleged[10] that forced labour is used at the Adola gold-mines (this report needs to be verified, but it is made more probable by the fact that Adola is in a remote and under populated area, while forced labour for vagrants is reported to be a custom). However many such abuses go on, the fact that a powerful section of opinion (their power was shown by the near-success of the attempted *coup* in 1960, which the radicals supported) opposes them so strongly made it seem always unlikely that any future régime would go back on the present Emperor's cautious but definite reform moves. The *coup* by the Armed Forces Committee in 1974 makes it seem even less likely.

But, as already stated, concern for human rights and individual liberties is not very developed in independent Africa, or indeed in most parts of the world. Radical young Ethiopians may oppose such institutions as slavery and sharecropping because they are 'backward', not because they are unjust – or even because they are tolerated, or have been tolerated, by an Emperor whose foreign policy they disapprove; they might approve equally oppressive but less 'backward' institutions later. Neither in Ethiopia nor anywhere else should slavery be seen in isolation, and its abolition should not be seen as a panacea for a country's particular ills.

When all this is borne in mind, however, Emperor Haile Selassie's name can be added to those of other slave-freeing rulers in history, such as Abraham Lincoln and Pedro II of Brazil.

*Notes*

1. R. Pankhurst, *An Introduction to the Economic History of Ethiopia* Chapter Thirty-one.
2. Margery Perham, *The Government of Ethiopia*, pp. 278 ff.
3. Ibid., pp. 227–31, 324 ff.
4. Ibid., p. 234.
5. Robert L. Hess, *Ethiopia: The Modernisation of Autocracy*, p. 24.
6. Ibid., pp. 145–9.
7. Perham, op. cit., p. 235.
8. Richard Greenfield, *Ethiopia: A New Political History*, p. 143.
9. Perham, op. cit., pp. 234–5.
10. G. A. Lipsley, *Ethiopia*, p. 149, 279.

*Chapter Eight*

# Colonisation and Forced Labour

Many decades have passed since the death of the League of Nations, but one of its agencies set up in 1919, the International Labour Organisation, still continues, and is very active today. It examines, and seeks to regulate, matters concerning wages, working conditions, trade unions, and other labour questions. The ILO may have been concerned to some extent with slavery, but it has been more concerned with forced labour, whose abolition was agreed upon by an ILO Convention (No. 29) in June 1930.

By that Convention, forced labour was defined as 'all work or service which is exacted from any person under the menace of any penalty and for which the said person has not offered himself voluntarily' (paragraph 2, 1). It is not the same thing as slavery, but it is often discussed in the same breath as slavery, and the history of Africa shows that the dividing-line between the two can be thin.

Labour scandals are a prominent part of the history of colonial rule. In Great Britain there were public scandals at the height of the colonial era about recruitment of Indian coolies, about Chinese coolies on the Rand, about 'Blackbirders' in Australia, and about many other cases of exploitation of individuals in many regions of the world. Loudest of all, and with good reason, was the international outcry over the Congo Free State, founded by King Leopold II of the Belgians in 1885 as a territory under his sovereignty to be ruled, ostensibly, as a humanitarian enterprise to bring 'civilisation' to the Congo basin and to end slavery, but actually run by him and his henchmen for the extortion of wealth on a vast scale from the area's natural resources, notably rubber. Not only was there forced labour on a large scale for porterage, but there was forcible collection of wild rubber (which took up nearly all a peasant's time and stopped him growing food), conscription for the local forces (whose atrocities committed while enforcing the collection of rubber were the main cause of international protests), and much else, making the sufferings of the Africans peculiarly great in the Free State. E. D.

Morel, a leader of the protest campaign, did not hesitate to compare the Congo oppression unfavourably with the Atlantic slave-trade.

Protests were also made against similar abuses in French Equatorial Africa and against the deadly use of forced labour there for the building of the railway from Brazzaville to Pointe Noire (1922–34). In Great Britain there were similar protests in the 1920s against compulsion or semi-compulsion of African labour in Kenya. Portuguese forced-labour practices in Africa have led to protests from the early twentieth century, if not earlier, until recent times. And these protests only uncovered for the European public a part of the reality.

Much of this story is of historical interest only, but it deserves a brief look so as to show how widely and how recently forced labour has been used in Africa; the areas where it still goes on are only a little behind the general practice of colonial and other authorities in Africa.

Under colonial rule there were three sorts of forced labour in Africa. First, there was communal or village labour for certain work for the local community or chief. Second, there was similar use of conscripted labour for local purposes by the colonial Administration. Third, there was recruitment by force of workers for large-scale public works' projects, or sometimes for private enterprises. This last form of compulsory labour has led to the worst abuses. There have also been abuses in the practice of having African taxpayers 'work off' taxes which they cannot pay, and in the use of convict labour, though the latter is not the same as forced labour of non-criminals.

Lord Hailey, in his *African Survey* (1938) commissioned by the British Government, described the use of the three main sorts of non-voluntary labour in the British, French, Belgian and Portuguese territories, and in South Africa. He dealt also with two other sources of complaint by Africans under colonial rule: forcible cultivation of crops, and official help given in non-forcible recruiting of workers for private employers.

Traditional communal labour was often accepted by villagers who had a true sense of community and social values in which the chief was important. It need not have been any more vexatious than another custom, that of farmers helping each other in turn with the harvest. But this labour for chiefs probably took on a new dimension when colonial powers gave the chiefs' powers greater than they had held by custom, in return for loyalty as agents of the Administration. Anyway, the Geneva Convention of 1930, already mentioned, called for restrictions on the use of compulsory labour for chiefs and its gradual abolition.

In the 1930s chiefs in Bechuanaland (now Botswana) could call out labour for several purposes, including even distraint of the cattle of hut-tax defaulters. However, in 1934 a Proclamation regulated such work. In Sierra Leone, the Forced Labour Ordinance of 1932 set out detailed provisions concerning personal services to recognised chiefs. But in 1924 the Paramount Chief of Barotseland, in what is now Zambia, agreed to give up his right to exact twelve days' unpaid labour a year, in return for an annual allowance of £2,500. By the time of Hailey's investigations, such services had been banned in Kenya, Tanganyika and The Gambia, and were of little importance in other British territories, though still important in some French ones.[1]

Colonial Administrations used and extended the tradition of unpaid communal labour. They told chiefs to provide workers for the maintenance, for example, of local roads, and regulations were made for the use of labour for these local projects; one, in the Belgian Congo in 1933, allowed the use of such labour for the maintenance of schools and village rest-houses as well as roads.[2]

The colonial powers depended on the extensive use of forced labour because they lacked funds to pay for voluntary labour. Also – and something hard to imagine in these days of widespread unemployment in Africa – there was a frequent shortage of voluntary labour for the work ordered by the colonisers: road and railway building, work in mines and on settlers' farms, and plenty of other work, porterage being particularly important and unpleasant work in the early colonial era (few can have seen the benefits of colonisation less than the 'native bearer', forced to carry officials, other travellers and their heavy luggage over vast distances for little reward). For all such purposes administrators, especially when they could not afford the wages and conditions which could attract voluntary workers, complained of a shortage of labour, as did private employers.

Legal provisions for the use of forced labour on public projects varied considerably. In Nigeria, where 'political labour', i.e. forced labour, had been used extensively in earlier years, an Ordinance of 1933 amended practice in accordance with the Geneva Convention, ratified by Great Britain, and outlawed all forced labour except for transport and for personal services to chiefs (who, in Nigeria, could be the powerful Emirs of the north). In Kenya, an Ordinance of 1922 allowed the use of compulsory labour on works sanctioned by the Colonial Secretary, for example, on the Uasin Gishu railway line. In that colony, too, the rules were altered after 1930. In other British territories, there were varying provisions for forced labour. In French Africa there was for long a labour tax called *prestation*, commutable for cash; it involved work for a specified period in each year – ten days in French Cameroon by an *Arrêté* (Ordinance) of 1936 – for a fixed wage, on projects such as roads and railways. The French also introduced conscription in their colonies, and a portion of each year's African conscripts, the *deuxième portion*, was employed on civilian projects.[3]

These regulations continued in force after the worst period of colonial exploitation was over. In the early days there was less regulation and even more suffering and death than in the later days, when there was plenty even so. In early colonial times, when conscription of porters was combined with forcible collection of ivory and rubber for export, oppression went to extremes. This, as already noted, was the case in Leopold II's Congo Free State. Both in the areas which formed the King's own *domaine* and in the larger areas which he handed over to concessionary companies, the aim of the 'state' was to collect as much rubber and ivory as possible, particularly rubber. The distinguishing feature of these concessionary companies in the Congo and in French Equatorial Africa (which was called the French Congo until 1910) was that they had a virtual monopoly of the purchase of these fruits of the forest, and almost complete power in every respect over the Africans. But even where they were not in control, the African's interests were, in the Free State, subordinated to the collection of rubber.

What this meant was described by Morel (in his book *Red Rubber* and other publications) and his supporters in Great Britain, where protests were at their strongest and eventually led to the creation of the Congo Reform Association. From the early 1890s horrific reports emerged from the Congo (notably from missionaries) of the massacring of villagers and the taking of hostages, who frequently died, to enforce the collection of fixed quantities of rubber to hand over to officials, who received bonuses increased in accordance with the lowness of the prices paid for the rubber. Food supplies were reduced by forced neglect of farms and by forced deliveries of food for soldiers and others; disease and demoralisation spread, so that over vast areas of the great Congo basin the population fell considerably. Sir Roger Casement, who as a British Consul reported on the crimes, and others estimated that during the Free State period the population of the region fell by over 1 million.[4]

In 1908, after years of international protest against Leopold IIs rule, the Congo Free State was turned into a Belgian colony. Some of the abuses of the earlier period stopped, and, with the development of Malaya's plantations, the Congo's rubber became less important. However, Africans continued to endure various forms of labour coercion. There was forcible cultivation of cotton in the 1920s – when Paul Schebesta, a German anthropologist who became famous for his writings of the Congo Pygmies, noted in the North-East Congo that a chief had had to threaten subordinate chiefs with prison to make them sow cotton in 1929 – and for long afterwards.[5] Porterage was also a burden until the building of roads and railways, which itself involved more forced labour. On the same visit, Schebesta noted: 'On all sides new road-building schemes were arranged, frequently causing a good deal of bad feeling among the natives, as they were always literally press-ganged for such work.'[6]

In the Free State period, many African workers died while building the Leopoldville–Matadi railway. Memories of this made it hard for the French, a quarter of a century later, to find labour for the Brazzaville–Pointe Noire or 'Congo–Ocean' railway. So the Governor-General told administrators to find workers from elsewhere in French Equatorial Africa, notably Saras from Chad and Bandas from Ubangi-Shari (now the Central African Republic). These migrants were badly affected by the Congo climate, and formed a considerable number of the 17,000 workers who died building the line (out of a labour force of 150,000). Fewer conscripted workers died in the later stages of the work, because of measures taken after an uproar in France.[7]

The only heartening aspect of these episodes, indeed, is the scandal that they caused in Europe. This could lead at least to the ordering of proper medical attention and rations for the forced labourers, or the enforcement of orders that were supposed to be already binding in these matters. Before the railway episode, there had been protests in France about the powers given to the concessionary companies in Equatorial Africa, and about the multiple oppressions of the Africans which (as in the Free State) resulted. But the protests were of limited use, for if the very worst crimes had ceased by about 1910 what went on afterwards seemed tolerable only in comparison with the worst period; the concessionary firms retained wide powers until the 1930s, and the Administration itself enforced rubber collection, cotton cultivation, and recruitment of forced labour.[8]

In the German colonies, forced labour led to a great deal of suffering; workers from the north imported for the plantations in the equatorial areas of Southern Cameroons died like flies in the strange climate, and it was officially ordered that every plantation should have its own cemetery.[9] The opposition in the Reichstag forced some improvement, with the result that in 1906 when the Germans built railways in Cameroon with forced labour there were some safeguards. The really deadly period of forced labour on railway construction in the territory was under French rule in the 1920s, when Njock, a place where the line had to be built through very hilly country, became a byword among Africans for a place from which one was likely not to return. For this and other work, agents of chiefs used to descend on villages suddenly and take away labourers, whose names might have been chosen on a mere whim by a chief.[10]

Forced labour was common all over French Africa, and had a new lease of life during the Second World War, when production for the war effort was considered essential and money was very scarce. But one of the first democratic reforms in the French Empire after the war was the abolition of forced labour in April 1946. The *deuxième portion du contingent* was not covered by the law voted then, but it ceased to be used for civilian work a few years later in practice, and by law in 1950.

The British record is less notorious than the French, but it is no cause for self-satisfaction. In Kenya forced labour was used for the building of railways, and the death-rate among workers aroused protests in Great Britain; in 1925 the use of forced labour was stopped on the Uasin-Gishu line, while labourers suffered less on the Thika-Nyeri and Yala-Kisumu lines. When one recalls that the Baro-Kano and Eastern Railways in Nigeria were also built with 'political labour', one sees what the building of Africa's railways cost.[11] In Kenya the white settlers were for long unable to recruit enough voluntary African labour themselves, and asked for official help. A circular in 1919, expressing the hope that officials would do all in their power to help the settlers find labour, led to strong protests.[12]

Recruitment of labour by the Administration for private employers in Africa was for long quite common; Chapter Nine will show how it remained common in Portuguese territories until recently (there officials actually helped private employers to find forced labour). The ILO Convention of 1930, which allowed several years for the abolition of forced labour for public works, outlawed immediately (paragraph 4, 1) its conscription for private employers. But there remained the question of recruiting by officials of labour for firms; in view of the officials' position, their recruitment of voluntary workers could in practice amount to compulsion. In the 1930s, however, such recruitment still went on in the Belgian Congo, though it had been criticised all the more strongly there because several officials were closely linked with companies. Official aid in recruiting workers for the South African gold-mines was also given for a time. Such practices, it is true, were not the only way in which colonial administration could be geared, sometimes consciously, to the interests of companies.

Hailey could report in the late 1930s that forced labour was generally being replaced by voluntary labour. To some extent, the colonial powers supported this tendency in applying the 1930 Convention. But the French and the British both felt that the emergency conditions of the Second World War overrode their obligations under the Convention, which included abolition of forced labour in the shortest possible time. After the loss to the Allies of the Malayan tin-mines, forced labour was introduced in the privately owned tin-mines in the Plateau in Nigeria though for underground work (in accordance with the Convention) it was not allowed. Forced labour was also recruited for private employers in Sierra Leone, Kenya, Northern Rhodesia, and even the minute Seychelles during the war, as well as in Nigeria and the French territories. In Kenya it was introduced in 1942 and soon affected 14,000 workers, but was suspended in 1943 after a food shortage and later re-imposed for sisal plantations only. Nigerian forced labourers could serve for up to four months per year. In Tanganyika 11,000 out of 18,000 workers on rubber plantations were conscripted during the Second World War. This emergency forced labour ended after the war.[13]

There remained provisions for natural disasters, forced food growing to prevent famine, etc., but these forced-labour provisions in British colonies were generally in abeyance at the time of the advance to self-government and independence. This was also a time of an influx to the towns and a growth in unemployment, which has continued until it has become a major problem in many parts of Africa. This, of course, has reduced one reason for the resort to forced labour. But one cannot assume that that is now a thing of the past. Many African governments want to involve their people in development and provide work for the urban unemployed – both excellent aims, but opening possibilities for coercion. In the French Congo and the Central African Republic, what amounted to forced labour was instituted before independence as a solution to the problem of urban unemployment. The idea is not new in Africa – it was enacted in Kenya in 1949 though not widely applied;[14] and it must tempt some of the more authoritarian governments. Can one be sure that all the people who do farm-training in the official party youth movements of Kenya, Malawi and other places are volunteers? And that the many sorts of regimentation in some countries such as Guinea do not include forced labour?

Apart from these questions, to be discussed further in Chapter Twelve, there are cases of recent large-scale use of forced labour, to be described briefly in the chapters which follow.

*Notes*

1. Lord Hailey, *An African Survey*, pp. 608-11.
2. Ibid., p. 612.
3. Ibid., pp. 613-28.
4. E. D. Morel, *Red Rubber*, passim.
5. Paul Schebesta, *My Pygmy and Negro Hosts* (English translation), p. 94.
6. Ibid., p. 29.
7. V. Thompson and R. Adloff, *The Emerging States of French Equatorial Africa*, pp. 12 ff., 140, 256.
8. Ibid., pp. 18-19.
9. H. Rudin, *Germans in the Cameroons*, p. 327.
10. E. Mveng, *Histoire du Cameroun*, p. 386.
11. Hailey, op. cit., p. 615.
12. K. Ingham, *A History of East Africa*, pp. 343 ff.
13. *Anti-Slavery Reporter* (October 1942, January 1943); Annual Reports of the Anti-Slavery Society for 1942-3 and 1943-4; Report of the *ad hoc* Committee on Forced Labour (ILO, 1953), pp. 540 ff.
14. Report of the *ad hoc* Committee, pp. 540-1.

*Chapter Nine*

# Forced Labour in the White South

Forced labour exacted by white employers in colonial Africa cannot be explained simply in terms of necessity. Besides that, there was the idea that the African had a *duty* to provide for the white man's needs, including his need for labourers. This idea still forms the basis of law and administration at the southern tip of the continent, in the Republic of South Africa.

There is no space here to describe all aspects of South Africa's 'Apartheid' policy. But it is useful to stress one aspect which sometimes receives less attention than, say, the gaoling of political opponents or the total ban on sexual relations between white and non-white people. This is the aspect of labour coercion. Apartheid is not aimed simply at segregation (so far as is possible) of the White, Coloured, Asian and 'Bantu' (black African) communities; it is also aimed at forcing the Africans to order their lives, and above all their work, to the convenience of white employers.

South Africa is a country of great wealth. The mines, producing, for example, gold on the Witwatersrand and diamonds at Kimberley, are the best-known source of its wealth, but not the only one. With all this production and large-scale industrialisation, a standard of living comparable to that of many European countries would be possible for all the 22 million people in South Africa – if the wealth were properly distributed. That it is not properly distributed is not a distinctive feature of South Africa; what is distinctive is that the difference between the minority, which on average lives very well indeed, and the majority, which includes many living at starvation level in a very wealthy land, coincides with the racial divide, and this not by historical accident, but by the deliberate intention of official policy and laws. For several decades, and particularly since the coming to power of the Afrikaner Nationalists in 1948, legislation and administration have aimed to keep the non-Whites, and above all the 'Bantu', as a servile group whose lives are geared to the needs of the white minority, with no right to any more wages, amenities of life or freedom than are needed to enable them to fill this role.

The 1970 Census counted 3,751,328 Whites, 2,018,453 Coloureds, 620,436 Asians and 15,057,952 black Africans. About half of the Whites are Boers (Afrikaners), the other half mainly British by descent. The historical differences between the two groups, of which the former are more numerous in the Transvaal and the Orange Free State and the latter in Cape Province and Natal, have given way to a considerable amount of unity in defence of the white 'way of life' and the Apartheid system, against the other racial communities. Of these, the Coloureds – the offspring of Afrikaner, Hottentot, Malay and other ancestors living in the days before the 'Immorality Act' – and the Asians used to have a less restricted life than the Africans, but their privileges have been steadily reduced. The 'Bantu' is fixed at the lowest level of the social hierarchy, with the function of providing cheap labour.

The Africans are deprived of the right to live in a large part of the country, the part including cities such as Johannesburg and other Rand towns such as Germiston and Springs, Pretoria, Durban, Cape Town and Port Elizabeth, and the mining and industrial centres. These are designated as 'white' areas, and in them Africans generally have only temporary and conditional rights of residence, dependent almost wholly on the labour demand. They have residence rights in the tribal 'homelands', now called 'Bantustans', such as the Transkei and Zululand; these, however, cover only 13 per cent of all the land area and are too poor to be able to support even a third of the 15 million people who are supposed to 'belong' to them. It is not, in fact, intended that the rest should live in the Bantustans; they are needed for the industries, mines, railways and domestic service of the Whites, and it is accepted that they live in the 'white' areas, but not that they should have real homes and a stable life there. They are kept in a permanent migrant status, their life in the towns and other white areas dependent on the work they can do there.

This work is generally unskilled, for the system of 'job reservation' excludes Africans from a large number of skilled jobs. It cannot easily be changed, because a man's life depends on his job. Advancement to a better job is restricted not only by job reservation but by the lack of educational opportunities. Wages are very low, far lower than those of white workers and, as several recent surveys have shown, often below the subsistence level. Efforts to improve wages and conditions are thwarted by the outlawing of strikes by Africans,

The 'White South' and Neighbours

by the unskilled (and therefore easily replaceable) character of most African labourers, and by the fact that a breach of a work contract by an African is considered a criminal offence. In addition to all this, African workers are forced to live in segregated areas, compounds at the mines, or 'townships' such as those which ring the smart and brash white city-centre of Johannesburg. Apart from the trouble this may cause to people who work some distance away, these African residential areas are districts of wretched housing and sanitation and are homes for all sorts of crime and vice. While life in the poorer quarters of the cities in independent Africa may in some ways be equally wretched, the situation of South Africa's poor urban Africans is distinctive because it is aggravated by segregation and regimentation, and because it continues in a particularly rich country.[1]

The life of Africans in the towns is governed by the Bantu (Urban Areas) Consolidation Act of 1945, intended to regulate that life in minute detail. Under it, no African may remain in an urban area for longer than seventy-two hours, unless he or she can prove to have been continually resident there since birth, or, with official permission, for fifteen years continuously; that he or she has worked there continuously for one employer for at least ten years, or has been allowed to remain there by a labour-bureau official; or that she is the wife or unmarried daughter, or he the son under eighteen years of age, of a person qualified to remain in the area. But measures to force Africans to work for white employers go further than this. A labour officer can forbid a man to take, or order him to be sacked from, a job, on the grounds of danger to the state or public 'or of a section thereof' or to 'public order'; then he can offer him another job or else tell him to leave the area.[2] He may be allowed to stay while a job is sought, but he must report to the local labour bureau. If, in any circumstances, a 'Bantu' has lost his job, and refuses to accept a new one when it is offered, he may be arrested as 'idle' after three such refusals, or after losing a job through misconduct, neglect, intemperance, or laziness, or after being sacked for misconduct.[3] In 1966 systematic efforts were begun to remove 'surplus' Africans from the towns, where already families were often prevented from joining the men. All this regimentation is enforced through the 'pass system', under which every African in the white areas must have his reference book, including several documents, with him all the time to present on demand. His few rights depend on all parts of the book (including the part set aside for monthly signatures by employers) being in order. The effect, as intended, is to ensure that Africans are in the 'white' areas on sufferance, which means that they must do a job there, and often a specified job, to avoid being 'endorsed out' – expelled – from the town to the poverty-stricken 'homelands'.[4]

This system has been described as massive use of forced labour. The description is fair, but it is important to be clear why. The mere fact that many individuals have to choose between a certain job and the gutter is not peculiar to South Africa, far from it, and it does not constitute a system of forced labour. Although the 1930 ILO Convention stated that forced labour was labour for which a man has 'not offered himself voluntarily', it referred only to *human* restrictions on voluntary engagement; many people have no choice at all, and not because of any coercive measures. What makes the South African system one of virtual forced labour is that it is not mere poverty, or lack of economic development, which restricts the individual's right to choose his job; it is legislation by the parliament at Cape Town. An individual may be forced to take, or keep, a job for fear, not only of the normal troubles of the unemployed, but also of expulsion from his home to a life of poverty. The regulations applied to Africans (and not to Whites) in South Africa's urban areas are stricter than the work-permit regulations applied by many countries to foreigners seeking employment; these are often able to seek new jobs, and stay without jobs for some time before becoming liable to expulsion.

In 1953 an *Ad Hoc* Committee on Forced Labour of the UN and the ILO considered the legislation of most countries of the world and, at unusual length, that of South Africa. It was eventually convinced:

'... of the existence of a legislative system applied only to the indigenous population and designed to maintain an insuperable barrier between these people and the inhabitants of European origin. The indirect effect of this legislation is to channel the bulk of the indigenous inhabitants into agriculture and manual work and thus to create a permanent, abundant and cheap labour force ... The ultimate consequence of the system is to compel the native population to contribute, by their labour, to the implementation of the economic policies of the country, but the compulsory and involuntary nature of this contribution results from the peculiar status and situation created by the special legislation applicable to the indigenous inhabitants alone, rather than from direct coercive measures designed to compel them to work, although such measures, which are the inevitable consequence of this status, were also found to exist. It is in this indirect sense, therefore, that in the Committee's view, a system of forced labour of significance to the national economy appears to exist in the Union of South Africa.'[5]

Since then, the regimentation aimed at this end has increased. In 1964 – the year in which the Verwoerd Government decided on the withdrawal of South Africa from the ILO (with effect from 11th March, 1966) – the Bantu Laws Amendment Act allowed the Minister of Bantu Affairs to apply the laws relating to urban Africans to new areas, to be called 'prescribed' areas, and made it possible for Africans found living illegally in such areas to be directed to jobs elsewhere. This further step towards full-scale forced labour had already been put into effect frequently, and chiefly in agricultural work. It is in this sort of work that South Africa's forced labour is found in its crudest form.

The rapid development of mining and industry has made farming less important for South Africa than in the days when the settlers of Dutch descent came to be generally known as farmers or *boers*. But these still form an important part of the white community and of the Nationalist Government's electorate. They own a large part of the land, most of the 87 per cent of the country reserved to the Whites being rural. The main crops grown are maize, wheat, sugar, grapes for the local wine, and fruit, including the oranges and apples sold abroad. All these are grown by unskilled African labourers, and for Africans farm labour is far more important, numerically, than any other sort of wage labour. In 1961 there were 1,441,470 African farm labourers, while a year earlier 3,400,000 Africans in all, about 30 per cent of the 'Bantu' population, lived on white farms. There are three sorts of farm labourer: tenants who have the use of land in return for labour, squatters who live on the land without formal agreement but are allowed to stay in return for labour, and wage labourers without use of land. The latter are again divided into registered and casual labourers.[6]

And then there is a category of workers whose situation has given rise to some of the biggest South African scandals: that of the Africans who work on white farms as part of punishment for offences. They are either convicts hired out by the prison authorities to farmers, or petty offenders allowed to 'volunteer' for farm work as an alternative to prosecution.

The hiring out of prisoners to private employers has been standard practice in many parts of the world, and in South Africa it dates back to 1889.[7] It is contrary to the 1930 Forced Labour Convention, which allows compulsory work for convicts but specifies that they must not be 'hired to or placed at the disposal of private individuals, companies or associations' (Paragraph 2, 2c). But in 1938 Field-Marshal Smuts, then Prime Minister, said that he did not defend the practice but it would be 'most awkward' to end it.[8] It continued, and became a most elaborate and well-organised system of supplying farmers with cheap and helpless labour. Placing of convicts at the disposal of private employers is open to many objections in any country, but the possibilities it opens are greatly increased in the context of Apartheid, as events have shown. Farmers have subscribed to have prisons specially built near farms, such as one at Leslie, Transvaal, opened in 1949 by the Minister of Justice.[9] In such cases, prison sentences could easily become a mere formality to be fulfilled in the transfer of labourers to farms. In 1957–9 farmers hired about 200,000 convicts a year, at wages of 9$d$ per day.[10] Earlier, it had been found that convicts were hired out to work for the railways and for gold-mining companies too.[11] But their employment on farms is the best organised and most notorious aspect of the hiring out of convict labour. Selected farmers are allowed to build prisons on their land, to government specifications, and official guards are provided. In 1963 there were twenty-five farm gaols, housing more than 9,000 long-term convicts. At first, only people serving sentences of under three months were sent to farms, but by the 1950s long-term prisoners were also included.[12]

The inclusion of long-term prisoners worsens one undesirable aspect of the convicts hiring system: that it places prisoners at the mercy of farmers. Sadistic ill-treatment by farmers and their African foremen has resulted; even where this does not occur, there can be no effective check on the farmer's treatment of the workers. The use of convicts also makes it easier for farmers to keep the wages of other labourers the lowest of all African wages. Their lowness is partly offset by the payment of some wages in kind, particularly food, but this in itself helps to keep the labourers tied to the farm, as they are in any case by the terms of the Masters and Servants Acts. The powers given by these Acts to farmers over all labourers have been compared with those of 'a feudal land-owner over his serfs'.[13] Obviously, convict labourers are more helpless still.

In practice, prisoners on farms report that they have had to work in wretched conditions. And even this is not the worst aspect of the system. In many cases people have been sent to work compulsorily on farms without even a semblance of judicial procedure, and this may be becoming a regular occurrence. Abusive though it is widely held to be, the hiring out of convict labour to private employers, even in a state where it is so easy to become a convict, cannot compare with forcible direction of labour independent of the courts.

In 1947 the Department of Bantu Affairs (as it is now called) agreed to a system by which people arrested for petty offences against the pass laws could choose to do farm labour for six or twelve months instead of facing prosecution. As the pass laws are so complex and vexatious it is easy to break them, and thousands do every day. The South African Government denied in 1953 that any of the people convicted of these offences were hired out to farmers,[14] but it seems that this was not necessary, as under the 1947 arrangement people went to work on the farms without any criminal conviction, and were not in fact given any choice. Supposedly volunteers, they were in reality simply sent to the farms in considerable numbers. This emerged when a Johannesburg lawyer, Joel Carlson, brought *habeas corpus* actions to free some of them. In 1954, however, the Secretary for Native Affairs issued General Circular No. 23, setting out a scheme 'to induce unemployed natives now roaming the streets in the various urban areas to accept unemployment outside such urban areas . . .'[15]

As a result, to take one or two examples, Nelson Langa, a street-cleaner at Johannesburg City Hall, was arrested as unemployed because he had no pass (despite his protests that he had a job), and was sent to work on a farm in the Bethal district. James Musa Sadika, a Johannesburg self-employed herbalist, was sent to work in the Nigel farming district because he objected to paying an extra sum of money for a new reference book.[16] Sadika and another forced labourer, George Dube, emerged (thanks to Carlson's efforts) to describe brutality on the farm, and the case became widely known; one man died, Sadika said, as a result of continual beatings, and apart from ill-treatment housing and sanitation for the workers was abysmal.[17]

After such cases, which aroused protests within South Africa, the system of 'voluntary' farm work in lieu of prosecution for petty offences was abolished in 1959. But, as an alternative, the Bantu Laws Amendment Act of 1964, allowing directions of Africans illegally living in 'prescribed' areas to new jobs, can be used to provide forced labour on farms. That this seems to be intended is shown by a case which was publicised in 1972.

A young man born in Johannesburg, arrested as an 'undesirable Bantu', spent a year in prison in another area, and on his release had 'Plaasarbeider/Farm Labourer' stamped in his reference book. Once he had been classified, by mere administrative decision, as a farm labourer, he could not work except on a farm. The Black Sash, an organisation of white women that helps victims of Apartheid laws, examined his case, but apparently felt unable to do much because such decisions, allocating people to particular sorts of work, are seldom revoked.[18] And in 1968 the Deputy Minister of Agricultural Development, Mr Vosloo, said that government policy was for farm labourers to stay in farm work, adding that if a man seeking a job in a town was known to be a farm labourer he would not be given a non-farm job. He even criticised some farmers for failing to register all their labourers and so making the policy harder to enforce. He did, however, remind farmers of their obligations to their employees, and said that there were still many farmers 'who pay hopelessly inadequate wages to their Bantu labourers';[19] but he did not seem to realise that administrative efforts to induce Africans to work on farms made it less necessary to offer proper wages and conditions.

The wages and conditions have remained poor, even by South African standards – in December 1970 it was estimated that a farm labourer in parts of the Transvaal received only 5 to 8 Rand and a bag of maize meal every month, and a casual labourer in the same areas only 20 cents per day – and this must be one good reason for the shortage of farm labourers, which was assessed in 1969 at 141,000.[20] The size of the shortage makes it all too probable that the quasi-legal and extra-legal methods of coercing people into farm labour are used frequently. The legal methods used under the 1964 Bantu Labour Act have been extended and refined. Not only had 188 farm labour control boards, on which officials and white farmers sit to direct labour to where it is needed, been set up by April 1972;[21] but the entire farm labour registration system has been centralised in Pretoria, with computers to record the full employment history of every African worker. For farm labourers, 1984 seems to have arrived. To escape from farm work, even if one is arbitrarily directed to it in the way mentioned above, must be very difficult, if not impossible.

And as if this increase in the use of forced labour were not enough – and the farmers it probably is not, for they have called for more direction of labour[22] – the system of farm work in lieu of imprisonment for petty offenders has been revived. A report in 1972 said that people arrested for minor offences against the pass laws and liquor laws may choose to work 'on parole' on farms rather than go to prison if they cannot pay their fines, and added that this seemed to be the same as the system denounced in the 1950s; it apparently had the same results, for in December 1971 a farmer was sentenced for grievous assault leading to the death of one such labourer, and it turned out that workers had been sent to his farm even though he had two previous convictions for assaulting labourers.[23]

It is on the farms that compulsory labour in South Africa takes its crudest form (and it is for farm labour that some independent African states have thought of similar measures as a 'solution' to the problem of migration to towns; see pp. 239–40). For urban and industrial labourers, Apartheid involves tight regimentation, which can at times tie a worker effectively to one employer, but as workers prefer such work to rural work coercion is not actually needed to bring them to the towns and mines. Indeed, it is often applied to keep people *out* of the urban areas and to preserve the mainly migrant nature of the work force.

Regulations aim, as already noted, to make urban workers migrants rather than urban residents, as far as possible. This policy is applied to workers from the Transkei, the Ciskei, Zululand and other 'Bantu homelands' within South Africa. But although those areas have thousands of unemployed people, immigrants from outside South Africa have been employed for decades, particularly on the mines. Three-quarters of the African work force (401,000) on the gold- and coal-mines run by members of the South African Chamber of Mines in 1970 came from outside South Africa.[24] There are foreign African workers in other urban and industrial jobs too, and some on farms. A number come from Lesotho and Botswana, former British protectorates now independent but economically tied to South Africa (particularly because of these migrant labourers). But most come either from Portuguese Mozambique or from Malawi, which in spite of its distance from South Africa has hundreds of thousands of its men working there, particularly on the mines.

This migration has for long been well organised and officially encouraged. Since many Mozambican and Malawian Africans go to work in South Africa voluntarily and illegally – besides those recruited through recognised channels – supporters of Apartheid claim that life cannot be so bad for Africans in South Africa after all. This is a hollow claim, for migrants go to South Africa out of necessity, work on the Rand being better than no work at all (the poverty of rural Malawi, Lesotho, Botswana and Mozambique is such that it is no great compliment to South Africa to say that it is marginally better in cash terms). Anyway, migrants do not intend to stay there, and can put up with Apartheid restrictions for a few years more easily than those who spend all their lives under them. But the propaganda value of the immigrants is, in any case, not their main value. Because of their situation, they are at the mercy of their employers, and their presence makes it harder for 'Bantu' workers as a whole to organise themselves. It is important for the régime that the workers should not do this, for when they do they can have some success; this happened after illegal strikes in Durban early in

8. Timbuktu – little remains of the former flourishing centre of learning and slave-trading.

9. Old Zanzibar, with the cathedral (top right) on the site of the former slave-market.

10. Rwanda: scene from a pastoral society of masters and serfs.

1973. Such things can be prevented more easily, and wages kept down more easily, when there are hundreds of thousands of foreign migrant labourers.

Labour migration is therefore an important part of the general labour regimentation in South Africa. It does not seem to be, in itself, an extra sort of exploitation. So many workers want to migrate for a few years to South Africa, for the reasons mentioned, that if any are actually coerced into going there, this is probably superfluous. But the reasons why they want to go are not entirely natural and inevitable. The British authorities in former Nyasaland either intended to provoke migration to the South African mines when they imposed taxes which could not be paid in any other way, or at least accepted this result of their taxation without resistance. Once it had started on a large scale, the migration made it harder to develop employment alternatives in Nyasaland, which would have been hard enough anyway, and so migration had to go on until today.

In Mozambique, where migration to South Africa is a well-established tradition among the Thonga people,[25] there are now, as in Malawi, more than enough recruits for officially organised migration, which has been handled for decades by the Witwatersrand Native Labour Association (now transformed into two companies which retain the well-known abbreviation of the old name, 'Wenela'). But it was not always so; at first 'recruitment' was a very polite word for the measures taken to bring Mozambicans to the Rand. A recent study (favourable to the Portuguese Government) says that 'Wenela' at first used 'questionable and illegal' recruiting methods, employing 'emigration police' who, as was no doubt intended, were confused by Africans with ordinary Portuguese police; later such behaviour stopped, and it became unnecessary.[26] But Eduardo Mondlane, the Mozambique revolutionary leader, said that the exploitation in the early days had been at the Portuguese end, recruiting for South Africa being another sort of labour coercion in Mozambique. He noted that the Portuguese were paid by 'Wenela' for each worker recruited, and the opportunities that this offered to an Administration used to recruiting of forced labour are obvious. So are the abuses made possible by the custom of payment of the workers' wages through the Mozambique Administration.[27] It is, indeed, most unlikely that this migration has always been wholly free and in accordance with the workers' interests, when it operated between two countries where labour coercion has been regarded as normal.

*Portuguese forced labour*
In the Portuguese colonies, forced labour was a normal part of life

for Africans until a few years ago, and it may be so still, for it is likely that the abolition of this form of oppression, ordered about the time that African revolts began, was carried out very imperfectly until the 1974 revolution and the great changes resulting in the Portuguese colonies.

Forced labour was one of the particular burdens imposed on the mass of 'natives'; and nearly all the Africans of Mozambique, Angola and Portuguese Guinea were of this 'native' status, only a few thousand becoming *'assimilado'* or *'civilizado'* and hence legally equal in rights to the white Portuguese. The conditions for attainment of this superior status were so stringent, involving the transformation of the African into a black Portuguese, and the number of schools available to give the necessary education were so few that it is clear that Portuguese colonial policy, which has an undeserved reputation for non-racialism, never intended more than a small handful of Africans to become *assimilados*.[28] The majority certainly could never hope to do so, and so remained subject, among other things, to recruitment for forced labour.

In 1961, after the outbreak of rebellion in Angola, Portugal belatedly abolished the distinction between 'natives' and *assimilados*. It has made similarly belated efforts to make up for the combined neglect and oppression from which the interior regions of Angola and Mozambique suffered for long after their conquest in the nineteenth century. These changes came far too late to stop the spirit of African revolt. Building of new schools and clinics cannot erase the memory of decades when very few of these were ever built and colonial rule meant mainly taxation and forced labour. Nor can the abolition of forced labour itself, carried out by measures in 1960 and 1961.

The results of forced labour before then are most fully recorded for Angola, the largest in area of Portugal's African territories but not the most populous (it has about 6 million people, while Mozambique has about 8 million). For centuries, the slave-trade devastated parts of Angola; Portugal ruled much of the coast but, contrary to official myth, no appreciable part of the interior before the late nineteenth century, and the interior was raided for slaves, with Africans of the Ovimbundu people and Portuguese half-castes handling the trade inland. The slave-trade was abolished in the Portuguese Empire in 1836, and slavery itself in 1876.[29] But various measures allowed ways of compelling Africans to work, so there was not much of a breathing space between slavery and *trabalho obrigatório*, permitted by a decree of 1899.

This decree obliged all Africans to do some sort of work, and while it did not allow unrestricted resort to forced labour it was taken as the basis for forcible recruiting of African labourers on a vast scale. Much of this was, for the next few decades, called 'contract labour'. The important aspect of this (not always made plain in accounts of Portuguese colonialism, which sometimes use the phrase as if labour contracts were themselves an evil) is that the 'contracts' in question were often not really contracts at all, as there was no true negotiation or mutual agreement. 'Contract labour' was commonly forced labour in disguise. This was made clear a few years after the 1899 decree by reports of conscription of 'contract' workers in Angola for work not only there but also on the Portuguese island of São Tomé in the Bight of Biafra.

These reports led to one of the major forced labour scandals of the colonial era. Three visitors to São Tomé found out about the appalling treatment of labourers there: Henry Nevinson, sent by *Harper's Magazine*;[30] Joseph Burtt, sent by the British firms of Cadbury, Fry and Rowntree, major importers of São Tomé cocoa; and William Cadbury, head of the same firm, who went himself to São Tomé, the nearby island of Principe, and Angola with Burtt in 1908.[31] It was this last visit by Cadbury and Burtt which led to the most spectacular protest at the exploitation of labourers on São Tomé and Principe, the two sister islands near the Equator which, at the turn of the century, grew a large part of the world's cocoa crop. The two Englishmen tried to persuade the owners of the cocoa plantations to employ voluntary rather than 'contract' labourers; when this failed, they sent a cable to England which led to a halt in purchases of São Tomé cocoa by the famous chocolate firm.[32] This was an expression of the Quaker social conscience of the Cadbury family, and its significance can only be grasped if one realises that a leading cocoa importer cut itself off from most of the world's cocoa supplies rather than continue to profit by forced labour. Such a gesture, at the height of the Edwardian imperialist era when forced labour was widely practised and accepted in African colonies, was remarkable.

Henry Nevinson had no doubt helped to bring about this result by his book, *A Modern Slavery*, based on his visit to Angola and the islands and published in 1906. In it, he said that in Angola workers were made to 'sign contracts' by trickery and then shipped to the islands, where they worked a seventeen-hour day on the cocoa plantations and, even though their contracts were supposed to be for only five years, they often stayed away indefinitely. Missionaries denounced this forced labour-recruiting in Angola, which was partly for work within that colony and partly for the cocoa islands;

recruiting agents were said to offer chiefs guns and other goods in return for workers delivered.

The Portuguese had ordered reforms in the treatment of labourers on the islands before the storm broke, but they were probably not applied seriously. As in the days of the slave-trade, in which São Tomé had also been important, the Portuguese were angered by British criticisms, and seem to have felt more resentful than attentive (they had resented and, so far as possible, ignored or evaded British efforts to stop their slave-trading in the nineteenth century; now they seem to have had a similar reaction to criticisms of forced labour). The fact that Great Britain was also an imperialist power and was at times thought to have designs on other European countries' territories made it easier for the Portuguese (as for Leopold II) to reject British protests over labour abuses as insincere. Certainly those abuses went on. The Cadbury's gesture, important though it was, brought about no serious improvement even on the islands concerned, much less in Angola and Mozambique.

Foreign reports of forced labour in Portuguese Africa went on: John Harris wrote a book on Portuguese slavery in 1913, and Edward Ross wrote a similar account in 1925. More important, some leading Portuguese decided that the system was intolerable. José Mendes Norton de Matos, appointed Governor of Angola in 1914, outlawed for a time the 'contract labour' system, and a decree of 1921 stated that voluntary labour was to be preferred, with good pay and conditions to attract it.[33] The decree did repeat earlier provisions for forced labour for public works; but as recruitment of forced labour for private employers was so important this decree would have made a great deal of difference if its intentions had been carried out; however, they were not. Forced labour for both government projects and private enterprises continued in Angola and elsewhere. In São Tomé and Principe, scandals in connection with foreign workers on cocoa plantations went on, as they did on the nearby Spanish island of Fernando Po. The Spanish planters employed labourers from Liberia and later from Nigeria, which gave them occasional difficulties with the Administrations of those countries. The Portuguese avoided these by recruiting labourers for São Tomé and Principe from other Portuguese territories, for example, Mozambique and the Cape Verde Islands as well as Angola. Immigrants from these three countries formed half the population of São Tomé in 1935. That they were still taken there under the old conditions was suggested by a report in 1950 by a visiting American missionary who saw about 250 workers being sent back to their homes in Mozambique, ill and aged, after twenty-five years' absence, and by other information reaching the Anti-Slavery Society, which took a close interest in Portuguese Africa.[34]

The Rural Labour Code approved by Decree No. 16,199 of 6th December, 1928, regularised the situation as regards forced labour for Africans under Portuguese rule. It banned forced labour but 'without prejudice to the discharge by ... natives of the moral obligation incumbent upon them to procure the means of subsistence by labour and thereby to promote the general interests of mankind' (Paragraph 3), and with some exceptions for government works.[35] These loopholes might have been enough in the context of the time, even if serious efforts had been made to apply the code. They were not; recruiting of labourers by Portuguese officials for private employers, outlawed by the same decree, went on, as it became clear that if not compelled, Africans preferred to work on their own farms rather than for white employers. European businesses in the colonies (not only the Portuguese ones) expected so much that no African would want to work for them if he did not have to. The Administration in Portuguese Africa helped the firms out of this difficulty by helping to recruit workers for them, and the power of the Administration was such that 'recruitment' is not really the right word. Anyway, forced labour was not seriously affected by the 1928 Labour Code.

In Mozambique a Circular from the Governor-General in 1942 said that Africans must, if able-bodied, prove that they lived by their work, or else be considered 'vagrants', liable to six months' forced labour on public works projects every year. This was clearly used as a pretext for the rounding up of Africans for allocation to private employers, because in 1947 a new Circular by the Governor-General condemned this explicitly, saying it had not been intended by the 1942 Circular.[36] The recruiting of labourers by officials for private employers, and the direct conscription of forced labourers for those employers, were similar practices that clearly went on together. In 1955 it was felt necessary to outlaw the former once again in Portuguese Africa and to increase the penalties for it. By the same law, forced labour was maintained for public works but under new restrictions and conditions.[37] The reality of life in Portuguese Africa, however, was far removed from the wording of the laws in force.

After a visit to Angola in 1954, Basil Davidson wrote a grim account of forced labour there, with the title *A Modern Slavery*, recalling Nevinson's revelations in 1906. He said that 'contract labour' went on in Angola and was still more like slavery than labour under genuine free contracts; 379,000 people were working under that system in Angola, and others had been sent to São Tomé and

Principe.³⁸ On those islands, the previous year, there had been riots by the long-established local half-caste community when its men had been told to register for contract labour; security forces fired on a crowd and were believed to have killed about 200 people.³⁹ By now, many of the immigrant workers on the islands came from another Portuguese island territory, the arid and poor Cape Verde Islands, while Davidson's report and others said that Angolans were still sent there. In Angola, Davidson reported, an African had to prove on inquiry that he was working then or had worked for six months of the previous year; if he could not, he was obliged to get work, in theory being free to apply for any vacancy or even to work on his own fields, but in practice being liable to conscription for forced labour. Private employers made thousands of applications every year to the Governor-General for contract labourers, and local administrators, such as the *chefes do posto* with whom Africans came most into contact, were told to find workers; chiefs and headmen were in turn told to recruit them, and could be punished for not providing them.⁴⁰

In such conditions, free labour contracts were not necessary for the recruiting of workers, and in fact there was general conscription of labour; sometimes men fled to avoid this and women and children were conscripted in their stead. Davidson found that the conditions of work – food, housing and transport – were better than in Nevinson's day, but the work was still very hard, especially the work on the roads. But perhaps most scandalous of all, in a way, was the situation in the diamond-mining area of north-east Lunda Province, where 5,000 of the 16,000 Angolan employees were admitted to be contract labourers. The Angola Diamond Company which owned the mines had a monopoly of labour recruitment over a large area of Northern Angola, so that the 'voluntary' character of the other 11,000 employees was open to question. Those 11,000 were paid less than the contract workers, and received no rations or housing. In theory, the contract labourers worked for one year only (long enough), but in practice they were often made to work for two or three years.⁴¹ While Davidson found that there were good medical services and dormitories at the mines, the power given to a private company to recruit forced labour on such a scale showed how little Portugal's own laws, much less international conventions, were heeded in what the Salazar régime insisted from 1951 onwards on calling 'overseas provinces of Portugal'. Another employer of forced labour in Angola in 1954 was the port authority of Lobito.

Besides forced labour on public works – still legal and enforceable on 'idle' Africans among others – and forced labour for private

FORCED LABOUR IN THE WHITE SOUTH 183

employers, there was also forced cultivation of crops, particularly cotton, and this was as harsh a burden as any other sort of labour coercion. The increase in the cotton crops of Angola and Mozambique from a very small quantity in the 1920s to 140,000 tons in the 1950s was due very much to orders forcing Africans to grow fixed quantities of it; over a million were thought to be forced to do this in Mozambique alone. Large European concessionary companies were responsible for producing the cotton, but it was Africans who grew it and sold it to the companies at prices dictated by the companies, below world prices. Farmers were forced to neglect food cultivation in order to grow the required quantities of cotton.[42] This was one way in which labour coercion kept Africans poor and made nonsense of the moralising about the value and importance of work. The sufferings due to forced labour were not limited to those endured by the workers on the work sites. Families were abandoned of necessity, and village and family life disrupted, when men were taken away to forced labour – and they could be taken far away, even if they stayed inside Angola and Mozambique, as both territories are vast – or forced to flee to avoid it (great numbers of Angolans fled to the Congo even before the war which began in 1961). Farming suffered; the fact that among Bantu peoples such as those of Angola and Mozambique the women do much of the farm work does not mean, as some Europeans have apparently thought, that the men have no work to do there and their absence is unimportant. The effects of forced labour and forced cultivation on people's minds can be imagined. It was considered a main cause of African revolt in Angola in 1961, as in 1902 when there was a major revolt in the Benguela Highlands.

The 1961 rising in Northern Angola was concentrated in areas of coffee farms, on which large numbers of forced labourers were believed to be at work to help grow Angola's major export commodity. This particular bloodstained rising was only a part, and in the end a fairly unimportant part, of the Angolan resistance, which has been continued more effectively in other areas by other leaders; and forced labour may not have been the only or major reason for the African risings in Angola and elsewhere. In Portuguese Guinea, where guerrilla war against the Portuguese was waged from 1963 with great success, until independence was declared in 1973 and conceded by Portugal in 1974, forced labour was relatively unimportant, there being no important cash crops or mines or settlers' enterprises (the complaint against Portugal brought by Ghana before the ILO did not mention any specific cases of forced labour in Portuguese Guinea). But the bitterness caused by forced labour and its contribution to the revolt against Portugal are clear from the writings of nationalist leaders, and are scarcely surprising. It may have been a realisation of the resentment it was causing, and of the danger that it might encourage Africans in Portuguese colonies to aspire to the independence achieved in other parts of Africa, that persuaded the Salazar régime to take action against forced labour in the late 1950s. This was also the result of a new colonial philosophy in Lisbon associated with the name of Adriano Moreira, and which believed in more rights, progress and equality for Africans – within a continued Portuguese empire.

In 1956 Salazar's Portugal ratified, with effect from 26th June, 1957, the 1930 Convention, under which ILO members agreed *inter alia* to abolish forced labour for private employers immediately and for public works as soon as possible. Then in 1959, with effect from 23rd November, 1960, it ratified the 1957 Convention on Abolition of Forced Labour. This new ILO Convention followed years of close examination of the situation in the 1950s by the organisation and its special *Ad Hoc* Committee on Forced Labour (1953). Unlike the 1930 Convention, it called for the total abolition of all forced labour, and bound all signatories to refrain from imposing forced labour as a penalty for striking or for political dissent, or as a means of mobilisation for economic development, or for any other reason.[43] Voted without opposition by the International Labour Conference on 25th June, 1957, this Convention (No. 105) bound all states adhering to it to abolish forced labour immediately. Portugal therefore became bound to do this on 23rd November, 1960.

Three months later, on 25th February, 1961, the Nkrumah Government in Ghana brought a complaint against Portugal before the ILO, alleging that forced labour on a large scale was normal in Angola, Mozambique, and São Tomé and Principe.[44] This led to a thorough investigation by an ILO commission, who published early in 1962 a detailed study of all aspects of forced labour in Portuguese Africa (its historical section alone is particularly useful, being the most complete historical account of laws and decrees governing Portuguese forced labour, though without any investigation of actual practice). The commission visited Angola and Mozambique in December 1961; its chairman was Paul Ruegger of Switzerland, the other two members being Enrique Armand-Ugon of Uruguay and an African – Isaac Forster, a leading Senegalese judge.

The Ghana Government's allegations included the use of forced labour in the diamond-mines and on the Benguela railway and at the harbours of Lobito and Luanda in Angola, and on the islands in the Gulf of Guinea. Its evidence included the report of the 1953

ILO/UN *Ad Hoc* Committee on Forced Labour, which had been unable to reach any definite conclusions about Portuguese forced labour but had suggested that rules on 'recruitment' made pressure possible and that the circumstances of the recruiting for São Tomé and Principe – such as the ban on migrant workers changing employers on the islands, and the legal provision that workers whose contracts had expired could be retained if there were no ships available to take them home – made it like forced labour. Other evidence included various books, such as Basil Davidson's *The African Awakening*; a report written a dozen years earlier by Captain Henrique Galvão, the opponent of the Salazar régime who won fame in 1961 by seizing the ship *Santa Maria* with other anti-Salazar Portuguese; and oral evidence, notable from Protestant missionaries, defenders for many decades of the Africans under Portuguese rule, and some Africans, for example the nationalist leader Marcelino dos Santos of Mozambique, and two students brought forward as witnesses by the Anti-Slavery Society.

After hearing these witnesses, considering the other evidence produced by Ghana, examining a very large number of Portuguese witnesses (including the Directors of Native Affairs of Angola and Mozambique), and making brief visits to Angola and Mozambique, the commission produced its long report, covering over 250 pages of the ILO *Official Bulletin* (Vol. XLV, No. 2, April 1962). During the year of the commission's work many things happened. A revolt broke out in Northern Angola on 15 March 1961, with fearful massacres by the insurgents followed by massive, indiscriminate reprisals. These events coloured some of the exchanges of notes on the forced labour question, and gave a new importance to the commission's findings. But the rising, a shock to the Portuguese, also led to the announcement of new reforms to accompany the suppression of the African rebellion. The formation of the ILO commission had provided another incentive for some of these reforms, which had become binding anyway in November 1960. So various measures to remove traces of forced labour were enacted while the Ruegger commission was sitting, and most had been published before its visit to Angola. Whether these hastily enacted decrees were due to the ratification of the 1957 Convention, to the formation of the commission, or to the rising in Angola, or to all three causes, they were carried out in good time to impress the commission.

The Portuguese, seizing the opportunity to impress the commission, co-operated in many ways with its work, sending many senior officials to testify before it, and facilitating its visit to Angola and Mozambique. The three commissioners were able to visit the Benguela railway and its forest reserves, the Angola Agricultural Company's coffee plantations, Lobito harbour, the National Cotton Company's territory in Mozambique, the recruitment centres and transit camps run by the Witwatersrand Native Labour Association in Mozambique, and many other places. They were allowed to talk not only to chiefs but also to ordinary Africans, workers at enterprises on the Commission's itinerary and labourers whom they happened to pass on their journeys, and to talk to them without officials or employers' representatives listening. This did not make the conditions of their fact-finding visit wholly satisfactory; but it showed that the Salazar régime had decided not to oppose this particular 'interference' in its colonial matters.

The commission's general conclusion was that Portugal had continued to practise forced labour or at least to tolerate it in contravention of the 1957 Convention after that had come into force in all Portuguese territories, but that it had since abrogated nearly all the provisions permitting forced labour, and that: 'The commission is fully satisfied of the *bona fides* of these changes of policy, legislation and practise and rejects as entirely without foundation the suggestion made in support of the complaint that "Portugal only ratified the Convention as a cover to continue her ruthless labour policies".'[45] The report, therefore, was to some extent an exoneration of the Portuguese. But a closer look at it shows that it was not such a complete exoneration as has been made out.

After dealing in turn with the various Ghanaian allegations and considering the evidence given on each one and what it had seen itself on its tour, the commission often found that the measures which had at least partly justified the allegations against Portugal had been repealed only a few months before, usually after the filing of the complaint. Moreover, on other occasions, though it did not say so, it clearly got the impression that practice had been far removed from the texts of laws and decrees. The Portuguese denied allegations that Africans not working as others' employees were commonly liable to conscription for forced labour or to be classed as 'idle', but this had been allowed in Mozambique until September 1961. The commission found that Africans said that they had been told to work by the authorities, and on visiting Luanda and Lobito harbours and Luanda railway station, where there were many recruited workers, it found that all recruited workers said they had been told to go to their work by the *chefe do posto*, or another local official, or a chief. Indeed, they had wanted to stay in their villages, but had been told to work for from nine to twelve months. Some of the workers came from quite distant areas, so that it was of little importance to them whether they were allowed, as the director of Lobito harbour said, to leave their jobs. Representatives of the enterprises concerned said that until July 1961 workers had been recruited for them by the authorities, via the chiefs. This was a virtual admission of many of the charges against Portugal, an admission that they were well-founded at the time of the filing of Ghana's complaint and until the conveniently timed reform.[46]

In Mozambique a worker at Beira harbour told the commissioners that he had been told to take the work by his chief, against his will; and the commission stopped on the road to interrogate road workers without warning, and found that four out of a dozen said that they had been forced to take the work by the *chefes do posto*. Later it was stated that the road company was being prosecuted.[47]

On cotton cultivation the commission found that provisions for compulsory growing had been abrogated on 2nd May, 1961. In Angola it was stated that this measure had led to an immediate fall in cotton production by one-quarter, a fact more eloquent than the statements of other witnesses who insisted that, in fact, there had never been compulsory cotton cultivation. Many Africans, certainly, said that they grew cotton voluntarily, but with the concessionary companies' powers now reduced there was more incentive to do this. The commission did not find out much about the labour camps at Baia dos Tigres in Southern Angola and other places, and did not observe anything to confirm the (detailed) allegations of people being sent there for refusing to be recruited for work, for protesting at forced labour or road work, or for being found without the right papers in police checks. But concealment, difficult in other cases, would have been quite easy for such abuses as these. The stringent 'vagrancy' laws which could justify such arbitrary action or at least facilitate it were not repealed in 1961 and the commission, while not condemning such provisions because they were not contrary to the Conventions, deprecated them in its report.

The Portuguese totally denied the general allegation that 'contract labour' was really forced labour, and said that recruiting was carried out under stringent safeguards. This raised the whole question of what 'recruitment' really meant. According to many witnesses, it was in fact conscription rather than recruitment, and the 'contracts' were not real contracts at all. The Portuguese official denials were modified by an admission that there had been complaints over recruiting in the Bembe district in northern Angola, where a witness spoke of regular conscription for coffee farms. In admitting these abuses (which they always said were punished), the Portuguese were half-admitting the substance of the complaints. On its visit, however, the commission found that the recruited workers on the Angola Agricultural Company's coffee farms had come voluntarily and benefited by good labour relations, while workers on the Zambezia Company's tea estates in Mozambique said that they had made free contracts. But employees of the Cassequel Agricultural Company in Angola seemed 'intimidated', and those of the Sena sugar estates said that chiefs could make people seek work.[48]

Allegations that the Diamond Company of Angola still found workers in the way described by Davidson a few years earlier were vehemently denied. But in Angola, where it visited the company's works, the commission heard that all the workers had originally been recruited, though only 9,000 out of 28,000 now were; that in July 1961 the Governor-General of Angola had said that the company should be told to start its own recruiting system and no longer depend on the authorities; and that the Governor of Lunda district had made an order on 28th October, 1961, to end certain actions by the authorities which 'may be regarded as compelling natives to work'. The company admitted that it had asked chiefs to provide workers, and that the recruiting agents still went through the chiefs, asking them to provide workers. A worker said that a chief could not compel people to go, but could work hard to persuade them to go to take up work for the company.[49]

The commission found no evidence of forced labour for the Benguela Railway Company, which it exonerated completely, or for the plantations. It found from workers and others that there was no forcible recruiting for the South African mines from Mozambique, and for work in the Portuguese territories it was told that all penal sanctions for breaches of work contracts had been abolished on 30th June, 1960 (such sanctions are still applied in South Africa).

The inquiry showed clearly that while the Ghana Government's case (which was drawn up rather carelessly at some points) was not wholly accurate, Portugal had in fact been practising labour coercion in roughly the way alleged, not only until the entry into force of the 1957 Convention but for months afterwards. It was clearly shown that officials and chiefs had helped recruit workers until then. The commission noted that Portugal had not ratified the ILO's Conventions on Recruitment of Indigenous Workers (1936) or on Contracts of Employment (Indigenous Workers) (1939), and said: 'It is precisely because of the part played in recruitment by public officers and chiefs that the employment of recruited labour in Portuguese Africa has been alleged to constitute, and has in the view of the commission in certain cases constituted, forced labour.'[50] However hard the commissioners tried to obtain freely expressed views from workers, they could not avoid the fact that the workers lived under a dictatorship and although what they said to the commission was not revealed, they could be punished quietly for talking to it. This fact makes the statements made about labour coercion to the commissioners all the more convincing, and probably such statements revealed only a small part of the reality.

The commission published a long list of enactments hastily made to bring the law and practice into conformity with the 1957 Convention: a Circular by the Angola Native Affairs Department on 31st August, 1961, calling on certain public authorities to end recruitment through the Administration; the abolition in Mozambique on 13th September, 1961, of the system allowing possible conscription for forced labour for those who could not prove that they had gainful employment; and others. The haste and convenient timing of these changes make one wonder whether the Portuguese were not simply concerned to create a good impression. The commission thought otherwise, and was convinced that the desire to change the situation was genuine. Was this naïve? People of those commissioners' long experience would not have been easily taken in, and the truth is probably that some Portuguese were determined on reform in various matters. The paternalistic movement for reform within a continued Portuguese Empire, already mentioned, was quite an important one and there had, in any case, always been officials who questioned the system of forced labour. The Angolan uprising provided a new argument for the proponents of reform. That the 'reformers' only wanted to ensure continued Portuguese rule was not something with which the ILO commission could concern itself.

The question is: how far did this desire to end forced labour and other abuses in colonial rule extend through the ranks of Portuguese officials and into those of businessmen and army officers? The commission knew full well that forced labour had always gone far beyond what the texts allowed and did, in fact, call for regular information about the application of the recent changes. The commission was convinced only of the genuine intentions of some Portuguese officials, and its report does not indicate at all that forced labour had wholly ceased in practice by 1961, never to return.

There are many reasons for doubting the fact that forced labour has ceased. War has been raging over considerable areas of Angola since 1961, Guinea–Bissau since 1963, and Mozambique since 1964. In war zones it would be hard for the new labour inspectors, appointed very recently, to enforce labour regulations, especially if they went against the wishes of the military commanders. In other areas, the labour inspectors seem to have been active and not ineffective, but can one imagine them penetrating the regroupment centres or *aldeamentos*, in which the people in war zones are resettled to isolate them from the guerrillas, and helping the people to make complaints against the local authorities who have martial-law powers over them? The war zones include some of the coffee-growing areas of Angola, and reports from there suggest that plantations are heavily guarded. This is, of course, to be expected in a military zone, but it raises doubts about the workers on the plantations. Are they likely to work there voluntarily in such conditions? The same conditions make their conscription easier. It has been alleged that forced labour on coffee farms still goes on in Angola. In 1971–2, in Holland, an 'Angola committee' publicised reports of labour conditions on coffee farms and urged a boycott of Angolan coffee. The action was reminiscent of Cadburys' boycott of São Tomé cocoa sixty years earlier. It had great success; imports of Angolan coffee, widely used for a drink indispensable to Dutchmen, were suspended in 1972, to the fury of the Portuguese. While some of the information gathered by the committee was many years old, and the United Nations' reference in 1970 to continued forced labour in Portuguese Africa, which it quoted, was vague, there are many reasons for accepting that there was much truth in the allegations.

A pro-Portuguese writer in *The Times* at the end of 1972 said that the formation of all-African co-operatives to farm coffee estates around Carmona had 'done much to eradicate the original reasons for the revolt in this area in 1961'.[51] Coming from a supporter of Lisbon, this is not saying very much. It suggests the possibility that plenty remains unchanged, and reports of very low wages for farm labourers increase one's suspicions. Who would work for very low wages behind barbed wire in a war zone if he had the choice? One wonders, also, about the Cabora Bassa scheme on the Zambezi in Mozambique. There is plenty of money in this ambitious hydro-electric dam scheme, which is intended to advance the economic and political interests of South Africa in particular, so that workers may be relatively well paid, but as the guerrillas are so close that roads to the dam site are often cut, it is possible to doubt that the workers have all been voluntary. The position of that project is now altered since the Portuguese coup of April 1974 has brought independence near for Mozambique.

Of course, workers may be compelled by factors other than legal or administrative force. In very poor areas, no actual compulsion may be needed to make people take even dangerous and low-paid jobs. The Cape Verdians who form much of the labour force on

São Tomé and Principe may often volunteer to leave their dry, infertile and poor islands for places where they can earn more money. The trend towards voluntary labour, noted by the ILO commission in Angola and Mozambique, was one to be expected; Angola, in particular, has had an increase in job opportunities in the past fifteen years, and normally people do not need to be made to seek paid jobs in modern Africa. Wage labour, once an imposition, may now be positively desired in Angola and Mozambique as much as anywhere else; however little they may like the Portuguese, the Africans must stay alive while the Portuguese are there, and there is no reason to doubt that they have the same employment preferences as other Africans. If that is so, mining companies, for example, probably do not use forced labour any more. However, the development of all aspects of Portuguese rule in Africa, including Portuguese labour policies, has been altered completely by the Lisbon coup d'état of 25 April 1974. when General António de Spínola and other army officers seized power. Besides ending 48 years of Fascist dictatorship under Carmona, Salazar and finally Caetano, the new military régime took immediate measures to end the wars in Portuguese Africa. These had become an extreme burden for Portugal and its people and General Spínola himself, who had commanded Portuguese forces in Guinea-Bissau had come to accept that a military effort to enforce continued colonial rule was futile. As President, Spínola apparently tried at first to see if a Portuguese-African Federation, which he had envisaged in a book published earlier, could be created. But later his régime, representative of many shades of opinion in Portugal, accepted independence for the African colonies.

As a result Guinea-Bissau, which had already proclaimed itself independent and been recognised by many countries, was formally conceded indepence by Portugal on 10 September 1974; about then negotiations about the transfer of power in Mozambique began; only in Angola, where the Portuguese were strongest and the African resistance weakest, did doubts remain for the time being about the future. Independence there, too, is probably only a matter of time, and the whole future of the 'White South' has certainly been altered now.

*Notes*

1. Among many writings on this subject, see *Industrialisation, Foreign Capital and Forced Labour in South Africa* by the UN Unit on Apartheid (United Nations, 1970); and Alex Hepple, *South Africa: Workers under Apartheid* (International Defence and Aid Fund, 1971).

2. Hepple, op. cit., p. 18.
3. Ibid., p. 19.
4. Ibid., p. 20.
5. Quoted in *Industrialisation, Foreign Capital and Forced Labour*, op. cit., Paragraph 46.
6. R. Ainslie, *Farm Labour in South Africa*, UN Unit on Apartheid (1971), p. 6.
7. Ibid.
8. *Anti-Slavery Reporter and Aborigines' Friend* (April 1939).
9. *Report of the* Ad Hoc *Committee on Forced Labour* (ILO, 1953), p. 375.
10. Ainslie, op. cit., p. 6.
11. *Report of the* Ad Hoc *Committee*, op. cit., p. 393.
12. Ainslie, op. cit., p. 7.
13. Ibid., p. 10.
14. Ibid.
15. Lewis Nkosi in *I Will Still be Moved*, ed. Marion Friedman, p. 65.
16. Ibid., pp. 65–7.
17. Ibid., p. 67.
18. *The Guardian* (4 October 1972).
19. *Bulletin* of the SRC Wages Commission (Natal University, Pietermaritzburg, undated).
20. *A Survey of Race Relations in South Africa, 1971* by the South African Institute of Race Relations, Johannesburg, p. 226.
21. *Bulletin* of the SRC Wages Commission (Natal University).
22. Ibid.
23. *Power, Privilege and Poverty*, Study Project on Christianity in Apartheid Society (Johannesburg 1972), pp. 92–3.
24. Ibid., pp. 93–5.
25. D. M. Abshire and M. A. Samuels (eds.), *Portuguese Africa: A Handbook*, p. 126.
26. Ibid., pp. 173–4.
27. E. Mondlane, *The Struggle for Mozambique*, pp. 91–2.
28. Ibid., pp. 40 ff.
29. Abshire and Samuels (eds.), p. 53.
30. F. Soremekun, 'Religion and Politics in Angola', in *Cahiers d'Études Africaines* (Paris, 1971), No. 43, p. 360.
31. Ibid., p. 363; *Anti-Slavery Reporter* (July 1939), p. 90.
32. William A. Cadbury in *Anti-Slavery Reporter* (October 1955), p. 43.
33. Soremekun, op. cit., p. 366.
34. *Anti-Slavery Reporter* (April 1952), p. 16.
35. ILO Commission *Report*, in ILO *Official Bulletin* Vol. XLV No. 2 (April 1962).
36. ILO Commission *Report*, pp. 215–17
37. Abshire and Samuels (eds.), p. 168.
38. Basil Davidson in *Anti-Slavery Reporter* (September 1954).
39. Ibid., p. 89.
40. Ibid., pp. 85 ff.
41. Ibid.
42. Mondlane, op. cit., pp. 83–5.
43. Text in ILO *Official Bulletin*, Vol. XL (1957), No. 1.
44. ILO Commission *Report*.
45. ILO Commission *Report*.

11. The Bilma Oasis, once on the route of caravans of salt and slaves.

12. At a Sahara watering point in northern Niger: are these African slaves from the south? Or children of such slaves?

13. South African contrasts: Modern white Johannesburg, oozing with money...

14. ...and the homes of some of those who produce the wealth.

46. ILO Commission *Report*, pp. 378–81.
47. ILO Commission *Report*, p. 389.
48. ILO Commission *Report*, pp. 463–97.
49. ILO Commission *Report*, pp. 519–28.
50. ILO Commission *Report*, p. 714.
51. Brig. Michael Calvert in *The Times* (27 December 1972).

*Chapter Ten*

# Forced Labour in Liberia

While they were in the dock for practising forced labour, and for much else, in their African possessions, the Portuguese made a counter-attack by alleging that the oldest of the modern independent states of black Africa, Liberia, practised forced labour. However poorly qualified the Portuguese were to make such criticisms, in this case, unfortunately, they were true.

Only ten years ago a quarter of all Liberia's wage labour force was forcibly recruited, and this situation may still prevail today. And the irony of such a situation in Liberia is too obvious to need emphasis. This republic on the West African coast was founded in 1847 by freed black ex-slaves from the USA, who had been settled there from 1822 by the American Colonisation Society.[1] The motto of the state is 'The Love of Liberty Brought Us Here'. Recently, it has been argued that the motto should be changed, for it relates only to the descendants of the black American settlers, who number no more than 15,000 out of a population of over 1 million, and suggests that Liberia is peculiarly their country, not the common country of all the inhabitants.

And that is, precisely, how Liberia has seemed to many of the indigenous Africans. The ruling caste is a small one, consisting of the descendants of the original settlers from America, of a few later settlers (including, as in Sierra Leone, people freed from slave-ships), and of indigenous Africans who married or were adopted into the ruling community. Although the amount of 'tribal' blood in that community is large, the term 'Americo-Liberian' is still used for the aristocracy which lives chiefly in the capital, Monrovia, and in other coastal towns like Buchanan and Greenville. It is a suitable term, for American culture is what distinguishes these people from the 'Aborigines' over whom they have wielded, since the foundation of their state, power comparable to that of the white settlers in Southern Africa.

For the Americo-Liberians, a version of American democracy has prevailed since 1847, with a Chief Executive, a Senate and House of Representatives, a Secretary of State and, usually, a First Lady. Until the long recent reign of President William V. S. Tubman (1944–71) the 'Tribesmen', as they are called, were excluded from this system and treated as subjects. Even in the 1960s they were still ruled as subjects, and liable to exactions, such as recruitment for forced labour, which the Americo-Liberians do not have to endure. For them, the politics of the Americo-Liberians in the nineteenth century, which involved the struggle for power between mulatto and black settlers, were of little importance. When the triumph of the Blacks ushered in generations of rule by the True Whig party, in power from 1878 until today, the settlers, under that rule, continued to treat the Tribesmen rather as contemporary British and French colonisers treated other interior peoples of Africa.

In fact, Liberia – although its bankruptcy and dependence on the outside world almost made it a victim of the Scramble for Africa – was also a partner in the Scramble, enforcing its hitherto incomplete control of the hinterland to prevent it from falling into British or French hands. Citizenship was granted to the Tribesmen by President Barclay in 1904, but they were conquered as surely as the Ashantis and Ibos were conquered. The process of conquest had begun much earlier, when the young American colony fought continual wars against the tribes of the interior, of which the most important were the Kpelle, Bassa, Kru, Grebo, Vai and Mandingo. The settlers had allies among the Tribesmen, but the only people from the hinterland who could attain equality with the Americo-Liberians and join them in the government of the country were those who were adopted into the ruling community, sometimes after being brought up by settler families on the coast (this practice, which has continued, sometimes led to scandalous exploitation of the children, as in Sierra Leone, where it was also common).[2]

Since the early twentieth century, when the government's control was established over the whole of Liberia, the 'Aborigines' have been in a colonial situation. They were ruled for decades through the chiefs and through settler officials, the administrative system being different from that of the coastal areas until 1964, when the interior like the coast was divided into counties.[3] Hut-tax, forced labour and requisitions of rice and other food were imposed on the interior peoples (only on them). With all this discrimination there went an attitude of superiority, shown by the use of the terms 'civilised' and 'uncivilised', which continued in spite of President Tubman's policy of 'unification' between the minority and the majority, and despite some extension of schools, hospitals and other amenities into interior regions once almost devoid of them.

Forced labour and other exactions were not ended by President Tubman's new policy towards the interior. A team of American investigators who went to Liberia in 1961-2 (at the invitation of its government and the US Agency for International Development, responsible for the USA's plentiful aid to Liberia) found that: 'With regard to taxation, land tenure, control over residence and movement, marriage and divorce, legal jurisdiction, access to educational and medical services, obligatory (no pay) labour services to local authorities, labour recruitment (forced labour with pay), and extra-legal exactions of money, rice and services, tribal Liberians in the hinterland are subject to a socio-legal system different from that of the Americo-Liberians.[4]

Another American writer, a few years later, said: 'Only during the Tubman Administration has an attempt been made to regularise and limit the use of compulsory labour.' This writer and others have noted Tubman's dismissals of several District Commissioners for robbery or brutality, his insistence on payment for at least some land seized from Tribesmen, his holding of Executive Council meetings in the interior, his recruitment of Tribesmen into the Administration, and the extension of the suffrage among them. But all this did not alter the structure and power of the True Whig party, which dominates the Americo-Liberians as they dominate the country. Since Tubman's death in July 1971 his successor, President William Tolbert, has announced further moves to give the Tribesmen real equality with the Americo-Liberians, and one hopes that this will bring to an end such forced labour as still exists.

The American investigators into Liberia's economic situation in 1961-2 found that labour recruitment was either paid, for foreign concessions and private Liberian farms; or unpaid, for public works projects, porterage and the private farms, often rubber farms, of government and local officials. There was also an extension of traditional communal unpaid labour, by which villagers had to work on the chiefs' and paramount chiefs' farms several times every year. Villagers who did this labour were almost certainly not included in the figure of about 20,000 Liberians recruited through their chiefs in 1960 for forced labour, mainly for local government projects and rubber plantations. This was a quarter of the labour force in the country (the wage labour force, that is to say; most men are subsistence farmers, as in other parts of Africa).

Chiefs were entrusted with the recruitment of forced labour, as they were in the French colonies. One chief was fined for failing to supply a porter during the rice harvest. Regular recruiting of forced labour during the harvest, when all hands are needed on the village farms, has been one of the most objectionable features of Liberian labour compulsion. Porterage was one of the deadliest forms of forced labour all over colonial Africa at one time, and it has remained a great burden for the 'aboriginal' Liberian, often forced to help carry a coastal official in his hammock up-country.

'Recruited' workers, according to the American report (entitled *Growth without Development*), were forced to work for two months, on pain of fines or sometimes worse, and were sometimes taken back for more periods of forced labour. Liberia had for decades flouted ILO Conventions daily, with the complicity of foreign private enterprise. Contrary to all Conventions against the use of forced labour by private employers, 'recruitment' was normal for the rubber farms, often owned by Americo-Liberians, and for the largest and most famous rubber plantation run by the Firestone Company of Akron, Ohio. Ever since Firestone signed, in 1925, three agreements with the Liberian Government, one of them giving the company a million-acre concession for exploitation of rubber on plantations, it had used forced labour recruited for it by the Administration. This helped it to become so rich in the first twenty years of its ninety-nine-year concession that the company came to dominate Liberia's economy and greatly influence its politics.

Firestone, whose main plantation is at Harbel, is less powerful than it was, but nevertheless still powerful. Ten years ago it still employed thousands of forced labourers. Forced labour on rubber plantations is not comparable to forcible gathering of wild rubber in the Congo Free State, but in Liberia it was, or is, particularly scandalous because Firestone could easily pay sufficient wages to attract voluntary labour. Here, however, the Liberian Government came in. Its members and officials could not afford, or did not wish, to raise the wages paid on their private rubber plantations, and so it prevented Firestone from raising its wages, which in the early 1960s were 35–40 cents per day (the US dollar is the currency of Liberia). While the name of Firestone has rightly become a byword for neo-colonialism, blame for forced labour in Liberia must be put where it belongs.[6]

Perhaps not even forced labour has caused so much hardship to 'uncivilised' Liberians as an extraordinary system of legalised robbery of rice and other crops. These, at the time of the American survey, were regularly taken without payment for officials (one of whom requisitioned a hundredweight of rice from each in one chiefdom), chiefs, soldiers and other agents of the Administration. The forced food levies have prevented Liberia, a rice-growing country, from becoming self-sufficient in that crop, and it has continued to import large amounts; naturally farmers will not grow more rice if it is going to be taken away from them. With all this considered, as well as the hut-tax and conscription into the Liberian Frontier Force, it seems that to call the Tribal Liberians' position 'colonial' was until very recently, and may still be, quite justified.

At the same time as the American investigators were in Liberia, gathering material for their report, the International Labour Organisation was also looking into forced labour in Liberia. That country had not ratified the 1957 Convention, but it had ratified the Convention of 1930 long ago; it had been in force in Liberia from 1st May, 1932, in theory. It was on the grounds of failing to abide by Convention No. 129 that the Portuguese brought their complaint against Liberia on 31st August, 1961. The fact that Portugal had not herself ratified that Convention until 1956, and that the substance of her accusations against Liberia lay in legislation up to that date, makes the righteous indignation of the Salazar régime seem fairly hollow, but it did not make the charges false, and any party to the 1930 Convention is allowed to bring a complaint about any other party's application or non-application of the Convention. The Liberian Government had not only failed to apply the Convention, but it had already, by 1961, aroused the ILO's suspicions by failing to send the required information about the application of it. So although the three-man commission appointed by the ILO found many of the detailed accusations brought by the Portuguese unconvincing, it decided to go ahead and look into the situation in Liberia, because there appeared to be serious 'discrepancies' between Liberia's laws and the 1930 Convention.

The commission, headed by a former judge of the International Court of Justice (Enrique Armand-Ugon of Uruguay), did not visit Liberia, but during 1962 heard witnesses and examined documents in Geneva. The three commissioners were interested in the state of the law in Liberia, and their attention was focused on the Liberian Code of Laws of 1956, and particularly on the Aborigines Law included there. An ILO Conference Committee and Committee of Experts had examined this and found that Sections 221 and 222 provided for forced labour in the hinterland for road-building and maintenance, with almost none of the safeguards laid down in the Convention, and Sections 240–8 allowed conscription for porterage, and not only for officials' needs. The commission noted this, as well as the most glaring of all breaches of the Convention, namely forced labour recruitment for private employers. The Liberian Government claimed that the Code of Laws was a collection of all past legislation not yet repealed, and that the inclusion of laws in it did not indicate that they were effectively in force; it added that those particular laws could not be in force, for they were contrary to the Constitution and to the law ratifying the Convention, and therefore automatically null and void. The commission was not impressed by this argument and found (Paragraph 416 of its report) that until the date of the filing of the complaint, Liberia's laws had been inconsistent with its obligations under the Convention.[7]

But, by the time of the report (signed on 4th February, 1963) several Acts had been passed to bring Liberian law into line with those obligations. One was passed on 24th May, 1961, and came into force (curiously enough) on 31st August, 1961. This Labour Practices Law regulated labour recruiting, and in particular made it an offence for chiefs, employers or recruiting agents to use force, the threat of force, misrepresentation or pressure in recruiting. But it did not make it an offence for officials (other than chiefs) to do so, and it allowed conscription for road-building and repair under conditions contrary to the Convention. It was found that this law did not repeal any of the measures about which the ILO was concerned. It was only during the investigation that these were repealed. The 1956 law allowing the conscription for road work just mentioned, and the laws on recruitment for porterage, were repealed by an Act of 25th January, 1962, and another of the 23rd May, 1962 (the former also repealed the legislation allowing forced cultivation). Between them, the two Acts had ended, by the time the report came out, most of the 'discrepancies' about which the commission would otherwise have complained in their report. Eventually, the commission criticised Liberia's earlier legislation, expressed satisfaction at the new measures, and pointed out a few remaining loop-holes, of which the most important, certainly, was the failure to make forcible recruitment an offence for officials other than chiefs.[8]

The American investigators did not mention either the ILO commission's report or the changes in the law, though their conclusions were dated 1966. This is a surprising and regrettable omission in a report which otherwise seems very thorough, but it is not one from which defenders of the Liberian record can take any comfort. On the contrary, the fact that the American investigators went to Liberia and reported on forced labour as they saw it, while the ILO commission stayed in Geneva and was interested in the text of the laws of the country, makes it hard to use the commission's findings as an answer to the fairly damning account given in the American report, *Growth without Development*. The authors of that work still felt it necessary to call for the end of 'recruitment' (as they called it, though they clearly meant forced labour and 'recruitment' does not usually mean that) even though the Liberian Government must surely have been most keen to let them know that it already had been abolished. In his book, *Liberia: The Evolution of Privilege*, J. Gus Liebenow also gives the impression that forced labour still goes on. The book is generally based on information going up to 1968, though on labour matters it draws on *Growth without Development* and, again, does not mention the ILO report. Until a detailed study of Liberian labour practices is published on the basis of thorough, on-the-spot investigations made after 1962, one can only say that it seems far from certain that the new measures hastily passed in that year have been put into effect.

Doubts are permissible because forced labour is only one facet of the general treatment of 'Tribesmen' as subject peoples rather than as full citizens. But this facet can change only slowly – though it undoubtedly is changing – because of the thirty-year period during which the 1930 ILO Convention was in force in theory but not in practice; and because a basis for forced labour exists in chiefs' traditional Administration (as in other parts of Africa but more so in Liberia because of the preservation of tribal society and of chiefs' power there). Government policy has been to keep the Africans of the hinterland under the control of the chiefs; the migration to the towns which has caused so much change in other parts of Africa has been discouraged in Liberia. *Growth without Development* claims that forced labour has helped to keep people tied to the villages and tradition, for it has prevented them from saving up enough money to be independent of the village community; abolition of forced labour would make the Africans of the hinterland more mobile and independent.[9] The chiefs have retained considerable local power, subject to the authority of Monrovia, and it would probably be difficult to prevent them from making extensive use of traditional communal labour, to which Liberians of the hinterland have been as accustomed as other Africans. The importance of chiefs in the recruiting of forced labour has been noted; abolishing it must go against the interests of the less scrupulous of them. Some must have complained loudly when in November 1962 Firestone stopped its programme of paying chiefs for recruited workers (this measure came just in time to be noted with approval by the ILO report (Paragraphs 445–6)).

As noted earlier, the Liberian owners of rubber farms also benefited from forced labour. It cannot have been easy, if it has been done, to persuade them to agree to its effective abolition. The Liberian ruling class, however, is sensitive to outside criticism. This was shown not only by the reaction to the ILO investigation, but by the much greater and more famous scandal of 1930, when Liberia was in the world's headlines for forcibly recruiting 'Aborigines' for work on the Spanish island of Fernando Po. As already recorded, conditions on the cocoa plantations of that island were very bad and many foreign workers died there. But it was the way in which they were recruited in Liberia that aroused protests, and in 1930 a League of Nations commission started to investigate the situation.

The commission, headed by a Scotsman (Dr Christie), found that Samuel Ross, appointed Postmaster-General in 1928, organised forcible recruitment in Monrovia and Montserrado Counties for Fernando Po; that a military expedition had been ordered in 1927 to capture 250 men for Ross; and that, in an incident in 1924 which became notorious as the 'Wedabo Beach Incident', Allen N. Yancy, Superintendent of Maryland County at that time but at the time of the inquiry Vice-President of Liberia, helped to recruit workers to go on a Spanish ship to Fernando Po, and threatened to burn a village if it did not find the 500 workers expected of it.[10] Besides exposing these facts, which had been well known for years in Liberia, the commission also condemned traditional slavery and the pawning system, which the government had decided, only a few years earlier, to allow to continue. The President, Charles D. B. King, and Congress promptly outlawed traditional slavery and pawning through an Act of 29th September, 1930. But the revelations about the shipments of people to Fernando Po forced him to resign soon afterwards, and Yancy naturally had to resign too. For years after this there was talk of annexation of Liberia, and it was perhaps resentment at the barrage of criticism by foreigners at a time when the country's independence was in jeopardy that led the Liberians to ignore the Forced Labour Convention for so long after ratifying it.

But the export of forced labourers to Fernando Po did end after 1930, and the Spanish recruiters turned to Eastern Nigeria for workers for the island. Foreign criticism is not ignored by Liberians. There is plenty of it, for the relatively few outsiders who write about Liberia note its poverty, corruption and class system, and they also note the great wealth it gets from iron-ore exports, which should enable Liberians to have a standard of living very high by African standards. This is the irony of the situation of the Liberian hinterland where the highest mountain, Mount Nimba, is almost solid iron-ore. Mining there by the LAMCO Joint Venture (a mainly Swedish concern) has made Liberia the third largest iron-ore exporter in the world; but the wealth obtained has been largely dissipated, and amenities for the interior people, such as proper health services, which the new wealth could easily pay for, lag behind those of other African countries. All this is seen by outsiders, and Liberia has a generally bad press. After some articles in the British press a few years ago, a Liberian diplomat in London was heard denouncing them: 'Diatribe after diatribe!'

Criticism in Africa is limited. President Sekou Touré's revolutionary régime in Guinea has always been on correct terms with the very different régime in neighbouring Liberia, both in Tubman's time and since his death. And although the Sierra Leone Creoles, comparable in many ways to the Americo-Liberians, have long since surrendered power over the country to the interior peoples who still have little of it in Liberia next door, the governments representing those peoples in Sierra Leone have been on generally good terms with Monrovia. But the contrast between the 'Tribal' Liberians' situation and that of other African peoples who had a similar subject status in the past is so obvious that it is hard to imagine the former being content with the real but limited 'Unification' policies of the Tubman Administration. Greatly outnumbered by 'Tribesmen' who are likely to be ever less content with any sort of discrimination, the ruling class has a long-term interest in peaceful reform, to which President Tolbert is more committed than his predecessor. If forced labour has not yet been effectively abolished as a part of this policy, one hopes its abolition will have priority, together with the abolition of forcible food levies and other *corvées* imposed for long on the hinterland peoples.

*Notes*

1. There are several books about Liberian history; one recent one is *Back to Africa* by Richard West.
2. J. Gus Liebenow, *Liberia: the Evolution of Privilege*, Chapters One and Two.
3. Ibid., p. 74.
4. Robert W. Clower, George Dalton, Michael Harwitz and A. A. Walters, *Growth Without Development*, p. 5.
5. Liebenow, op. cit., p. 55.
6. Clower *et al.*, op. cit., pp. 17–20, 89, 149–51, 157–9, 259–60, 273, 297–8, 335.
7. See full text of the report on the complaint by Portugal of forced labour in Liberia: ILO *Official Bulletin* (Geneva, April 1963), Vol. XLVI, No. 2.
8. ILO Commission *Report*, pp. 222, 417.
9. Clower *et al.*, op. cit., p. 335.
10. George W. Brown, *The Economic History of Liberia*, pp. 149 ff.

*Chapter Eleven*

# Modern Exploitation

Slavery and forced labour, as the last few chapters have shown, are not so different in practice as they seem on paper. In particular, when money changes hands for the recruitment of forced labour, something like slave-trading easily results. And such payment has been common; only in 1962 did Firestone stop paying chiefs for recruiting forced labour for its rubber plantations in Liberia.

But there is an important difference in Africa between residual slavery, a survival from pre-colonial times, and forced labour, which has been mainly the result of colonisation. Traditional slavery and servitude may have been reinforced or otherwise altered by colonial rule, but they did not originate as a result of colonisation. Forced labour, however, did (apart from the relatively small traditional forced labour for chiefs). Compulsory labour for building railways and roads, for working on plantations and in mines, for porterage, and for wild rubber collection and for forcible crop-growing was part of the 'development' of the colonies for the benefit of Europe.

This economic exploitation, of which forced labour was for long seen by Europeans as a necessary part, was concentrated in certain regions of the continent. Generally speaking, the inland regions, which did not have mines, saw less of this colonial economic activity. Often it was in these regions, treated as 'backwaters' or as labour reserves or otherwise 'neglected' by the colonial economic set-up, that traditional social hierarchies survived best. The Moors and Tuareg with their slaves, and the Hutus and Tutsis of Rwanda and Burundi, are examples; the territories of the former produced nothing of value to Europe in colonial times, and those of the latter nothing except a little coffee. It has been stressed often enough in this book that the absence in their home areas of the economic opportunities created by colonisation is one reason for people of traditionally subject status to remain in their situation.

But Africans in such situations do not always live in the poorer areas least touched by 'modernisation'. For example, the Osu caste

Africa and its Towns

system in Eastern Nigeria lasted very well, even while that region was becoming one of the most 'modernised' in Africa, with large-scale commercial activity at the famous Onitsha market and elsewhere, with millions converted to Christianity and given a Western-style education, with good communications, and, after the Second World War, with plenty of political activity.

But the economic centres of Africa, and the areas near them, differ in many ways from the more 'neglected' regions of the continent. On the one hand, there are areas, like Eastern Nigeria, Ghana's cocoa-farming districts, the Zambia–Zaire copperbelt or Buganda, where towns, cash crops such as cocoa and coffee, and often mines are concentrated, together with almost all amenities – schools, roads, hospitals. On the other hand, there are areas like Mauritania,

Mali, Rwanda or Malawi, where almost all the assets just mentioned are lacking and where there are few means of livelihood except small-scale farming and stockbreeding. The fact that some traditions widely regarded as 'backward' survive very well in these less endowed areas is not their major problem. They have an unfair share of all Africa's problems; they are, in general, places from which people migrate to the less poor areas.

Such regional inequalities, and their consequences, are found all over the world. Ireland is an outstanding example of a poor region providing generations of migrant labourers for a near-by industrially developed area. Southern Italy is another. The difficulties of such places in Europe are exceeded in comparable areas of Africa.

Labour migration has always provided an opportunity for all sorts of exploitation, and this will certainly be a serious danger for decades to come in Africa, for migration is now a part of life for millions of Africans. Hundreds of thousands of Malawians have migrated to work in South Africa, often travelling over a thousand miles. Workers from Mali, Upper Volta and Niger travel similar distances, by lorry or on foot, to Southern Ghana and the Ivory Coast. Probably millions of families all over Africa depend for a part of their income on regular money-orders from sons working far away. And migration is certain to increase, impelled by what has been called the 'revolution of rising expectations'. A modern peasant in Mali or Malawi migrates not because he is actually poorer there than his grandfather who stayed at home, but because he knows, as his grandfather did not, of opportunities for earning more money in other places, and because he and his family want things which their ancestors did not know they were missing: education, European goods, and a generally less hard and austere life. In places like Mali, improvement of life at home often necessitates leaving home for many years.

Migration is only one result of this increasing desire for a better life. Indeed, much of the African scene can be explained by the spread of this desire – for schooling, for improved health, for better food and water, for good clothes, and for gadgets such as transistor radios, bicycles and record players. It is inevitable that this desire should spread, because the Europeans have provided a standard for Africans' emulation, and nationalism has encouraged an urge towards progress. That this progress should be seen so commonly in terms of following the West is regretted by many Africans, but seems for the moment unavoidable. Also regrettable and unavoidable is the fact that 'rising expectations' can make all means of making money seem tolerable. The mercenary nature of modernised African society is blatant, and many aspects of it, such as the prevalence of official bribery ('dash'), are widely and properly regretted. But poor communities struggling to improve their position naturally tend to concentrate on the making of money and to forget other considerations more obvious to those who already have enough. 'If you're gonna be straight you're gonna be poor,' said Italian immigrants in the USA, who for that reason helped or admired Al Capone and other gangsters. Similarly, corrupt politicians and smart operators of many sorts may often be accepted, even admired, by the African public.

So modern changes in Africa make new sorts of exploitation possible in two ways. First, the desire for a better life can make people ready to submit to almost anything in the hope of having it, and they become still more vulnerable if they migrate. Second, exploiters of various sorts, including petty slave-dealers, can benefit to some extent from the generally broad-minded public attitude to money-making. Not that such means of making money are approved by all, even by the majority; the climate of opinion simply makes them easier. Many of the recent scandals involving slave-dealing and similar crimes can be explained best in this way.

*Petty slave-dealing*
Courts in many parts of Africa frequently handle cases of petty slave-dealing as an extension of the crime of kidnapping. Possibly many other cases never come to court, for law enforcement is inadequate in much of the continent and public opinion, which can make fear of lynching or other rough justice a greater deterrent to crime than the police and the courts, is not always aroused even by such vicious crimes as these. Many of them have occurred in Nigeria, as one would expect, since that country has a quarter of the population of black Africa.

In the late 1950s there was a horrid case in the region of Abakaliki in Eastern Nigeria (now in East Central State). Dozens of small girls were sold for £60 each to dealers who took them to a secret place which the police eventually discovered. Thirty of the children were found; some were sent to a Child Welfare Centre in Calabar because their parents could not be traced, others were returned to their families; but the parents were also prosecuted.[1] This was not the only occasion of parents selling their children or agreeing to their sale. Possibly the girls in this case were to be brought up as prostitutes, but in other parts of Africa children are bought for certain religious purposes. The Abakaliki case occurred in one of the less poor regions of Nigeria, though the area concerned is less developed than other parts of Iboland.

Eastern Nigeria was the scene of countless tragedies in the war a few years later, but although the war led to the fearful famine with which the memory of the ill-fated Biafra will always be linked, it is remarkable that such things as trafficking in children were not more commonly reported then (though they probably did occur).

A few years before the Abakaliki crime there was another, perhaps slightly less appalling crime, in the area of Abeokuta, an important Yoruba town in the Western Region (now the Western State). In 1954 some non-resident children were reported to be working on farms in the area, and it was revealed that one villager had enticed fifteen children, whom he had met at the motor-park in the region's metropolis of Ibadan, to work for farmers. The dealer said that the children's parents had agreed, but parents who came to reclaim a number of the children denied this. Later George Oul was sentenced to three years' hard labour for child-stealing.[2]

In Lagos, whose rapidly growing population and poverty and shortages provide the occasion for all sorts of crime, there was one criminal in the 1950s who had no less than *twenty-five* convictions for slave-dealing. This shows not only persistence in his crime, which suggests no lack of opportunities and rewards, but also an incredible leniency on the part of the authorities, still British in those days. He was Karimu Adisa, a carpenter of Yaba, a district of the Nigerian Federal capital. On the twenty-fifth occasion he was sentenced to ten years' hard labour for child-stealing.[3]

Other cases which have been reported from time to time in the Nigerian press (in 1963 sixty-nine cases of kidnapping were reported to the police, forty-nine involving slave-dealing)[4] have not necessarily involved children, the easiest victims. At Ikeja, in Lagos, two brothers were charged in 1961 with selling a man of twenty-five for £300; at Ibadan, in the same year, a herbalist named Aminu Amao was said to have sold a woman of thirty to a police officer for £250, telling her that she was being given to a friend in marriage so that she could have children by him.[5] It seems incredible that people in a major city could feel able to detain and sell adults without detection.

Such crimes are not confined to the cities, but these, of which Lagos and Ibadan are the largest in Nigeria, are a favourable setting for them, because of the greater anonymity and less restricted life there and the demoralising struggle for a better existence. In Nigeria Lagos is also favourable because it is near a frontier, the frontier of Dahomey, and several kidnappers have taken their victims across it, making success easier. In the autumn of 1972 public opinion in Lagos, which had failed to prevent many such kidnappings from taking place, became thoroughly aroused after it was reported that children were being stolen for sale, and some suspects were lynched. The Dahomean authorities sent a special armed corps of frontier police to stop kidnappers from crossing the border with children, and set up a special office to receive tip-offs.[6]

The public no doubt had a good deal to reveal in tip-offs in this case and in others. It is clear from all the cases of slave-dealing which come to court that the criminals enjoy a great deal of complicity; most dreadfully, sometimes, of the parents of their victims, and, obviously, of the people who buy the victims for farm labour or other purposes but probably also of many ordinary people. One probable reason, a tolerant attitude to methods of making money, has been mentioned already. Another is the feeling, expressed in many contexts in Africa, that one's family is mainly responsible for one's fate; if this is assumed then there seems little need to fuss about, say, kidnapping if the victim's family either takes no action or even gives its approval.

It also seems that people generally rely on each other, rather than on the authorities, to prevent crime. The fact that the children at the Ibadan motor-park could be so easily enticed away into slavery is revealing. In West Africa children roam everywhere with remarkable freedom, and seem often to have none of the fear of possible child-snatchers which is instilled into European children ('don't talk to strangers'). And yet such crimes do occur in Africa, as in Europe, and children who hang around places like motor-parks are obvious victims. This shows that in African communities, where people tend to know each other better than in European ones, it is assumed that neighbours and friends will see that no harm befalls the children. Usually this is either effective or unnecessary, but sometimes, no doubt, it fails.

There is another factor, too. Besides the few parents who actually sell their children, there are others who confide them to people for varying periods, sometimes for money. The former action is certainly not approved in Africa, where children are loved as much as anywhere else if not more so, though if parents do it the reaction may be: 'It's their business.' But the latter action, of putting one's children in someone else's care, is regarded as normal or even commendable for poor families. This must surely make kidnapping easier, and slave-dealing too.

Petty slave-dealing is no doubt helped by all these factors in all parts of Africa where it occurs. To take one or two examples which were brought to the notice of the Anti-Slavery Society, apart from those in Nigeria: in 1955 three Africans, a Ugandan and two

Rwandans, were convicted at Entebbe (Uganda) in two separate cases of slave-dealing, the Rwandans receiving nine-month sentences for offering two of their fellow-countrymen for sale.[7] Ten years later, thirty Kenyan boys were put to work for two years in forest saw-mills across the border in Tanzania. This case, which reached the British press, was not a clear-cut one; although it was suspected that the boys, who had worked without pay, had been forced to work at the saw-mills, and the two governments co-operated to have them freed, the Anti-Slavery Society said they seemed 'in excellent health and spirits on their return after two years of what can hardly have amounted to forced labour'.[8] It seems odd, however, that they should have agreed to do such work away from home for two years without pay, and that the employer should have thought of recruiting across the border; and it is probable that the young workers were in fact recruited on false promises of good wages, which their parents may have believed.

Even if it was a true case of slave-dealing, this case is not the worst case of petty dealing in human beings in modern Africa. Most horrible, certainly, are the cases of kidnapping and buying of people for religious rituals, including ritual killing. When slave-dealing in Nigeria was arousing concern not long before independence, this was said to be one of the reasons for it. Sometimes, no doubt, the 'ritual' purposes are not very different from the sex crimes for which kidnapping takes place in Europe. But stealing or buying of victims for genuine, though obviously illegal, religious purposes certainly occurs from time to time, even in areas where Christianity and Islam have been established for generations. Most adherents of the traditional religions in Africa will certainly have nothing to do with such practices, which may be the work of small sects comparable to the 'leopard-men' operating in Eastern Nigeria twenty years ago. The general hostility, by people of all religions, to such practices makes them clandestine and dangerous at times.

This seems to be the case, in some places and at some times, in Sierra Leone. Kidnapping of children for ritual crimes has occurred there, and slave-dealing in the interior, reported in 1964 by a member of the Anti-Slavery Society, seems to be partly for ritual purposes, including human sacrifice and cannibalism. That such things do occur from time to time has been shown by a number of court cases, including one in Freetown in 1964. The Anti-Slavery Society's informant said that people did not sell their own tribesmen, and that victims could be people away from their homes; here are opportunities for slave-dealers.[9]

While such occasional crimes should not be exaggerated, in Sierra

Leone Christian and semi-Victorian superficial culture do seem to coexist with well-preserved traditional practices, mostly innocuous but not all. This is suggested by a spectacular political scandal in 1973, when the Minister of Information, Mr Alimamy Khazali, was dismissed just before being put on trial for murder and trafficking in a human being. The evidence suggested that he had been involved in the sale of a man for a ritual killing.[10]

A most hideous case of this kind was reliably reported to me in 1972 in Douala, the largest city of Cameroon and a typical new African city with a rapidly growing, heterogeneous and often poor population. Its people, the indigenous Duala tribe and the immigrants who now greatly outnumber them, are mainly Christian, but some Dualas still practise a sort of witchcraft called *ekong*. It is believed that this enables a sorcerer to kill someone and then revive him as a sort of half-human being who is his slave for various ritual purposes. It is difficult to say what lies behind this belief, which is also found in the West Indies, where the sorcerer's half-human slave is called a 'zombie' (the belief may have come from the Cameroon area). What seems certain is that children are sold to sorcerers for them to do whatever the magic actually involves; and in this case, where the police happily intervened, some children were said to have tried to sell another child of their family for *ekong* treatment. One hesitates to believe such a blood-chilling story, but it appears to be true.

While the need for money, increased by the ostentatious example of those who already have it, is no doubt the basic reason for such unnatural crimes, it is obvious all the same that there is no alternative to treating them as crimes, by police methods. Slave-dealing of this sort cannot be treated with the caution with which domestic slavery among people like the Moors must be approached; it is, and should always be, treated as a police matter. The only problem here lies in the deficiencies of the police force in many parts of Africa; their methods, combining violence with inefficiency, are often defective, they are often distracted by political and 'security' matters, and they often lack sufficient funds and men.

*Poverty and pawning*
The practices described in this chapter are called 'modern exploitation', not because they happen only in modern conditions, but in order to distinguish them from slavery as a traditional institution and to suggest that modern change in Africa, notably the spreading desire for a better life for oneself and one's children, is an important reason for the prevalence of such crimes. The practice of 'pawning'

of human beings, usually regarded as one of the practices resembling slavery, can be regarded in the same way.

The placing of one person by another in the keeping of a third, in return for cash or credit, was common in pre-colonial Africa. In the Yoruba system of *iwofa*, one could put oneself or a relative, usually a child, temporarily in pawn, as security for a debt or to raise money for trading or other purposes.[11] Placing oneself or someone else in pawn for debt has been common in Africa, and although banned by colonial and successor governments may not have been suppressed. In 1923 in Liberia the President yielded to pressure from chiefs in the interior and officially approved the traditional pawning system, but seven years later in response to pressure from the League of Nations he had to have it abolished by Congress.[12]

On the tragic occasions when families facing starvation in times of famine have exchanged their children for money, it has probably been – at least in intention – pawning rather than sale, with the parents intending to reclaim the children when times were better. Probably such things have often happened in times of hardship and still do; it is a natural way of trying to save both oneself and one's children, and one cannot criticise it in cases where there are no effective relief operations. However, it is obviously appalling that the people with whom children are placed in pawn should exploit them and demand large payments for their 'redemption'.

Probably many real cases of pawning are reflected in a fictional case in *Efuru*, a novel by Flora Nwapa, the Eastern Nigerian author. Written in 1966, this novel is set in the old, unchanged Iboland, with scarcely any reference to Christianity and other modern changes which have so affected the Ibos. At one point in the story, a family ruined by a flood puts its daughter at the disposal of the heroine, Efuru, who looks after her and employs her as a servant, paying £10 to the family which, in this story, never reclaims its child. This is treated as being something quite normal.[13]

'Sham adoption' of children is regarded as similar to pawning; it is another way in which hard-pressed families can exchange their children for cash, probably with the hope of reclaiming them later. Fraud in the adoption of children is a fairly widespread crime. In 1969 in a reply to the UN Questionnaire on slavery, issued five years earlier, the Government of Ghana said that sham adoption was one practice related to slavery which went on in Ghana.[14] No doubt it goes on in other African countries too. But it is not so easy to say exactly when it happens, still less to decide what to do about it.

In the African context, it is probably very difficult to devise and apply effective rules on fostering and adoption, because people are so used to informal arrangements for caring for others' children on a temporary, semi-permanent or permanent basis. It is a common observation that the European-style 'nuclear family' of father, mother and children matters less in Africa, where nephews, cousins and other more distant relatives can belong to the family circle as much as the immediate offspring. People may look after relatives' children not only when these are orphaned, but if their parents either abandon them, or want to leave them behind when going abroad to study, or fall into such poverty that they cannot care for all their children. It seems strange to Europeans that families can part with their children like this, even if only for a few years, but it does not show lack of affection. Sometimes it is due to a desire to secure what is felt to be the best future for the children. In one case known to me, a Cameroonian woman placed her two daughters in the care of an unmarried and childless sister who lived in France, so that she could take them there and see to their education; she now does so, treating the children as her own for a few years, but not thinking for a moment in terms of actual adoption, fostering or anything formal. This probably happens quite often for the same purpose, to give children a good education.

When such casual arrangements are common, and are not necessarily harmful to the children, the enforcement of laws laying down stringent terms for adoption and fostering is probably impossible. It may even be undesirable, for the informal customs have their good side. In practice, tighter control would mean that forms had to be filled in and fees paid whenever a child was sent to country-cousins for the holidays, and one can imagine what efforts to enforce this would mean. It would probably help rather than hinder the unscrupulous 'foster-parents' who are the real danger: people who care little for the children and are interested only in the money. Normally parents will need no encouragement to avoid such operators, who are liable to be found in any country to exploit poor families, but in times of great hardship they may take the risk of agreeing to fostering or adoption by such people. But even prevention of this, though very desirable, is likely to be hard in practice without efforts to enforce regulations of the sort just mentioned. Heavy sentences for people convicted of really blatant exploitation in this way could help, but the only real solution lies in an effective system of relief for families in exceptional difficulty, and it is hard to see official efforts at present doing better in this respect than the 'extended family' already does.

## MODERN EXPLOITATION 213

*Sacrifices for schooling*
Some occasions for exploitation of children could be removed if blind faith in the value of Western-style education were to become less widespread. All over Africa, in English-speaking, French-speaking and other countries, there is a great demand for more schooling, generally for more schooling of the Western type now established in Africa, leading often to the GCE or the *baccalauréat*. This is part of a general desire for what is European, which many Africans deplore but few are prepared to turn against (except in two countries: Tanzania and Guinea). The fact that so many school-leavers are unemployed does not, it seems, make many doubt the value of their schooling; after all, in times of high unemployment every individual thinks he will be among the lucky ones with a job. At present, it is felt that a child deprived of schooling aimed at the exams now taken is suffering a very cruel deprivation, and that sacrifices to give a child such an education are admirable. And such sacrifices really are made. Parents may part with a child for years to secure an education for him. So they do in other parts of the world, of course, but it is not the same for African parents as for, say, a British diplomatic family that leaves its children in England, going to a boarding school there, while it has no fixed British address. The African family may hand over a son or daughter almost entirely to others who, because they have more money or live in a big town or in Europe, can provide for his or her schooling.

The Cameroonian example mentioned above is probably one of many. Not all others may work out so well. A recent white visitor to Ethiopia met peasants in that very poor country who asked him to take away their children, to look after and educate them. This may reveal a lack of judgement that could make exploitation of children possible, not only in Ethiopia (where there has, since then, been serious famine to worsen the normal poverty).

Such things have happened, and over quite a long period, in Sierra Leone and Liberia. As in other African countries, but from a much earlier date (in the nineteenth century), the African – or, in this case, African-descended – people of European education and culture have been emulated by other Africans. One result has been that, from the early years of the two settlements of Westernised ex-slave communities, Africans of the hinterland have sent children to be brought up, and often virtually adopted, by those communities. They have become members of the families of Sierra Leone Creoles or Americo-Liberians, but have also worked as unpaid servants for them in return for board and education. While the result has been the provision of many benefits for sons of penniless parents in the interior (the idea that Western education is the passport to a better life is not baseless, however exaggerated), some of the children concerned have been exploited cruelly.

Such occurrences in Freetown and Monrovia remind one of the exploitation of foreign *au pair* domestic servants in Great Britain. This does not often happen to African girls in Europe, but in 1973 there was a scandal over the ill-treatment of Ghanaian girls employed as servants in Lebanon. Their employment there was presumably an outcome of the decades-old presence of Lebanese businessmen in most West African countries, including Ghana. The military régime there outlawed the employment of Ghanaian girls under seventeen outside Ghana as servants, clerical workers, artisans or apprentices after the scandal, and many returned.[15]

*Long-distance traffic*
The Ghanaian girls exploited by employers in Lebanon were far from being the first Africans to suffer exploitation in Arab countries, as earlier chapters have shown. Tens of millions of Africans have been transported into slavery in those countries or in the New World. Mention has already been made[16] of a residual traffic in slaves to Arabia in recent times; and in other ways, too, Africans have sometimes been taken into slavery or similar conditions over long distances.

Kidnapped children from the fringes of the Sahara have probably been taken far into the desert to be made slaves. A recent report on the trafficking of kidnapped Senegalese might refer to this, though it seems to link this kidnapping with the slave-trade carried out under cover of the Mecca pilgrimage, and it is probably exaggerated.

In 1960 it was reported that slaves were taken up the Niger from Eastern Nigeria to what was then French West Africa. In the House of Lords debate on slavery on 14th July, 1960, Lord Faringdon said that he had heard a few years before of many boys being taken up the river to be sold to farmers in French territory; and Lord Lansdowne, Joint Parliamentary Under-Secretary of State at the Foreign Office, said that he had heard of this and, while feeling optimistic that it could be stopped, did not deny that it still went on.[17] Unfortunately, Lansdowne did not say more about what he knew, and he confused matters by saying he knew of the traffic in question from having lived in French *Equatorial* Africa. Even if he was referring to the traffic to Fernando Po, also mentioned by Faringdon (see below), this was puzzling. The Anti-Slavery Society did not unearth any more about what must have been quite elaborate slaving

MODERN EXPLOITATION 215

operations. The report was credible to some extent because the Tuareg and Kurteys[18], traditional slave-owners, live on the Niger not very far above the Niger-Nigeria border. But Tuareg have enslaved local people, the Bela, without much difficulty, and one wonders why they would have needed slaves who, having been taken upriver for 800 miles, must have been very expensive. It is more likely that such an elaborate, risky and expensive slaving operation was attempted once or twice and was not a regular occurrence.

Lord Faringdon also referred to Eastern Nigerian girls being sold to men on the Spanish island of Fernando Po, and this sounds more plausible, though they may not have been taken for sale against their will; they could have been prostitutes recruited by a white-slaver for the large numbers of Nigerian workers on the island. Such a transaction seems more possible in view of the known scandals surrounding the recruitment of the labourers themselves. The Spanish cocoa-planters on the island used Liberian workers in the first part of this century, until the scandal over the conditions of their shipment, very reminiscent of the old slave-trade, stopped it about 1930.[19] After that, the main source of labour for Fernando Po was nearby Eastern Nigeria. Scandals arose over this, too, but now they tended to relate to the treatment on the island of the migrant workers, which had always been bad.[20] The British and Spanish authorities made agreements to regulate the recruitment and treatment of the workers, but these may not have been fully applied. There were probably illegal shipments of labourers from Eastern Nigeria, Fernando Po being quite near Calabar across a stretch of water easily crossed by canoes, as there certainly were from the coast of British Cameroons, even nearer to the island. In 1931 canoe-men in the creeks around Tiko were recruiting workers, telling them at first they would work elsewhere in Southern Cameroons, but then revealing, when the boat was well out to sea, that they were in fact going to Fernando Po; there the workers on arrival were made to sign contracts for work which they were told would be domestic service or craft apprenticeship, but was in fact on a plantation.[21] Similar illegal recruiting was done on the coast of French Cameroon. But Ibos and other Eastern Nigerians formed the bulk of the labour force and of the whole population on Fernando Po, and still do. The labour conditions there have recently led to Nigerian protests; after a recruiting agreement signed with Equatorial Guinea, of which Fernando Po is now a part, expired early in 1973, Nigeria stopped recruitment and there were accusations of near-slavery treatment.

Most Nigerian and Cameroonian labourers on Fernando Po in

recent decades have probably gone there voluntarily, for work there offers opportunities that many have lacked at home; Eastern Nigeria now suffers more than ever from unemployment. In general, very few Africans today suffer from forcible transportation to work in distant places, compared with the millions who migrate voluntarily over great distances. Migration in Africa need not always involve great distances; a large number of the immigrants who swell the populations of Lagos and Ibadan are from other parts of Yorubaland, and migrant farm and city labourers in Sierra Leone move mainly within that country. But long-distance migration is important in many countries, including those from which many migrants go, such as Mali, Upper Volta and Malawi. The reasons for which they are willing to migrate were indicated earlier in this chapter; whether they are motivated by sheer necessity or simply by a desire for a less hand-to-mouth life, there is no reason to doubt that they are generally very willing, even eager, to go.

This does not mean that migrant labourers do not suffer from many sorts of exploitation. It would be interesting to see if there is any organisation behind the illegal immigration of Malawians and others to South Africa, which goes on at the same time as legal immigration. The regimentation of Africans there makes it quite probable that some organisation exists to help illegal immigrants escape official checks. Such checks may not be very thorough, for many illegal immigrant workers do seem to get in, and this may be tacitly tolerated, for it must help employers; workers whose situation is technically irregular are more helplessly dependent on employers than any others.

In independent Africa, where frontiers are often mere lines on a map and passports and visas are not taken seriously by everyone, a great number of migrant workers are probably in a technically irregular situation. This makes them vulnerable if a government suddenly decides, like Busia's Government did in Ghana in 1969, to enforce paper rules about passports and permits in a situation where such things have been generally ignored. On that occasion, hundreds of thousands of immigrants from Nigeria, Niger, Togo and other countries were brutally expelled. This is not the only time a new African state has decided, absurdly enough, to enforce immigration rules on European lines for a territory whose frontiers are in practice wide open, instead of welcoming this fact as a sign of 'African unity' already existing. But mass expulsions like Busia's are rare. Migrant labourers who come without papers may be vulnerable and easily exploitable for that reason, but they are inevitably so anyway, because they are badly in need of money and are often in no position to pick and choose. This is true of migrant workers everywhere; the very fact that they travel so far to work shows that they are willing to take any work offered.

In independent Africa, as in Southern Africa, a survey of who organises long-distance migration, and how, might show interesting results. But for independent Africa it might simply show that migrants move as individuals, paying their own way and travelling by lorry or 'bush taxi'. Where more elaborate, and more sinister, organisation is found is in migration to Europe from West Africa.

This migration is nearly always to France, which has millions of immigrant workers – particularly Italians, Portuguese, Spaniards and Algerians, but also West Africans, tens of thousands of them from the countries which are the nearest to France, and which are among the poorest of the black African countries. Many come from Senegal, where, it is said, village headmen select 'volunteers' and tell them to go to Europe, and find work so that they can send money back to the village. Others come from Mali (a particularly wretched country) and from Mauritania. In France it is these immigrants who do the dirtiest, least pleasant, most dangerous and lowest-paid jobs (nearly all the dustmen of Paris are black Africans).

In France the African workers suffer from very poor housing, in the *bidonvilles* (shanty towns) around Paris if they are lucky, and generally have a very hard life. Since their employers may know that they came illegally they can threaten to turn them over to the police if they protest against working conditions. But the workers accept all this because they can at least earn money which they could not have earned back at home, and send some to their families there.

What these workers endure after reaching France may be exceeded by what they suffer to get there. Comparisons with the slave-trade were made in 1972 after one major scandal over the 'importing' of labourers.

On 14th July of that year a lorry broke down on the road near Aix-les-Bains after crossing into France from Italy, and the French driver went to the police for help, saying he was carrying 'perishable goods'. The lorry was opened and the 'goods' emerged: fifty-nine Malians, 'half naked and dizzy with hunger and thirst', said one report.[22] Interpol began investigating and it was reported that an organised racket for the transporting of Africans to France in conditions like this was run by an Italian and two African brothers, one in Tunis and the other in Paris. The Italian police said that hundreds of Africans had been recruited in Mali, the Ivory Coast and Senegal by Frenchmen who promised them secure and well-paid jobs in France and persuaded them to agree to their first few months' wages being docked for the cost of the journey. They were then taken to France via Italy.[23]

The many other reports which have appeared in the French press confirm that illegal immigration of Africans is organised on a large scale. According to a report in *Le Monde*, the migrants are usually Senegalese and come mainly from one tribe in Senegal, the Soninke or Sarakolle. Men of that tribe assemble in Dakar where they contact the organisers of the migration, to whom they pay vast sums somehow accumulated, for travel expenses and false passports and other things. In the end, up to four times the normal airfare may have to be paid. Workers pay this because they want to go to France at any cost and are prevented from doing so in the normal way by the travel regulations of the French and Senegalese Governments. Sometimes they stow away in ships, but often they travel to Spain and then try to cross the frontier into France (Portuguese workers heading for France without *papiers* do the same). Terrible reports emerge of such migrants freezing to death in the Pyrenees or drowning in the Bidassoa River. Others have to live off charity in Spain after failing to reach France.

While the operators of these rackets are criminals who exploit the migrant workers mercilessly, the comparison between them and slave-traders must not be pressed too closely, for the modern migrants do leave voluntarily, though no doubt fooled by 'recruiters' (how, by the way, do these operate so freely in independent African states?). Investigators into the illegal immigration rackets find that the 'victims' are unwilling to help them; they want to work in France, and the racketeers do them a service by helping them to get there, even though it is for money, not out of charity. While one must be disgusted at the criminals involved in these operations, one must remember that they meet a need and that the people they exploit do not want them to be discouraged too much. The same is true of the operators of illegal immigrant ships across the English Channel, which transport Indians, Pakistanis and Bengalis above all. Whatever British xenophobes may think, the illegal immigrants do not travel across Asia and Europe, and pay vast sums for the crossing to England, just for fun. So long as the great gap between the rich and poor countries remains, sheer necessity will make many people want to leave those desperately poor countries, and other Third World countries, to earn money in Europe for themselves and their families. Until that gap is bridged, illegal immigration will go on, to England and France and other rich countries. If one has the interests of the people concerned really at heart one should not regret the illegal immigration, but only the fact that it is necessary.

*Notes*

1. *Anti-Slavery Reporter and Aborigines' Friend* (June 1960).
2. Ibid., referring to letters from Chief Secretary's Office, Lagos, on 10th January, 1955 and 25th June, 1956.
3. Ibid., referring to Reuter Report of 12th October, 1957.
4. *The Anti-Slavery Society: Its Task Today*, p. 18.
5. *Anti-Slavery Reporter* (March 1962).
6. *West Africa* (2nd October, 1972).
7. *Anti-Slavery Reporter* (January 1956).
8. *The Anti-Slavery Society: Its Task Today*, p. 19.
9. Ibid.
10. *West Africa* (22nd July, 1974).
11. R. Smith, *Kingdoms of the Yoruba*, pp. 118–19.
12. G. Brown, *The Economic History of Liberia*, pp. 156–7.
13. Flora Nwapa, *Efuru*.
14. Anti-Slavery Society Annual Report, 1969–70.
15. *West Africa* (26th February, 1973).
16. See Chapter Six.
17. Parliamentary Debates, House of Lords, Vol. 225, No. 104, 14th July 1960 (London, HMSO).
18. See Chapters Two and Three.
19. See Chapter Ten.
20. *Anti-Slavery Reporter* (for example April 1939 and March 1962).
21. Report on the Administration of the Cameroons under British Mandate for 1931, Paragraph 187.
22. *Africa* (Sept. 1972), quoting *The Guardian*.
23. Ibid.

*Chapter Twelve*

# Action on Slavery

The preceding chapters have tried to show two things. First, that yes, there is some slavery in Africa still. Second, that so many sorts of slavery and related practices exist (even more if forced labour is included) that merely to state that there is slavery is not very helpful. Investigation into all these practices reveals a complex picture.

First, since slavery as a social class, caste or group, established as part of society, has existed for centuries over much of Africa, it is not surprising that traces of the old sort of slavery survive. They are particularly noticeable in the Sahara Desert and on its fringes, among peoples such as the Moors and Tuareg. There, slavery has lasted because it could not be drastically abolished without upsetting the whole nomadic way of life. Traces are also found in Ethiopia, where slavery was abolished only thirty years ago, in black Africa (especially the Sahelian regions of West Africa), and in Northern Nigeria and Northern Cameroon (in the latter area unambiguous chattel slavery on a small but not negligible scale lasted until a few years ago).

But, in all these cases, it is difficult to say when a slave is really a slave. It is apparently very rare for a slave to be still bought and sold. Generally, it is hard to tell how far those who seem to be slaves, but who under the laws of the countries concerned cannot be so, really are slaves. Many seem to be no different from their ancestors whose slave status was beyond doubt. If they are officially called 'servants' or 'retainers', are they not in fact really slaves? Often, indeed, they may be called slaves, but, in Northern Nigeria for example, so can people of the traditionally slave-community who are not in anything like a servile relationship to anyone.

A black Tuareg who looks after the nomads' herds and helps in domestic work in the tents, who calls himself a 'slave' and is so called by everyone else, and who is treated as property even if treated well and never sold, may seem to be unambiguously a slave. But a visiting official will be told that there are no slaves, only servants. Perhaps the master is prepared, however unwilling, to make this true by letting his slaves/ex-slaves/freedmen/servants leave if they want to. But often they would never want to take an opportunity to leave. What are they, then? Slaves, servants, or what?

Generally, something like true slavery seems to exist more obviously in regions nearer to the Sahara, though not necessarily in it. About Mauritania there can be no serious doubt. The ultimate sign that slaves are treated as property is that they cannot marry and have their own family lives; their children belong to their masters. They are truly slaves, and they may number hundreds of thousands.

Slaves have had a less degraded, less obviously servile status among the Tuareg and the Fulani. But buying and selling of slaves has occurred among the former in recent times, even if only rarely. There are other signs that Tuareg slaves, including many of the 'Bela' people on the Niger, are regarded on all sides as real slaves. So were many sections of the nomadic and settled Fulani, and many people in the states founded by the Fulanis in pre-colonial times. Slavery of an unambiguous sort lasted in Ethiopia until Emperor Haile Selassie abolished it (probably almost wholly successfully but perhaps not yet completely since Ethiopia, like the West African savanna, has recently suffered serious drought and famine, and this may well have led to some slave-dealing.)

In Ethiopia, however, and in the Sahelian states further west, old tribal slavery is, or was, supplemented by something else. For centuries large-scale raiding for slaves for the state itself and for individuals in the state took place, making slavery more of an organised economic venture than a traditional social distinction. The difference is hard to define, but clearly the large-scale enslavement typified by raids on the Pagans of what is now Northern Nigeria in the nineteenth century, and on the peoples of South-Western Ethiopia in the twentieth, was different from the old slave-castes of the Tuareg, the 'cattle Fulani' and the Gurage. It is mainly of historical interest; but where slavery was important in well-established old states whose social system is still partly intact, traces of it remain strong. The Kanuri of Bornu are an outstanding example of this. But social attitudes like those of slave societies can easily survive long after individuals have ceased being anyone's slaves. This is common in Hausaland.

In such cases it is always hard to tell just when slavery ended. It would be easy to find great numbers of white Americans whose attitudes to Negroes differ not at all from those of their slave-owning ancestors; but there is no slavery unless it happens that some

Negroes are still considered as belonging to *individual* white men. A whole community may be treated worse than slaves by others, but only individuals can actually be slaves, and they are so only if they are slaves of a particular owner, not of 'society' or the upper classes. The essence of slavery is a personal relationship, which may not be at all close but is clear; the large Southern plantation-owner might not have known any of his slaves personally, but they were his slaves, not the state's, nor a company's. Governments, of course, have had slaves, but then governments can be treated legally as human individuals for ownership of any sorts of property. Generally, it is safe to say that in Africa people are slaves only if they are *someone's* slaves.

This is why the oppressive labour system in South Africa is not real slavery except, perhaps, on some farms, where 'labour relations' may indeed approach the master–slave relationship. And there, serfdom may be a better term than slavery. As mentioned in the introduction, serfdom can be taken to mean a state of *personal* subordination which is not that of a piece of property but is still different from the subordination of a worker to an employer by its personal nature. Traditional serfdom has survived better than traditional slavery, as in the position of the Pygmies and of the Hutus in Burundi and (until recently) in Rwanda. In the same category one may place subordinate castes like the Osu among the Ibos. There, however, people are collectively treated as inferiors and socially relegated, rather than being subject as individuals to other individuals, or as tribes to other tribes. The distinction between serfs and a subject caste is not always clear, however.

These subtle varieties of slavery and related practices may include, at times, virtual enslavement of women due to institutions such as the bride-price. But it seems that on the whole the bride-price does not involve anything like slavery, and the abuses of it which come nearer to that can be classified, perhaps, with individual slavery activities.

Those activities form a separate category altogether. Kidnapping of individuals by other individuals for use or sale as slaves is to be distinguished (it is not always) from old-established slavery. It is the distinction between isolated actions, always criminal, to take people from freedom into captivity, and general customs in which some people are relegated to slave status. Cases of individual capturing and sale of slaves occur in many parts of Africa; probably many more occur than come to court. They need not have any connection with traditional slavery. Where this survives such crimes are made easier, as in Mauritania. But they also occur in parts of Nigeria where traditional slavery is no longer significant. The frequency of such crimes in Africa may be due as much to the difficulties of law enforcement and the general poverty of the people as to traditional slavery. Comparable crimes occur in other parts of the world. The same observations apply to trafficking in human beings under the guise of child adoption, something believed to go on in Great Britain to some extent.

Lastly, there are labour practices which come near to the verge of slavery and slave-dealing. Forced labour is one (is, not was). So is the exploitation of migrant workers, with, however, the important difference that the victims of this are, if naïve, at least willing rather than forced.

If the answer to the question, 'Is there still slavery in Africa?' is so complicated, the answer to the other question, 'What can be done about the slavery that still goes on?' is even more so.

One must first remember that much has changed and that, as Rattray said in connection with Ashanti slavery, any ideas based on the old Atlantic slave-trade days should be dismissed. There can be no suggestion of reviving Great Britain's nineteenth-century role in worldwide action against slavery and the slave-trade. The days have long since passed when British warships could sail to Calabar to force the ruler to stop selling slaves, or when British diplomatic pressure could force the Bey of Tunis to abolish slavery itself. Such actions, though prompted by genuine concern to end slavery, were also a part of Great Britain's determination to act as the world's policeman, a role which she cannot play now. The British Government certainly encouraged Haile Selassie's abolition of slavery, but even before 1935 she could do little more than merely encourage.

Anyway, conditions in Africa are such as to make stronger action inappropriate in most cases, even if it were possible. Whatever action is possible is the responsibility of African states first and foremost. Doubts have been expressed about their capacity for it, but there is little justification for such doubts now. In fact, some pre-colonial African states began to take action against slavery as well as the slave-trade. Tunis had abolished both by 1846, when the French who ruled near-by Algeria were still permitting slavery. Madagascar's warrior Queen Ranavalona had begun to abolish slavery before the French conquest in 1895–6. These rulers certainly acted under outside pressure, but so did those of France and, notably, Portugal in the abolition of slavery. And in modern African states, which are only in a very few cases pre-colonial states revived, the situation has been totally transformed. Economic changes, of dubious benefit in many cases, have certainly changed the old societies greatly, and the colonial authorities have done much to end slavery. Pressure on the new rulers of Africa is more likely to be for stronger action against the remnants of traditional slavery than the reverse.

Those who believe with the old faith in 'Western civilisation' and fear an abandonment of this by independent Africa are very wide of the mark. Whatever failures and crimes the ruling classes in modern Africa can be accused of, no one can accuse them of the 'crime' of lack of respect for Western values and culture. It is their worship of these things that is more plausibly regarded by many as a crime. The educated classes in Africa are typically ashamed of their traditions rather than too proud of them, too keen to reproduce in their countries all the trappings of European life rather than too careless of them. In ex-French Africa, notably, official publications and many official actions, and the efforts of many other educated people, seem aimed to make their countries seem as un-African, as much like France (and like Neuilly, not Corsica) as possible. The 'English-speaking' élites may have fewer complexes about the African tradition and African character of their countries, but sensitivities are generally in the same direction (also, to some extent, in Ethiopia).

Because of this, no one need fear any show of complacency towards slavery, serfdom and other such practices in any African country. Such things are essentially 'backward', and therefore more likely to be regarded with shame than with defensive pride. 'Feudal' is a deadly word of abuse in Africa, and much of the old social order in Ethiopia is so described, notably the power of the landlords, the grossly unjust distribution of land, and the burdens imposed on the peasants. When a system is not only oppressive but 'backward', it will never be accepted complacently in Africa. In Ethiopia, where Haile Selassie's régime has done much in the way of reform, the most vocal and strongest opposition to it, which triumphed in 1974, comes from men thinking it did not do enough. In Mauritania, an outpost of traditional slavery, radical opposition leaders accuse the Ould Daddah régime of reforming the country's 'backward' character too slowly, rather than too fast. Such critics will always remain important in such countries, especially in times of political crisis. Landlords and nobles may sometimes seem all-powerful but, like the colonial régimes, they dig their own graves by encouraging people to go to school. The number of young educated Ethiopians, typically hostile to the imperial régime and sometimes so hostile as to say that the Italians cannot have been so bad after all, is increasing yearly. So is the number of Mauritanians humiliated by their country's situation and hostile to its régime.

Any non-Africans shocked by certain traditional institutions in Africa can be sure that the people of that country know about them and that many will be even more shocked. One result of the shame felt about 'backward' traditions is, of course, that their existence is merely denied. But another can be the taking of some action, and hasty and ill-planned action is just as likely as inaction. In a continent where a foreigner's remarks about slum houses and beggars could bring bulldozers into the slums and police vans to the beggars' pavements in a short time, mention made of something regarded as even more shameful, such as slavery, is unlikely to be disregarded. It is even necessary to be cautious, for fear of encouraging the wrong sort of action. Germaine Tillion has done well to warn anti-slavery campaigners that African governments are so opposed to slavery that they need to be advised to go easily rather than to do more. Do such campaigners want to encourage armed expeditions with tanks and aircraft against a few nomads who have a few aged slaves?

Revival of anti-slavery 'gunboat diplomacy', if it were possible, would be an unacceptable idea for another reason, too: that the situations in question do not allow the possibility of quick and easy reform. Among the Moors, whose nomadic life has always depended on the work of slaves and *haratin* in the camps and at the oasis farms, a social revolution like that which happened in French Guinea just before independence is unlikely to happen and cannot easily be provoked from outside. The present régime in Mauritania may be very closely tied with the nomadic aristocracy, with the President's own relations having what outsiders consider to be 'slaves' though the law does not, but any régime would have to take them into account. And the reasons for going slowly in altering the nomads' social system are not only political. A radical reform, if it were possible, could well lead to a decline in nomadic life and large-scale emigration to the towns. This might be an inevitable and acceptable result, but it should surely be foreseen and provided for. What work is available in Mauritania and neighbouring countries for people who abandon farming and stockbreeding? Very little at present. Even for slaves the alternative to the present way of life may not always be worth considering.

The same applies to the Tuareg and their 'Bela' slaves or serfs in Mali and Niger. Slavery among them is in any case milder than among the Moors, for slaves are allowed to have their own family life, and slavery has been on the decline for decades. Complete emancipation must be slowed down by the economic considerations just mentioned, perhaps even more pressing in Mali and Niger than in Mauritania. In normal times the only practical alternative to farming and herding for most people of those countries, the nomads included, is migration to the local cities or to Ghana, the Ivory Coast or Nigeria – or, sometimes, to France. And the past few years have been even worse than normal because of the drought disaster. Not until the middle of 1973 did the world at large know of the plight of the Sahelian countries of West Africa, where millions of cattle were killed by the drought and the vanishing of pasture, and thousands of human beings died of hunger and thirst before ill-prepared emergency aid began to flow in. As a result of the rainless years, the advance of the desert, the failure of crops and the threat of famine, vast numbers of nomads and others converged on the Niger River or moved further south into Ghana or Nigeria. Nomadic life was totally disrupted (with herdsmen driven to sell pregnant cows for slaughter) and it will take many years for it to be re-established; until then destitute nomads can do little more than hang around cities like Niamey in makeshift settlements and wait for relief, or go to work as night-watchmen in Nigeria as so many Tuareg have done. All this happened on the same scale in Upper Volta and in the two countries where slavery still continues or had continued until recently – Chad and Mauritania.

In such a crisis as this the nomads' traditional slavery is scarcely the matter requiring the most attention. For slaves as for other members of the Moorish and Tuareg communities, and for the more-or-less serf class among the Toubou and the 'cattle Fulani', staying alive is the main problem; to some extent it always is, of course, but now it is an unusually serious problem, and it will be for years to come.

To some degree, indeed, the nomadic way of life may now have been totally wrecked because of the destruction of both beasts and pasture, and in such circumstances many former slaves and serfs may now be 'free'. It would be difficult to contend that this was worth the price. Even if the 'sedentarisation' of all nomads were a beneficial result of the disaster, it would be a small benefit compared with the suffering caused to millions, whatever happened to the slaves. In fact, it is a very dubious assumption – based partly, one suspects, on city-bred Africans' shame about the camel-borne nomads who seem so picturesque to Europeans – that all nomads must eventually lead settled lives. Where is the land for them to farm all the year round and graze their flocks without transhumance? And where will meat come from if nomads cannot adapt to less nomadic stockbreeding? Anyway, is their way of life really such that they need to be forced, if necessary, to give it up? The problems of health and education, still serious for millions of settled Africans, can be tackled for nomads without making them give up their nomadic way of life.

If the problem of slavery in the Sahara and Sahel has not been 'solved' in the most terrible way by the famine, no doubt it could merit attention when some recovery has set in. Even then, however, the region concerned will be among the world's poorest, and the impossibility of considering slavery in that region outside its context of general poverty has already been stressed often enough. As Germaine Tillion suggested in the pamphlet *The Problem of Slavery*, slavery in Saharan and sub-Saharan Africa can best be dealt with in an international effort at economic development. What the development should involve can only be decided after careful study; it could include, where appropriate, new wells, efforts to improve pasture, possible restocking of herds (to be tried with caution), improvement of marketing of cattle and meat, aid for preservation of meat and milk (have refrigerated lorries been considered?), introduction of improved cattle feed and means to store and preserve it, improved veterinary attention, and efforts to improve yields on farms and make large food reserves both easier and less necessary. Irrigation, by canals from the rivers or tanks like those of India and Somalia, is a high priority whose neglect since independence is scandalous. Improved medical services for nomads, difficult but not impossible, are also needed.

The success of a large-scale programme like this would depend on close co-operation among states who cannot manage on their own and on financial and technical assistance from outside sources. Such co-operation might achieve what states like Mali and Chad, small (in population, not area) and bankrupt, could not achieve. Outside aid could come from many countries, including Great Britain, which has so much experience to draw on in the matters of irrigation and drought prevention in, notably, the Indian sub-continent. In fact, France would probably provide most of the aid. But the important fact is not who sends it, but that the needs of the local people should be carefully noted and should be the only criterion for the aid-givers. Outside aid, though indispensable for such a poor region, should not lead the local government to relax their own efforts; these could include, not new taxation of the destitute local population, but efforts to create real regional co-operation.

If a programme of real economic improvements for Mauritania, Mali and the other Sahelian and semi-Saharan countries were successful, the context in which slavery continues would be altered. An assured and sufficient diet for all farmers and herders all the year round, rain or no rain, would make life less precarious and people less dependent on a social system which involves degrading treatment for many. Slaves who were ill-treated could escape more easily if they were less likely to starve by doing so, and in escaping they would prevent ill-treatment of others, and slavery would in the end die out except for 'servants' who chose to remain with their masters although free to leave. If farming at the oases or by the Niger could yield more, slave or serf farmers could, while still helping to feed the nomads, have more for themselves and so improve their general situation. And proper economic development could, of course, make life easier for those who chose to stay in the nomads' tents, or at the nomads' oasis and riverside farms, as 'slaves' or 'servants' or whatever they would be called; they could be more truly free to go or stay if life were made better for them in either case.

This is the way to approach the sitation in West Africa where slavery continues. It is not an easy or quick approach, for even the minimal aim of an assured constant diet for all is a major one for this vast and poor region, now more destitute than ever.

Although its abolition can only be aided by cautious means, slavery in these regions has many features which make it desirable that it should end. There is no cause to be sentimental about nomadic life, still less about the lot of slaves in that life. They are condemned from birth to carry out the most menial work, the hardest and the most boring. They have little or no choice in the matter and cannot easily escape. Among the Moors they cannot marry, cannot have their own home life or family life; they can only breed children who belong to their master. The Moors' slavery is peculiarly degrading from that point of view.

If it continues to die out as it has been doing among the Tuareg and may have done altogether among the Toubou, this type of slavery may turn into a sort of caste system, or perhaps something like the position of the ex-slave elements among the Wodaabe Fulani and the Wolofs, or the Kamadja among the Toubou. Such people, it appears, are still considered inferior socially, but they no longer belong to others to the extent that slaves do. The difference between a slave and a socially despised serf who does all the hard work may seem slight to outsiders, but it is real enough. Centuries of inequality breed attitudes, among both dominators and dominated, which tend to last a long time; the USA is a good example, especially the South. So if Moorish and Tuareg slavery disappears, it will probably give way, and quite possibly is giving way on a large scale, to something which looks to the visitor rather like slavery; the ex-slaves may do much of the work slaves have always done, people may still call them slaves, social relations may be very much as they were. But, if nobody can any longer claim rights over anyone by calling him 'my slave', if the serfs or whatever they are can run their own lives and rear their own families to some extent, then the change is important.

The distinguishing feature of slavery, as already mentioned, is that one *individual* is felt to belong to another. In a sense, peoples can never be enslaved, only individuals. A Southern American employer who regards his Negro employees just as his ancestors regarded his slaves, and so far as possible treats them similarly, is still essentially different from a slave-owner if he cannot treat any individual black employee as belonging to him. It is this change which must be hoped for in places like Mauritania in the foreseeable future, not true freedom and equality with a decent standard of living added; that is an aim which at present seems very remote.

Such a change, however important, leaves people looking very much as before in their relations with each other. Emirs' slaves in Northern Nigeria, freed by law, often remained in their rulers' courts in the offices they held before; for decades after the abolition of slavery Ibos knew who was of slave descent and who was not, and treated people accordingly. The same thing has happened in other parts of Africa. This fact must raise doubts for some about the reality of emancipation. Probably many of the doubts about Ethiopia's reforms are due to this. All reports on that country suggest that anyone looking for radical change will be disappointed; ex-slaves are more likely to live as serfs, servants and clients of those who are still masters in many real senses, than to turn overnight, or even over a generation, into the equals of their former masters. But, if individuals are no longer owned and controlled as slaves were, the essential change, as far as ending slavery is concerned, has been made. It is simply difficult to tell, at times, when it happens. All this is true of the Hausa states and Bornu, and the other old states which, like Ethiopia, had slavery on a large and well-organised scale in pre-colonial times.

It is important not to be deceived by appearances which often outlast the reality behind them. When the Asantehene in Ghana holds official ceremonies, he is accompanied by traditional office-holders called 'executioners'; but they do not execute anybody. So an Emir may have retainers who look very like slaves to some, but the appearance may be wholly deceptive; nowadays, probably, it always is.

The traces of slavery which outlast the institution can be quite noticeable. In Northern Nigeria distinctive facial marks are still seen, and in Bornu, at least sometimes, shaved heads distinguish the ex-slave caste. But, as already mentioned, the late Prime Minister of

Nigeria, Sir Abubakar Tafawa Balewa, had the facial marks which traditionally indicate slave status, and may have been called *bawa* by old Hausas, but did not in fact belong to anybody.

However essentially different it may be from slavery, serfdom cannot be regarded in most cases as permanently satisfactory. It is another sort of inequality in which some individuals are under others' control from birth, and are relegated to a position in which they must usually stay. In general, Africa does not have the scandals of large-scale landlords, *latifundia* owners, and exploiters of *peons* and sharecroppers which are so prevalent in Asia and Latin America. But Ethiopia has its big landlords, including princes and the Coptic Church, whose power over the peasants often amounts to the crudest and most thorough exploitation – through exaction of 75 per cent shares in crops, for example. This is one part of Africa comparable to certain areas of Asia and Latin America. The need for reform is admitted in Ethiopia, but land reform was opposed strongly until the 1974 revolution. This is not a case where outside intervention of any sort is useful except to keep up the pressure; unless, of course, the Ethiopian Government requested aid for compensation of land-owners, which could certainly be given.

Other sorts of serfdom are rather different, but the example of Rwanda and Burundi shows that they are not taken lightly by the people most concerned. In one of those small mountain states in the heart of Africa the traditional serf group, the majority, has rebelled successfully; in the other, it has tried to do the same, without success; in both blood has flowed on a vast scale. After the 1972–3 bloodbath, Burundi is probably beyond any possibility of peaceful reform, and it is hard for an outsider to suggest how the traditional clientage system, involving for example tending by the client of the lord's cattle, could be reformed, and what difference such reforms would make.

A better standard of living could probably remove some of the causes of inequality in such countries as Rwanda and Burundi, as well as in those where slavery has not yet died out. The frustration which led to the revolution in Rwanda was doubtless due to realisation of that country's great poverty as well as to other causes. In Guinea, the other African country which has had a full-scale social revolution (like Rwanda's it was on the eve of independence), it is similarly reasonable to suppose that economic discontent caused the rising by the less favoured classes, which included actual slaves. Such occurrences, incidentally, are further proof that beliefs in Africans' unlimited resignation to poverty and inequality are absurd. Proof of this has appeared in the Portuguese colonies and to some extent in South Africa. As for independent Africa, however, it is not easy to think of large regions of organised inequality and oppression quite like pre-revolution Guinea and Rwanda, apart from the Saharan and Sahelian slave areas, the rather special case of Ethiopia, and, of course, Burundi. Tribal serfdom and clientage on a smaller scale, such as exists in some Somali clans or in relations between Pygmies and their Bantu neighbours, is not really similar.

Traditional tribal institutions such as these should not concern the outside world too much. African educated opinion, as already indicated, is likely to be over aware of such 'primitive' situations rather than the reverse. A tribal set-up well adapted to local conditions will probably not change if the conditions remain the same, but it probably will if the conditions change, and such change is likely to be encouraged by African governments. A situation like the division of labour between Pygmies and their farming neighbours is not so cruel, nor so likely to be accepted with complacency, that it merits serious attention by the world at large. It seems to work reasonably well and to fit in with local conditions of life for what is, in addition, a fairly small number of people.

In a case where a group is still regarded as socially inferior, even though it is not effectively kept in a menial position, probably only preaching and education, backed up by law as far as possible, can bring about changes. What has been said recently in Great Britain about the impossibility of changing human relations by Acts of Parliament is generally true, whether or not it justifies the total absence of such measures as the Race Relations Acts. An outstanding African example is that of the Osu community in Nigeria's East-Central State. Discrimination against members of this former religious slave-caste is banned by law, but cannot be stopped while the general prejudice goes on, as it does. This is a matter for the Churches and others who have unofficial influence over opinions. Similarly, Islamic thinkers and preachers are the people best able to encourage acceptance as equals of former slaves in many countries, and those of the Coptic Church (if such a thing can be imagined in that hidebound Church) in Ethiopia. It would be a mistake to leave all such things to governments which try to keep too much in their hands already.

Does all this mean that outside opinion and outside activity is useless or irrelevant? No, the outside world, or rather that small part of it which cares seriously about African affairs, has a right to concern itself with matters like slavery, and it can encourage elements in the African states in favour of reform and discourage those against reform. Journalists, writers and demonstrators can all do this usefully from time to time. But the most effective practitioner of 'foreign interference' is the well-informed outsider, who may often be a churchman or a university man.

The abolition of slavery in the Lamidate of Rei Bouba in Northern Cameroon seems to be a clear example of success by a campaigner of this sort, who in that case was a missionary, Halfdan Endresen. He made repeated protests against the continued enslavement of about 50,000 people by a traditional ruler who really did regard them as his own property; his protests were reasonable but firm, and based on his close knowledge of the area. He was allowed to revisit Cameroon several times, and made two visits to investigate progress in the emancipation of slaves which had begun about 1969 and almost certainly owed much to his efforts.

The Cameroon Government showed a reasonable attitude towards Endresen's protests, though it can be as sensitive as any other African government to outside criticism. This was no doubt because Endresen spoke from close knowledge and a sincere desire to see a wrong righted, without any political or racial bias. Many critics of African governments lack these qualifications, and resentment of them is often understandable. But resentment is regrettable because African and other governments have no right to expect all outsiders, or all outsiders except small groups of experts, to avoid commenting on their countries or confine their comments to praise. The world is smaller than it was, concern about countries other than one's own is spreading in an almost wholly welcome way, and African states are no more perfect and no more entitled to expect people to call them perfect than any others. If Etniopian landlords oppress serfs, or South African farmers oppress convict labourers, there is no reason why a Swiss or a Japanese should not mention the fact.

As for the question of whether such comment is useful, there is no generally valid answer; the the belief that foreign criticism 'only makes thing worse' is almost certainly wrong in many cases, though not all. Sometimes, when a government is exceptionally sensitive and really is capable of punishing its own people for what foreigners say, silence may be the right answer; but just as often silence will encourage those who believe in oppressive policies and discourage those who urge restraint because of 'world opinion'. Criticism which really is likely to do harm rather than good is criticism based either on serious ignorance or on a commitment to the total overthrow of a régime. Such a commitment may be justified, but if one has it one cannot expect attention to be paid to detailed criticisms – a reference to forced labour in Ethiopia's gold-mines, for example, is unlikely to achieve much if it comes in the middle of an article denouncing Haile Selassie as a feudalist stooge of the USA and calling for revolution against him.

With these provisos, I believe that unofficial opinion in Great Britain and other countries does at least no harm, and can do some good, in efforts at reform of oppressive systems in other parts of the world, Africa included. Where slavery is concerned, such opinion has been centralised and spread by the Anti-Slavery Society above all. On the basis of its 150 years of existence, the Society believes that Western opinion is definitely important, even though slavery and related practices must now be the responsibility of African governments first and foremost.

The Anti-Slavery Society also believes, however, that governmental action is very important, and particularly inter-governmental action. It is possible to doubt that international efforts would justify the faith the Society puts in them. But if there is any official pressure for the abolition of slavery and related practices it should certainly be international rather than national, for neither Great Britain nor any other country can now fill the former British role, and it would be inappropriate for them to try. And there are a few ways in which an international body could help.

Such a body could, first of all, verify progress made in states which have only recently abolished slavery or where there is reason to believe that it still goes on. The states which signed the Anti-Slavery Convention of 1926 and the Supplementary Convention of 1956 admitted in doing so that slavery was a matter of international concern and not simply a domestic matter. They were therefore bound to answer the worldwide questionnaire on slavery sent out by Dr Mohammed Awad, the Egyptian educationist appointed in 1964 as the UNs Special Rapporteur on Slavery. The creation of this post, which Dr Awad held until his death in 1972, was the result of a resolution of the UN Economic and Social Council in July 1963, and showed the extent of concern about continued slavery. Not many governments in countries where slavery is reported to continue sent very helpful replies to the Awad questionnaire, and the replies published in 1965 and 1971 are not a great source of knowledge on the subject.* Nor had Awad any power to take serious action on the replies. The Anti-Slavery Society has therefore suggested, over the years, that a permanent UN agency concerned with slavery should be set up, which could, as a start, ask for reports from the governments which are parties to the Convention and Supplementary Convention.

* See Report by UN Special Rapporteur on Slavery, UN Document E/4168 of 1966.

From the point of view of information this would be useful; and it could lead to some action (but here, the question of what action could be possible, and where, arises again). Reminders about failures in the programme of emancipation of slaves would no doubt be more useful if they came from a United Nations' agency rather than a private body (even of the Anti-Slavery Society's eminence), but only if they also took into account all the problems involved in the abolition of slavery. Otherwise, all that happened would be exchanges of letters in which the Government of Mauritania (for example) denied that there was any slavery in its country while the agency called for measures impossible to implement. The agency might, however, be able to offer detailed help and even technical assistance to governments which were trying to end slavery effectively, helping them solve resultant problems.

It is doubtful whether slave-trading occurs on a scale sufficient to merit such an agency's attention. As Chapter Six showed, residual trafficking in slaves to Arabia may possibly go on from time to time but, since the abolition of slavery began in Arabia, there seems to be no possibility of large-scale slave-traffic. If any slave-trading does occur it is a police matter; foreign ships' masters and other foreigners hearing of such cases can always help local police deal with them, and special international police efforts are called for only if the traffic is of serious proportions. If slaves are still shipped across the Red Sea, more co-operation in police efforts to stop this may be needed; and in the Sahara, kidnapping seems to be frequent enough to require more efforts in common by the states among whom the Sahara is (on the map) divided.

The sad fate of the girl Aouicha, abducted into slavery across the unmarked Algeria–Mauritania frontier, suggests that more efforts are needed to stop kidnapping and to reclaim the victims. But one major reason for hastening the effective abolition of slavery in that area is that, while it goes on, kidnapping is made easier. Because of the number of nomadic camps (some of which may be ready to buy slaves) and the difficulty of policing such a large and empty area, it would be very difficult to stop such kidnappings; but it would be worthwhile to try more serious efforts through co-operation among the countries concerned.

In the same area, in a desert section of Mali near the frontiers of Mauritania and Algeria, the Taoudeni salt-mines might repay a little investigation, to find out if slaves still work there and, if so, under what conditions. Tuareg slaves have traditionally dug for salt during nomadic migrations, but not for very long each year; if salt at Taoudeni is dug by passing nomads for limited periods, even if the work is in fact done by slaves, this may be no worse than the general condition of the slaves. But if the mines are permanently exploited in a systematic way by slave-labour it is a different matter. In that case, co-operation in police action would be called for. But it is not certain exactly how the salt-mines at Taoudeni are exploited now, when they are probably much less important than they used to be.

Kidnapping in Africa is generally due to poverty and to the inadequacy of police forces. International aid cannot do much for either problem, except by helping in economic development whose eventual success, if any, in raising the standard of life could have other incidental benefits. International aid, as already mentioned, is also sure to be needed for serious economic development, with priority to food supplies, in the Sahara and Sahel. But if such development aided by other countries may help end slavery and related practices one day, proclaiming this as the main aim, or even as one of the aims, would not be helpful. It would cause resentment which would be partly justified, for slavery cannot really be seen as the number one problem facing the people of Mauritania and Mali, and any foreign suggestion that the people must be properly fed in order to end slavery would be justly criticised.

The chief purpose of international action, and particularly of a new international agency, would be to gather information about slavery. The mere existence of an office under the United Nations doing this would be a constant reminder to governments about the slavery question. It could also recommend action in certain cases but the question is not one that can be dealt with by an international body as the drug traffic and white slavery are.

There are some practices 'related to slavery' which cannot really be dealt with even as police matters, for they depend partly on economic need and partly on social attitudes, and repressive action, particularly the sort of repressive action common in all too many African states, can do little about those things. They include abuses in the adoption of children, which lead to their virtual enslavement at the worst, and debt bondage. They also include the activities of money-lenders and the sort of bondage in which they can hold people. Rural money-lenders, often charging exorbitant interest rates, are certainly common in Africa; in the towns people are often heavily in debt to such people, but there, unlike in the country, it may be less easy to exert pressure on a debtor. In rural areas it is quite possible that farmers have to work for creditors in a form of quasi-debt-slavery. If so, there is no easy way of preventing such things as long as people are likely to need more ready cash than the meagre amounts the average farmer has. Laws fixing interest rates can be evaded very easily, and it may be equally easy to conceal the fact that a man is working for another in order to work off a private debt.

Shortages of all sorts are the basic reason for the difficulty of preventing abuses by money-lenders and certain offences involving the custody of children, such as 'sham adoption'. To some extent, social attitudes are also involved; it may not always be sheer physical need which leads to rash borrowing or to 'pawning' of children and other people – it may arise from the desire for Western goods, such as Western-style clothes, or education, which are desirable but not absolutely essential. This is probably rare, but if it occurs a decline in the widespread blind faith in all that is European could make it occur less often.

Public opinion is involved in questions affecting the status of women. The trend is probably against betrothal of children, which makes some crudely financial marriage-transactions possible, and in favour of marriage by consent between adults. This does not prevent the 'bride-price' from being deformed into an institution very different from what it was traditionally; it may often be accurate to talk of 'buying' a wife. But the serious abuse comes in such dealings involving a wife who is an unwilling partner, and if, as probably happens most often, a girl objects neither to her prospective husband nor to the bride-price he must pay for her, it is not like slave-purchase. Such questions concern Churches, schools, individuals and public opinion, rather than local or foreign governments. The important thing seems to be to continue the trend against betrothal of small children, though it must be remembered how normal this has been throughout the world for thousands of years and how difficult it must be to persuade people of what Europeans had not fully accepted only a few generations ago.

While various ways of attempting to dispose of the lives and work of others which are often regarded as near to slavery can only be dealt with by public opinion in the countries concerned, any exploitation in the field of labour comes within the province of the International Labour Organisation.

The ILO can deal with any question of forced labour, low wages, bad working conditions, irregular recruitment or other labour abuses which arise in its member states, which include most countries of the world. Its members admit by their membership that their labour policies are not their concern alone, and the ILO can investigate, expose and criticise them. It cannot do more, certainly, and it cannot prevent a country from leaving the Organisation in response to criticism, as South Africa did in 1966. This,

ACTION ON SLAVERY 237

however, did not absolve South Africa of all international obligations in labour matters, some of which arise from membership of the United Nations, whose Economic and Social Council has dealt with South African labour questions since 1966. It is, in fact, difficult for a country to avoid determined efforts to expose its labour policies; even press and other unofficial exposures can lead to an ILO investigation, which is always painstaking.

The limits of the ILO's powers have been shown not only by South Africa's withdrawal but also by the doubts expressed over the abolition of forced labour in Portuguese Africa and in Liberia after the ILO investigations in 1961-3. In both cases, legislation was hastily passed to end forced labour while the investigation was going on. This was in itself a welcome consequence of the inquiries, but it suggests a desire to avoid criticism rather than actually to end forced labour. Nobody can doubt that many reforms have been made in both the Portuguese colonies and Liberia, but it is possible to doubt that forced labour has really ended in either (though the Portuguese revolution must have altered things greatly), and if it has not, there is not much the ILO can really do.

What can anyone else do? This question is often asked about South Africa, Rhodesia and the Portuguese colonies. One possible answer is that certain aspects of the ultra-colonialist régimes in the southern part of Africa could be considered separately, and protest or boycott action could be applied to that particular abuse. This approach might be particularly suitable in labour questions. In South Africa the facts about exploitation of farm labourers, sometimes involving virtual forced labour, are well known, and foreign opponents of Apartheid could find out what exported fruit is grown at the farms involved and then organise a boycott campaign directly relating to the farmers growing that fruit. Something of the sort has already been done by the Dutch Angola Committee, which has succeeded in cutting imports of Angolan coffee in protest (at least partly) at the exploitation of labourers on the coffee farms.

The trade boycott is a weapon most effective when aimed at the conditions in which the boycotted articles are produced, not the political régime as a whole. A classic case is that of the California Grapes Boycott in the USA, whose aim was to improve the conditions of the workers in the vineyards, an aim which was at least partly achieved. A general boycott of South African goods will not bring down the Apartheid régime – probably nobody thinks it will, as long as the boycott campaign remains a private one and governments are not interested; but a campaign to boycott South African apples could lead to improved conditions for workers on apple farms.

It is almost certainly wrong to suggest that small improvements in a general situation of oppression are not worth seeking because they reduce the desire for real change. The white South African view, that the more the 'Bantu' are given the more they will want, is nearer the mark. The strikes in 1973 and the wage rises which had to be conceded afterwards alarmed Pretoria, and a forced increase in wages and improvement in conditions for farm labourers would cause similar alarm. As de Tocqueville said, the most dangerous moment for a bad government comes when it begins to improve itself; then what people have tolerated because there seemed no hope of anything better comes to appear intolerable because improvement seems possible. Hence those who generally oppose the Apartheid and white Rhodesian régimes need have no hesitation in opposing particular crimes of those régimes, such as forced labour. Not only would the ending of this be of immediate and practical benefit for the victims; it would whet the appetite for more reform.

All this is stated on the assumption that the South African and Rhodesian Governments are unlikely to carry out any serious reforms in the situation of their black subjects themselves, except under pressure. Both governments seem so determined to hold on to power over the African population that anything which might weaken that hold is certain to be opposed. Even concessions in the application of labour coercion could well be seen as a fatal surrender, because this coercion is so essential to the South African system. The situation in Angola and Mozambique is, of course, modified by the wars there. In response to the successes of the guerrillas, the Portuguese were before the 1974 coup already making concessions of a sort which the South Africans, not under similar pressure, would not dream of. Now the Portuguese revolution and its sequel may make forced labour and all aspects of Portuguese rule in Africa a thing of the past very soon. When that happens the white South African and Rhodesian régimes will be under stronger pressure than ever.

Any sort of exploitation involved in migration of workers is a matter for the ILO, which has dealt with such situations for many decades. It could examine migration from other countries to South Africa, and migration within independent Africa. While the poverty of certain regions which forces workers to migrate is obviously to be regretted in every way, the migration itself can hardly be regretted while its causes remain, and exploitation suffered by migrant labourers is commonly accepted by them as worth enduring for the money that can be eventually earned. This does not absolve authorities from seeing that migrant labourers are treated in accordance with ILO recommendations, but while such labourers want decent treatment they do not want closer control over their migration, so that the causes of migration are what need to be most closely examined. This is true of the much-publicised illegal immigration into France, whose organisers are certainly criminal types but only take advantage of Africans' desperate need to migrate to find work; that desperate need is the only really intolerable side of the matter.

The ILO has not finished dealing with forced labour in Africa yet. Several independent states have introduced forced labour in ways which would have made some colonial governments blush. In 1973 the bureau of the ruling party in Zaire decided that every citizen of the country was automatically a member of the party and therefore liable to do party duties, such as forced labour once a week, on Saturdays. While all the population was to do this forced labour, those who could not prove that they were employed were obliged to seek work (this was like one former enactment in Mozambique); and urban unemployed and prisoners were to be put to work on farms near the capital, Kinshasa. As most Africans are self-employed, a large portion of the population may have become liable to direction to jobs on South African lines, depending on the whims of the police and the militants of President Mobutu's party; while instead of serious efforts to find who was employed or unemployed in towns there have probably been indiscriminate round-ups of people for work on the farms around Kinshasa. It is not clear what force the decisions of the party have, but it does seem that this programme of forced labour is being applied at least in part. And this, irony of ironies, is in the country which was once Leopold II's Congo Free State and the scene of forced labour and exploitation on a massive scale.

Other countries have tried to stop the 'drift to the towns' by adopting definitions of 'vagrancy' worthy of 17th-century Europe and trying to deport *en masse* people so defined from the towns to the rural areas; in 1972 Cameroon introduced such a measure. And all ex-French and ex-Belgian countries try to enforce on their people a system of police controls and regimentation with *papiers* or *pièces* (identity cards, etc.), with the apparent aim of directing everyone's life and movements in a way quite impracticable on a large scale in those countries but opening possibilities for many sorts of petty oppression.

Most African states are one-party states which talk much of 'mobilising' the people. Apart from Zaire, where it is undisguised, one wonders how much coercion this 'mobilisation' of the people, ostensibly for the work of development, usually involves. Are the youth corps which do farm training apart from acting as political strong-arm boys composed entirely of volunteers? President Nyerere of Tanzania, rightly praised for his egalitarian ideals and his belief in starting development from the poorest level in the rural areas (rather than concentrating on a few grandiose projects), seems to have convinced so many people with his talk of *Ujamaa*, 'self-reliance', that the special '*Ujamaa* villages' set up in this spirit have escaped close attention from the outside world. In fact it is said that some of these villages, which are co-operatives with a large degree of collective ownership, are established by coercion.

But at least this is possibly not Nyerere's wish, and at least he made any coercion of the Tanzanian people which goes on serve some clear purpose. In many other African states the argument (tenable in theory) that individual freedom must be suppressed for the sake of development seems little more than an excuse for extending the irresponsible power of the ruling régime. It is far from being proved that suppression of freedom and improvement of living standards commonly go together in Africa. The suppression of freedom is very general, and includes forced labour in some places. In fact, individual liberty is at a low premium in much of independent Africa. Forced labour does not occur only in Ethiopia (where its importance is discussed in Chapter Ten); if it did, it could be written off as one more relic of the past in two antiquarian states. That it has been introduced in Zaire, a new state now engaged in rapid expansion and beloved of foreign business, a state full of modern ideals to some extent, shows that labour coercion is a thing of the present and future. So are other sorts of oppression in all too many states.

It is a pity to end on such a pessimistic note, but unfortunately a book on modern slavery in Africa must end by pointing out that, while slavery of the old sort is no longer very important, other sorts of oppression and coercion whose justification in the name of economic development is hard to accept, are common there. Such slavery as remains will probably be gone before very long, and Africans and others would be ill-advised to regard it as a serious scandal, threat or danger. More serious is the danger of ever-increasing power for governments, perhaps unaccompanied by benefits for the people. Most Africans are glad to be free of slavery because freedom is appreciated in Africa as much as anywhere else. They will not, in the long run, accept attempts at state regimentation that burden them just as slavery usually did. Slavery is largely a thing of the past; for Africa the future is more important, and for the future the question is whether independence will be followed by a fuller and a freer life for the African people.

*Index*

# Index

Aden, 135–6, 137, 139, 147
Algeria, 31, 36, 43, 44, 47, 48, 52–3, 234
Amharas, 150–1, 153
Angola, 124–5, 178, 179, 181–2, 183–9, 190, 191, 237–8
Anti-Slavery Society, 48, 74, 126, 139, 141, 142, 144, 147, 148, 156, 181, 185, 233–4
Apartheid, 167–77
Arabia, 24, 128, 129–31, Ch. 6, 152, 234
Arabs and Arabic-speaking peoples, 20, 21–2, 42, 101, 128–32, Ch. 6
Ashanti, 84–5, 117

Bakongo, 95, 114
Bamileke, 94–5
Belgium, 97, 162–3, 164
Bemba, 105
Benin, 90, 112, 114
Berbers, 20, 21–2, 23
Bornu, 46, 50, 56–7, 60, 62, 64–6, 67, 126
Botswana, 161
Brazil, 110–11, 119–20, 122–3, 124, 134
Bride-price, 103–7, 222
Britain, 48, 56, 57, 58–68, 73, 100, 102–3, 118, 119, 120–6, 126–8, 129–31, 134–7, 140, 143, 144, 147, 148, 160, 161, 162, 164, 165, 179, 218, 223, 227, 233
Burundi, 97–9, 230–1

Cameroon(s), 62–4, 70–6, 93–5, 105, 117, 162, 163–4, 212, 215, 232, 239
Cape Verde Islands, 115, 180, 182, 191

Central African Republic, 80, 163, 165
Chaamba, 52–3
Chad, 50–2, 64, 163, 226
Chagga, 102
Congo (ex-Belgian), v. Zaire
Congo (ex-French), 163, 165
Congo Free State, 96, 125, 130, 131, 159–60, 162, 239
Cuba, 122, 124, 125, 134

Dahomey, 112, 117, 124, 125–6, 207–8
Denmark, 119, 122
Douala and Duala people, 93–4, 123, 125, 210

Efiks, 91, 112, 115, 123
Egypt, 127
Equatorial Africa, French, 142, 160, 162, 163
Eritrea, 145, 151, 155
Ethiopia, 139, 141, 142, 148, Ch. 7, 221, 224, 229–30, 231, 240

Fanti, 112
Fernando Po, 123, 180, 200, 215
Firestone, 196, 199, 203
Forced Labour, 157, Ch. 8, Ch. 9, Ch. 10, 236–40
de Foucauld, Charles, 36, 42
France, 26, 29, 31, 36, 41, 42–4, 48, 52, 64, 68–9, 70, 72–4, 77–9, 80, 94, 119, 122–3, 125, 126, 128–9, 142, 160, 161–5, 217–18, 224, 227, 239
Fulani, 25, 56, 62, 68, 69–79

Gabon, 107

## 244 INDEX

Gallas, 150-1, 153
Germany, 71-2, 94, 102, 125, 131, 163-4
Ghana, 84-5, 183, 184, 211, 214, 216, 229
Guinea, 76-9, 165, 201, 213, 225, 230
Guinea-Bissau, 115, 125, 178, 183-4, 189
Gurage, 100, 156, 221

Haile Selassi, 150, 153-4, 221, 223, 224
Haiti, 111, 120
Haratin, 24, 28, 38-9, 50-1, 53, 225
Hausa people and Hausaland, 46, 48, 56-62, 65-8
Hutu, 97-9, 203, 222

Ibibios, 91, 104
Ibos, 90-3, 117-18, 119, 123, 124, 211, 222
ILO, 159, 164, 184-91, 196, 197-9, 236-7, 238-9
India, 128, 131, 152
Italy, 49-50, 153-4, 217
Ivory Coast, 205, 217

Kamba, 106, 131-2
Kano, 34, 36, 46, 56, 60, 62
Kanuri, 50, 56, 64-6, 117, 221
Kenya, 106, 131-2, 153, 160, 161, 164, 165, 209
Kufra, 46, 50, 141
Kurtey, 79-80

Lagos, 124, 125, 207
League of Nations, 63-4, 72-3, 102, 153, 159, 200, 211
Liberia, 124-5, 180, Ch. 10, 203, 211, 213-14, 237, 240
Libya, 42, 48-50
Livingstone, David, 121, 129-30
Lozi, 103, 106
Luba, 95-6
Lugard, Lord, 58-9, 60, 62, 73, 156
Lunda, 96

Madagascar, 129, 131, 223
Malawi, 130, 131, 176-7, 205, 216
Mali, 24, 25, 34-46, 79, 141-2, 205, 216, 217-18, 225-6, 234

Mauritania, Ch. 1, 38, 48, 111-12, 204, 217, 221, 224-5, 226, 229, 234
Mauritius, 111, 128, 131
Mende, 86-7
Moors, Ch. 1, 38-9, 40, 48, 203, 225, 230
Morocco, 21, 47, 48, 141
Moshi, 57, 68
Mozambique 129, 130-1, 178, 180-1, 183, 184-9, 190, 191, 238
Muscat and Oman, 128-9, 136-7, 138, 139, 145, 148

Netherlands, 119, 122, 190
Ngoni, 102-3
Niger, 34-46, 79-80, 142, 205, 225-6
Nigeria, 46, 56-68, 69, 87-93, 105-6, 121, 124, 141, 143-4, 145-6, 163, 164, 165, 180, 200, 203-4, 206-8, 209, 211, 214-16, 221, 226, 229-30, 231
Nupe, 57, 117
Nyamwezi, 102

Osu, 90-3, 203-4, 222, 231

Persian Gulf States, 136, 140, 147-8
Portugal, 111-12, 114, 115, 119, 122, 124-5, 128, 129, 130, 164, 177-91, 197, 237-8
Pygmies, 96-7, 222, 231

Red Sea, 139-40, 152, 234
Reguibats, 23, 26, 48
Rei Bouba, 73-5
Réunion, 111, 128, 129
Rhodesia, 237-8
Rwanda, 97-8, 203, 209, 230-1

Sahara Desert, Ch. 1, Ch. 2, 221, 234-5
Sahel, Ch. 1, several refs; Ch. 2, several refs.; Ch. 3; 221, 226-8, 235
Sao Tome, 114, 115, 125, 179, 181-2, 184, 191
Saudi Arabia, 42, 136, 137, 139, 140-6
Senegal, 24, 70, 119, 217-18
Senussi, 42, 49-50, 126
Seychelles, 111, 131, 165
Shuwa Arabs, 63-4

Sierra Leone, 85–7, 114, 115, 122, 124, 161, 165, 194, 201, 209–10, 213–14
Sokoto, 58, 62
Somalis and Somalia, 100–1, 139, 151, 155
Soninke, 25, 218
South Africa, 115, 164–5, 167–77, 216, 236–8
South Yemen, 147
Spain, 21, 111, 119, 122–3, 218
Spanish Sahara, 21, 23, 30, 141
Sudan, 126–8, 130, 141, 142, 143–4, 153, 156

Tanganyika and Tanzania, 102, 130, 148, 161, 165, 209, 213, 240
Taoudeni, 25, 27, 234–5
Tibesti, 50–2
Timbuktu 35, 36, 41, 46, 142
Toubous, 50–3
Tripoli, 46, 126
Tuareg, 34–46, 68, 79, 141–2, 203, 215, 221, 225–6, 230, 234–5

Tukulor, 25, 68, 70
Tunisia, 46, 47, 126, 223
Turkey, 48, 128
Tutsi, 97–9, 203, 222

Uganda, 131, 208–9
United Nations, 72, 74, 142–3, 147, 233–5, 237
Upper Volta, 57, 142, 205, 216, 226
USA 110–11, 119–20, 122–3, 140, 193, 195, 221–2

West Indies, 111, 116, 123–4, 210
Wilberforce, William, 120–1
Wolofs, 69, 70, 228

Yao, 130
Yemen, 136, 140, 146
Yorubas, 87–90, 112, 119, 124, 211

Zaire (ex-Belgian Congo), 96, 161, 162–3, 164, 183, 239, 240
Zambia, 130, 161, 165
Zanzibar, 129–31, 138

For Product Safety Concerns and Information please contact our EU representative  GPSR@taylorandfrancis.com
Taylor & Francis Verlag GmbH, Kaufingerstraße 24, 80331 München, Germany

www.ingramcontent.com/pod-product-compliance
Lightning Source LLC
Chambersburg PA
CBHW062137300426
44115CB00012BA/1957